Games and
Simulations
in Action

Woburn Educational Series
General Editor: Peter Gordon,
Institute of Education, University of London

Games and Simulations in Action
Alec Davison & Peter Gordon

The Education of the Gifted Child
David Hopkinson

Slow Learners: A Break in the Circle
Diane Griffin

The Middle School: High Road or Dead End?
John Burrows

Music in Education
Malcolm Carlton

Games and Simulations in Action

Alec Davison and Peter Gordon

The Woburn Press

We would like to express our thanks to the following for allowing us to make use of their photographs:
Noeline Kelly (Photograph 1), Greater London Council Photographic Unit (Photographs 2–7).

The People G.R.I.D. was inspired by Margot Brown of OXFAM, to whom thanks are due, and the graphics of *Raftonbury* were by Richard Plum.

All other illustrations and cover by SUE HENRY.

First published 1978 in Great Britain by
THE WOBURN PRESS
11 Gainsborough Road, London, E11 1RS, England

and in the United States of America by
THE WOBURN PRESS
c/o Biblio Distribution Centre
81 Adams Drive, P.O. Box 327, Totowa, N.J. 07511

ISBN 0 7130 0150 X (Case)
ISBN 0 7130 4002 5 (Paper)

Printed in Great Britain by
Chapel River Press, Andover, Hants

Contents

1
Within the Experience

Breed or Breathe?

'. . . and remember, it's the future of the world that's at stake.' Laughter and an immediate babel of talk. The briefing and stimulus session was over. Slides had been shown, statistics and examples given and the instructions for the activity spelt out. Around the edge of a House Room in a split site North London comprehensive school fifty or so first year sixth formers were scattered in groups of four and five. There were students of all subject disciplines who were working together for the first time. Each group sat around one of twelve tables on which were prominently displayed a series of illustrated cards denoting a geographical area such as China, India and Pakistan, North America, Britain and Western Europe, and Australasia, so that in all, spaceship earth was totally represented. Each area had been given units of population and units of food, as they were known in that year. The aim of these sixth formers, as heads of state of such territories, was to feed their people and to keep them fed until the year 2000. The question at stake was to *Breed or Breathe?*

The co-ed groups, themselves a variety of nationalities and colours, were reminding each other of the rules of the game and recapitulating the information about their area. This included what territories it covered, its politics, what agriculture it sustained, what resources it included, how much of these was committed to industry and defence and what were its current estimates of food wastage or storage. To represent these each area had been given units of industry, units of resources and units of industrial products. It was a while before groups could assimilate their problem and decide what their national policy must be should they have an insufficiency or an excess of food for their population.

8   Tentatively two or three delegates from each area wandered round to other tables and began some quite jovial bargaining. Foreign accents, often highly artificial, were assumed by many of the participants—the spirit of Peter Sellers was especially evident. Many had to check again on the rules and the teacher-controller advised. Population and industry units could not be exchanged; it is assumed that factories cannot be moved and that no one wants more population. Food, resources and industrial product units could be traded between areas on a one to one basis. These provided the means of bargaining and negotiation. There was also a control bank manned by two sixth formers; here a coloured map of the world indicated the twelve areas and a store of units in cards of all denominations were held. It was possible for any territory to gain from the bank further industrial product units: one resource unit plus one industrial unit must be traded at the bank to gain two industrial products—products coming in real life from resources being processed. But as the industry itself is not consumed in the process it is only the resources that the bank will actually keep in return for the products.

By now this first 'round' of play was in full swing. It was to represent the five years from 1975–1980. Ten minutes of negotiation were allowed. Only North America, Southern Africa and Australasia had food surpluses to start with so there was ample motivation for decisions and negotiation. Those left at the tables bargained with delegates from other areas, when enquiries showed that they had something to offer. Some delegates negotiated purely at a playing card level to start with. 'I'll have one of those for one of those.' Others gave elaborate scenarios of why politically or culturally it would be good for the countries to join in some kind of partnership and what this might promise for future co-operation. Some players took their cues from others and argued from the faint knowledge that they had of world issues: one or two of the girls giggled to each other and did little this round.

In the midst of this global bazaar the controller sounded the bell and all delegates returned to their territories to work out how they stood. Any area that had more food than population had to return to the bank such food surplus for it would 'go bad'. Most areas were short of food, some like India, South East Asia and China importantly so. A shortage in most other areas indicated malnutrition not starvation. So now decisions had to be made. Each territory was given by the controller a pink sheet with a choice of options open to it. There was a choice of the country investigating a policy of cutting down wastage, either in manufacturing or in improved storage, or initiating a birth control programme. Countries could choose both, one or neither of these options, the players imagining what the countries might do in reality. They had to write down their choice on an option form that was their record of choices throughout the morning. Each area was also then given a green effects card. This indicated the population increase that would occur in the 1980–1985 period, based on actual United Nations predictions, plus any individual increase or decrease in food, resources and industry units. Thus the Middle East lost 10 food units because the sardine catch lessened in the Eastern Mediterranean as a result of the building of the Aswan dam: yet it gained an extra 15 population units. India and Pakistan gained 140 population units plus an additional 25 units because the projected drop in birth rate failed to materialize. However, it did gain an increase in 100 food units because a higher yielding cereal strain was introduced and there was a trial marketing of new C.S.M. and Vita Soy cereal foods.

9   A delegate from each country went to the bank to gain or lose its various units. At the same time the results of its decision in the options were taken into account. If it had opted for greater birth control then it lost 10% of its proposed population increase; if it reduced wastage in manufacturing then the industrialised countries gained 10 food units and the third world countries if they improved storage gained 20 food units. Now each area had a time to evaluate its situation and to work out a strategy of what its policies must be. A great deal of higher mathematics seemed to follow and some countries which were startlingly under-fed decided to be more aggressive in approach; several groups planned to change the rules—even if not to cheat, for the controller had warned everyone at the start that cheating would be so easy as to make a nonsense of the morning's work.

The controller now called a press conference for a brief public report from each area to learn how it stood and whether there were any national policies or proposals that it wished to make known. Fifteen minutes were allowed for this. During that sequence some delegates maintained their accents, generating both laughter and ribald comments, others had little to say, while others were justifying a range of devious tactics. The U.S.S.R. and East Europe proposed the drawing together of the world into a united world government with greater international sharing. This met with a suspicious reception from North America, Britain and West Europe, who were aware that the Soviet Premier's five year plan for cultivation of barren regions had failed owing to poor weather, when the bell went. Time had run out and, as in life, events march on. The second trading round started.

Some of the unit cards for 'Breed or Breathe'

10 It was observable how the atmosphere had changed. Most delegates were now in greater earnest; some had exchanged with those who had previously remained at base; many had a plan of action agreed by the group and wanted to push that through. Australia was under great pressure from many countries to accept a mass influx of immigrants. This was resisted most firmly by its head of state already very conscious that supplies of gold and lead were exhausted and energy resources were depleted. North and Central Africa had declared war on Southern Africa and were trying to work out the consequences in terms of units. Central and South America were putting enormous pressure on Western Europe to make the Pope alter his views on contraception. Throughout the room there were pockets of great disputation and less aimless shopping about. But some chiefly attempted to make more industrial products through trade and barter. Those not so deeply engaged were involved in listening to others who were.

The bell sounded and reassessments were made at the end of the second round. Some countries had effected little trade and their situation was now at crisis point: others had accepted a lower standard of nutrition by agreeing on one food unit to every two population units. Now the controller gave out the printed pink option sheets for the next five year cycle. As well as increased birth control and wastage elimination three further alternatives were offered:

Disarmament: more countries have nuclear weapons, food shortage is creating tension, safety would indicate a disarmament pact; does the area join it?
Pollution: can resources be committed to clearing up land, sea and air; will other countries agree to take part?
Water: shortages are acute all over the world, can conservation be practised or should major engineering works be initiated?

After area discussions all options were marked on the sheet. Every group had now a sufficient number of players involved in the issues to be rigorously engaged.

The controller then gave each area its green effects card for 1985–90. Japan gained 6 extra population units, but lost five food units because of the decrease in fish catch due to a global increase in sea pollution, and also lost ten industry units because air pollution brought a rise in killer smogs: this meant work hours lost through sickness and many deaths—so one population unit was lost also. India gained 200 food units because more and better fertilisers were used on the land, though that consumed 10 industry and 5 resources units which were now quite scarce for the country. China gained 160 food units because its hilly areas were opened up to cultivation, though that used 5 industry and 5 resources units; but it lost 10 of these food units because of the decline in fish catches from sea pollution. And so on for each country.

Delegates went back to sort out all the changes in units and also to discover the effects of the options—either losses in population because of birth control or gains in food units because of reduction in wastage; gains in resources and industry units because of disarmament; and gains in food units because of water conservation or better pollution control, though the latter meant that industry and resource units would be lost. Again countries had to reassess their situation and prepare new policies. This time, some were ready with firm proposals for the press conference when each area reported back. Britain and Western Europe, whose

11 population was still increasing, had had an outbreak of typhoid because of water contamination, a killer smog and great losses of food because increasing industrialization throughout the rest of the world diminished the demand for goods produced in this area. These countries now urged for world government along with U.S.S.R., Eastern Europe and North America all of whom had had to impose food-rationing and had lost resource units as lead, platinum and gold deposits were exhausted. But China this time strongly opposed, having had a good five year cycle and having negotiated with South East Asia to share in this in return for annexation. The press conference grew most heated as the implications were explored, with various power blocks and alliances being made. The bell sounded in the thick of things and the third bargaining period, 1985–90, was instantly engaged.

There were far more high politics involved this time as area sided with area. Some of the strategems were most ingenious, some highly fantastic. Two additional 'local' wars broke out, China annexing Japan, and the U.S.S.R. occupying the Middle East. All units were pooled in those territories but the players found that this only resulted in a super-

'Breed or Breathe' in action

12 abundance of industrial products but no more food. Many countries decided to give up industry and concentrate on food production but the game only allowed for an exchange of food units. As no one would exchange food and everyone was in need there was an urge by many players to want to change the rules. Science and industry would create more food even if more could not be grown, most players thought. But the teacher stood firm, knowing that this was due to happen in the next round, and the bell rang.

For two more rounds the game continued. The choice of options grew even wider; countries could deindustrialize, committing resources for food production; they could impose a diet of staple food reducing growth in non-essential crops; they could battle with falling energy levels by restricting consumption or put new untried nuclear reactors into use; they could take positive steps about a more equal distribution of wealth; they could use new, very powerful but untested pesticides; they could ration all oil and petrol productions, and they could resort to total war, if they were still armed. Meanwhile the effects had multiplied. Some were positive, like the new methods discovered for purifying and recycling water, the new animal foods developed by cultivation of protein growth on petroleum, the reclamation of the Sahara Desert and the break-through of synthetic food. But these were set against the dire effects of the exhaustion of most minerals and energy, the creep of pollution and outbreaks of diseases, smogs, new pests and bacteria. The consequences of earlier decisions and options were now built into each area's brief so that if action had not been wisely taken on critical issues beforehand the effects were now magnified.

During this period the sixth form groups varied in approach. Some quietly pursued their own line, attempting to balance out food with population at a consistent nutritious level; some by now were blasé and rather tired with so much decision-making and intensive debate; others were deeply involved in creating pressure and winning their way in the most hair-raising negotiations. Bloody and scarred, yet with multi-millions still alive and thriving on restricted diet and in a simple egalitarian society, the nations in 2000 A.D. experienced world government, severely imposed universal rationing, enormous bureaucracy and obligatory sterilization of parents after two children. The problems had not been solved, for the co-operation was as yet enforced by the super powers, with passions mounting high; but the experience had been rich.

The controller sounded a final bell and a short belated break was called for. He felt the game had gone well. 'It's always so different. This is the third year I've used it for starting off the year's work in General Studies. It brings everybody together in a bumper working morning—which I'm only allowed once a term—and it raises practically every important issue about ethics, morality, politics, religion, economics and the purpose of life. It's good to have physicists here working with those studying English Literature and both alongside others who are retaking the Certificate of Secondary Education. Most of the sixth form staff have played it now so they can pick it up in their specialisms over the term.' Ten minutes later the debate was renewed with an hour's evaluation. Most had never previously pictured the headlong rush of events that were bringing about such problems. They had enjoyed so much the experience of determining power that they were optimistic that government and not war would win through. They were more concerned to examine the game and question its doomsday bias. Everyone was encouraged to read one of

13 the library books especially gathered. There was a general feeling of expectation, of where do we go from here?

The Dream Game

The group consisted of twenty eight mixed ability second formers, boys and girls who had been together for four terms, a student teacher and their form teacher. This was a double period timetabled for religious education in a Central London Church of England school experimenting with a more affective and effective approach to religious studies. Desks had been stacked and pushed to the edge during break and the chairs were in a circle. Last term the class had looked at worship and belief in primitive societies: now in the spring term the class was moving into an exploration of myth in several early civilizations.

Already there had been five minutes of spoken warm-up exercises in pairs in the circle, involving re-telling stories and trying to make up the most fantastic lie and get away with it. Now the pairs moved into fours and each quartet was asked to tell a communal story with every person speaking in turn but only one word at a time starting with 'Last—night—I—dreamed . . .' In two minutes the class had volunteered a variety of dreams. The mistress then asked them to discuss in groups why they thought that we had dreams at all, and why they took the form that they did. Within five minutes groups were well into sharing particular dreams, talking about nightmares and embellishing rumours of dreams that they had heard of, often through films and television. The class pooled its findings. Some talked about cheese the night before, others suggested prophecies and warnings, some thought they reflected our worries or our hopes, others that our minds were working without constraints; one or two had read of scientific experiments which examined how much we dreamt every night: a few claimed that they never dreamt at all. However, all agreed that there were good and bad dreams and that dreams were full of feelings.

The teacher now proposed that each group would make up a dream and show it to everyone else. The aim would be to see if they could work out why the dreamer was experiencing that kind of dream and what it might mean to him. So that no one would have to show their own personal dream and also to help structure it, she was going to give out a series of cards which everyone could interpret in his own way. First of all each group had to decide which pupil was going to be the dreamer because he or she would be the stage manager of the whole affair. The teacher then went to each group in turn and allowed the dreamer to pick one of eight red cards, which were facing downwards. These were the archetypal central roles that he would see himself in during the dream—such as hero, heroine, priestess, sorcerer, witch, mother, ogre, father . . . The boy dreamer in the noisy corner group got *Trickster— sometimes helpful, sometimes underhand.* Then the teacher explained that everyone else in the dream was to be an aspect of the real dreamer himself; they were different facets of his character now embodied in a different role. The rest of the class were allowed to pick a blue card from the pack. The pupils in the corner group received *a Burglar, Someone of no importance* and *a Saint.* There was plenty of reaction and laughter to these. Next the teacher talked about the overriding feeling of the dream, whether it was a joyful one, or fearful, whether it was dominantly angry or indecisive. It was this feeling that had to go back to something that had happened to the dreamer in real life that day and

14   was the hidden spring of the dream. The dreamers all chose one of eight purple cards and the corner group had *Grief—loss, failure or disappointment.*

The teacher now explained that a dream was frequently dramatic, that there were often tensions between opposites and that it was the dominant emotion, just given out, that would determine whether the conflict was resolved happily or unhappily. These were eight black cards with such conflicts as the battle of life and death, the conflict of overwhelming good with irredeemable evil, of the masculine against the feminine, of childhood against growing up. The corner group picked out *the real against the romantic.* Finally, the teacher described how in a dream certain objects often kept reappearing and disappearing and had a power well beyond what they represented. The class of pupils had already explored the concept of symbolism and had then invented situations where an object was used symbolically. Now each dreamer had to choose two symbols, a yellow card of man-made symbols and a green card of natural symbols. The corner group chose *Maze, a Labyrinth* and a *Lion.*

By now all the groups were champing at the bit, having begun to work things out as the cards were allocated. Preparation time was limited to half an hour and the groups were told that once they had an idea they were to work it out in action and not only through discussion. The dream had to start and finish with the dreamer asleep by himself. After a minute or two some groups were in great debate about how to include all the elements; another had as its symbol a wheel and all was literally to revolve around that; one group had the Quest as its task and started from the dreamer setting out; a group mainly of girls were using a great deal of movement, and a group mainly of the class comics were attempting to make it very dream-like, and surrealistic, with nothing seeming to relate to anything; most of the others had held on to a strong story line.

Model for any action maze

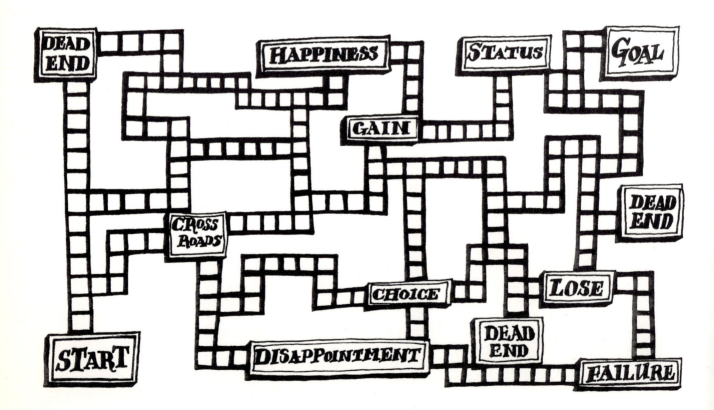

15

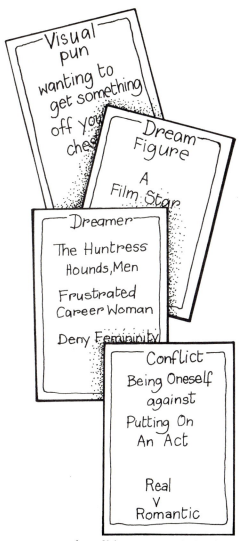

Some stimulus cards for 'The Dream Machine'

The corner group were only talking around the issues, while all about them was a bustle of activity. The student teacher came over and they explained their cards. They couldn't get anywhere with *the real against the romantic.* 'Well let's start with the dominant emotion then . . . what about the grief, why are you sad?' Suggestions were made about losing football matches, or getting into trouble at school or home. Then one of the boys came up with, 'How if he's lost his mother—she's left the family and the boy's living with his dad . . .' 'Yes, and then he's working out what he *really* thinks of her and what he *says* he thinks of her . . . the romantic bit . . . for she's let them all down, after all.' They were now under way and the student was asked to join them, because they wanted a girl. The card she picked from the pack was *a Tramp, a down-and-out, a slut;* they had some fun with that.

In the next fifteen minutes they had worked intensively and had imagined the dreamer waking into his dream as a fairground barker, a trickster, selling genuine golden lockets with a lion crest on the front. Inside was a portrait and lock of hair of a beautiful woman—the dreamer's mother. The four other aspects of himself approached him in their different ways to purchase a locket and each in turn they were swindled as a last minute switch was made, so they actually bought a fake, worthless trash, which they discovered in walking away. But the fourth aspect, the burglar, pick-pocketed the real locket just before he left.

16 Great despair from the trickster as he discovered this. He set out on a journey to look for the burglar, seeking out the characters at the fair. But they all joined hands to make a maze through which the dreamer had to go each time to find the next aspect. Each in turn rejected him, having once been fooled, until he came to the burglar. As he implored him to return the only thing that had any value to him the dream fades away and he wakes up.

The other groups were strangely held with the power of the enactment. They were soon discussing the loss of the boy's mother and how he must have had mixed feelings about her. They also touched on guilt and blame. They only gleaned part of the other ideas the boys had been exploring and in places they saw more into it than the boys had intended. The explanation by the boys was quite complex and they surprised themselves with how deep they had gone. One of the girls blurted out, 'Oh, I see, you were all meant to be parts of Brian's mixed feelings.' No one talked about the quality of the enactment; there were more interesting issues to pursue. Each dream was evaluated in this way. Other dreams had a more fairy-tale quality: one was incredibly myth-like with an Emperor in a tree, like the Cheshire cat, and a ritual sacrifice that kept changing at the foot of it. The class went out buzzing with chat, 'Can we do it again, miss?'

The teacher explained. 'This kind of thing gives me an insight into their thinking. Some are still very much seeing things only in concrete terms, others are clearly now able to begin to cope with abstractions. It shows how disparate their grasp of any religious concepts must be. I've tried to get into dreams before but lacked any structured way in and it got rather chaotic. Also it wasn't stretching enough. I've tried this game with half a dozen classes now, in English and religious education. It's an excellent way into story telling, myth and symbolic action. Every time it's totally different. It seems to me that myth, like a dream, is a structuring of an unknown, a mystery, but the structuring gives meaning and understanding. I'll let them have another go—it seems to get more mythical the second time around.'

Who Cares?

They had not been an easy group. Thirty young school leavers from six neighbouring London schools had volunteered to take part in a six day residential experience of informal social education in the country. Some of the more awkward participants had been 'encouraged' to take part by their schools, perhaps for a week of peace; others had opted without knowing what it was about but wanted a break from home. Half the group came from single sex schools, a third were on probation and a different third were first generation immigrants. They had not come to be educated but for a bit of fun.

By the end of the third day of visits, occasional speakers, discussions and some creative activities, a trust was developing between the group and the three leaders, whom they had met only once before at a briefing session; some genuine friendships were gently burgeoning amongst the members. Each day, in order to explore some of the situations that were being raised under the generic theme of 'Communication', simple pair and small group simulations had been set up. Although no one claimed to have done this kind of thing before at school, and everyone was apprehensive and inarticulate at first, they were now accepting it as a normal element of the week. On the third evening three of the Health

17 Education Council's short trigger films on adolescent relationships were shown and the discussion went on well after cocoa time until lights out.

On the fourth day a whole morning of simulation was planned. All members were in jeans and ten minutes of hectic physical limber soon saw everyone working together embodying in abstract form the theme of 'human networks.' Then the leader set up brief spoken work in pairs. A was a fifth former who had had a magazine confiscated earlier in the term by a teacher, B, who said it was pornographic. A now wanted it back. Could he persuade the teacher to return it? This was an easy fun situation. A second problem now had A as an anxious parent, worried about the company his son was keeping, and waiting up at 11.30 pm for B, the 15 year old, to come home from an evening out. What happened? This took longer. In talking them through afterwards the players could see what a wide range of ways there were to deal with such situations. In each case the fact that our behaviour had effects on others outside the immediate relationship was explored.

This led to the introduction of *Who Cares?* which explores the network of our interpersonal relationships. Everyone was given an information card about a person who lived in West Green, a new inner city estate; half were teenage roles, half adults. For several hours the players were going to stand in other people's shoes. The cards were given out carefully so that none would trespass on what was known about individuals in the group; yet some cards were given to help certain players identify with an attitude that it was thought might have been helpful to them. Other cards were given to those who would be the centre of the activities and keep it in play. Groups of fours were made by bringing together those who had the same coloured cards: these were three families, each with parents and two young people, a group of school fifth formers, some of the staff of the school, a group of those who had left school and were either at work or in further education, and several groups of social agencies. A placard was placed close to every group indicating *The Johnstone Family* or *West Green School Staff Room:* players had their names boldly printed on stick-on labels which they wore prominently for later reference.

The cards were studied. Each outlined a little of the person's biography and indicated some of his pattern of social relationships. A range of problems had been built into every situation, some minor and others major. Some parental relationships were happy, others less so. The agencies varied in their range of experience, understanding and awareness; some were blinkered in doctrinaire or fashionable attitudes. Without knowing it, however, every card in some way indicated a relationship with a never-present central character, Helen Johnstone, a 15 year old fifth former, very moody of late. The course leaders and a visitor had taken some of the more difficult parental and agency roles but all helped a good half dozen of the groups who were having difficulty in reading the cards.

On the reverse of the cards three encounters were outlined; the first two were essentially to help everybody to climb into the situation and to begin making the person himself. There was a feeling of great trepidation all round and much clutching of cards. This was the most difficult of all the participation they had been called to make so far. The leader set off the first encounter, which involved a simple task needing some kind of persuasion. In every group A and B, perhaps the two parents, were in dialogue, and C and D, often the teenagers. This ran for five minutes and was in general a lukewarm experience, unfortunately with much reference back to the cards. Some players, however, were

18 beginning to pick up clues and cues within the relationship.

The second encounter involved all four players within their groups, either at a family meal, or in a professional meeting. Here matters began to catch fire, for there was by now at least one person in each group who was inside the situation and was prepared to take some action. In the Barnet family there was civil war. Mr. Barnet, a tobacconist, had no time for the family and his wife could not cope; the eldest son was a tearaway and the daughter was depressed. For the social agencies this was a known problem family. The Jennings family were on better terms yet their eldest son was not able to speak his worries. The more middle class Johnstone family were in conflict; there had been a mother-daughter row some months previously and now an unsuccessful attempt to patch things up had been made. Helen, their youngest daughter, had still not arrived home. Meanwhile in the school staff room the more experimental staff members were trying to propose a new personal relationships dimension to the curriculum in the face of some unwillingness from the headmaster. The social agencies—a doctor, a youth leader, a student welfare officer and a youth advisory counsellor—were all considering the problems of West Green amongst young people. Both groups of young people met to make proposals about facilities in the youth club and school that might help the lonely or those with problems. But built into these situations were the private concerns of the individuals: one or two began to put out feelers for help, not with much success. This encounter ran for well over ten minutes and by the end of it people were much more secure, though some were still having difficulties in maintaining the situation.

Now the controller opened the situation out. For the next half an hour anyone could meet with anyone else, unless already engaged in conversation, and the third encounters on the card suggested a range of people whom the person would be likely to know. At this point the animation increased and the temperature went up. Frequent bouts of hearty laughter were a reaction to the developing feeling of earnestness. More people were consulted who could listen or advise; parents consulted agencies, or visited the school; friends met, some of the agencies went visiting and interaction gave rise to a host of new situations and issues. Many of these new interviews went on for ten minutes or more; often there was a referring back to the original family to seek for help. Some people met with no understanding and only had further demands and pressures placed on them. One or two were 'outraged' by events and disclosures in role.

During this session, the leader, as a police officer, visited Mr. Johnstone to break the news of the discovery of his daughter in West Green Canal, a suspected suicide. In turn Mr. Johnstone broke this to his wife and the news slowly spread. There was genuine shock. Eventually the leader called for silence and read an article as it appeared in the local newspaper a week later about the death of Helen Johnstone. All players returned to their original groups to take what line of action would have been thought fit. At this point there was a coffee break but players were pledged to maintain confidences.

When everyone returned two meetings had been convened. The youth leader gathered all the young people into the youth club to make proposals for greater help with young people's emotional needs in the light of the recent death. Meanwhile, under pressure, the headmaster had convened a meeting for parents to see what more the school ought to be doing in its concern for the welfare of its pupils. All players continued to stay in role. For forty-five minutes both discussions ranged deeply and

'Whole self involvement': a teachers' workshop explores 'The Dream Machine'

23 In the *Dream Game* the boy was a most powerful instrument of communication in hinting at the sense of the dream world. One group went as far as expressive dance but even the more self-conscious boys' group by a simple use of moving and interlocking arms suggested the labyrinth and the nightmare.

The other simulations were more traditional but involved a great deal of non-verbal communication. In both cases there was movement between situations, often with an increasing sense of a real person behind the attitude, especially in *Who Cares?*

This all helped generate the dynamic. In *Breed or Breathe?* it was barter and political negotiation, gesture and rhetoric. The attitudes in all the groups demanded certain bodily expression which was not merely acting, as there was essentially no 'show', but an enacting of a need or a relationship or a personalised task. In turn the involvement suggested new ideas and new tactics.

The whole self in the situation and not merely an intellect thinking about a situation can produce very different solutions. Relevant action can stimulate thought; many young people think better on their feet and feel less stultified in some form of activity. It may only be legitimate movement between desks and then some form of personal encounter. But the encounter is invariably more telling if there is a more physical awareness—if the angry 'delegate' does thump the desk—and the actual permitted freedom of choosing which encounter to enter next helps reinforce the gains in social terms.

The contribution of the emotions and feelings as the motor of the activity has been stressed. Without any engagement of the feelings the work will disintegrate. Whereas in the customary classroom situation this is easily passed over by moving on to exercises in books or work from the board, in simulation it is fatal. The game *has* to be played for any personal learning to follow and this is why each of the three situations prepared the way by exercises, warm up or discussion for initial involvement in the topic. There must be a willing suspension of disbelief. This calls for an imaginative response but one that pupils know from the play of childhood, so it is not too remote. Yet it can seem to pupils to be inappropriate to the classroom and it has to be made permissible again—which takes trust and confidence. Because this is a more vulnerable situation in many ways, if it 'works' then the feeling of personal satisfaction can be all the greater. It is a self confirmation, a self validation—even though it was seemingly behind a role.

Talk

As well as the action, the other distinguishing feature of all three experiences is the enormous commitment to talk. Sometimes this is loud and boisterous with argument and debate in whole groups or pairs. But at other times the earnestness of the encounter makes for an intentness that reduces sound to a concentrated hum. Yet everyone throughout the class is talking. And there is talk of all kinds.

Some of the talk is superficial as pupils fumble for a direction, a way into their experience through the limitation presented by the role. Others launch in boldly with stereotypes for an initial effect. There is talk in order to arrive at a decision, where a transactional bargain has to be made and both parties satisfied; talk that is sensitive, probing and imagining how one would deal in real life with that situation. In some talk the pupil is 'representing' a concern or a country; or a human being some way away from his actual self.

Much of the talk is out of role, concerning the game or simulation, or about a friend or the teacher. Roles break in laughter or embarrassment, or after the conclusion of an encounter, to talk about it.

At times people propose changes in the rules or are in doubt about procedures. People find their own levels but they can stretch themselves in surprising ways.

Little of this talk is teacher-directed. The leader has set the experience in motion and may control the 'rounds' or the overall structure but he can also sit out completely and listen with a creative ear. There is encounter and communication all about him and from that, learning will come if the teacher trusts in the value of talk at all. Learning will come in ways that he cannot prescribe because it comes from the state of the pupil at that particular moment.

In the pair situations there is little else that the participant can do, except talk and listen. Without the teacher noticeably listening or cajoling, he can try out more experimental situations and approaches; he can risk attitudes in any language style without failing in appropriateness or correctness.

In the small group situations much can be gained from listening as well as from contributing; the gauge of the activity and learning is often the teacher's perceptions of how much non-speakers' attention is being held—especially if the teacher is silent too. Even in whole class 'meetings', 'conferences' or 'protests' where the teacher is not in a central role, the structure can support others in new ways. Often after a double period there has been so much earnest talk that participants are exhausted and turn to other kinds of study with pleasure. But, like movement and action, the talk is self-validating; it is the mechanism for our quest for meanings and understanding. Although many would now claim that a no talking situation is without validity to the individual, many teachers still are troubled by gossip. The situation of a good simulation is to provoke discovery, to generate talk that is purposeful and exploratory.

Problems and Decisions

Simulations revel in problems—whether it is solving every major world issue in two hours, as in *Breed or Breathe?*, or dealing with the thorniest of dilemmas in the personal relationships of *Who Cares?* Its structures are geared towards making the participants decide and usually within the next fifteen minutes. Urgent real-life decisions are also made under such pressure as any politician will confirm—though he has sometimes spent many years trying to understand them. Nevertheless, however much they can be caricatured, simulations enable young people to make decisions, yet within the safety of a controlled experiment. In this way some kind of rehearsal for living is possible. New behaviour can be tried out and be appraised by the group. Its consequences can be traced in theory in ways impossible in real life. This is why practically every major training scheme in the country is now involved in human inter-relationships from trade union leaders to nursery nurses, industrial executives to Sunday school teachers, all will use sessions of role play, often video taped or observed.

There is also the planning strategy—the give and take of suggestions and counter suggestions. In the *Dream Game* much of the time was spent in planning, in taking up ideas, rejecting them, relooking at earlier suggestions, despairing and rediscovering. These are real decisions to make the activity or task work; problem-solving in the group in order to facilitate the suspension of disbelief. Without coming to conclusions the activity will not move on. The fact that the teacher might be 'neutral' or engaged in one encounter may leave about two dozen other encounters going on all round her to cope with themselves. The decisions are theirs.

We know from our adult experience how much being placed in situations of responsibility where we have to cope with frequent decision-making gives us confidence in coping with more. Simulation, if reality is impossible, is the next best way to preparing pupils for work situations, as all careers materials now indicate. This can also be seen with materials for moral education which are centrally focused on the enactment of human problems.

Clearly, not all pupils will find the decision-making of simulation easy. But it will be worth the struggle, because responsibility comes only with practice and a democracy can only genuinely be made of participants. This needs rehearsal.

Creativity

Unless a simulation is mere manipulation, like painting by numbers, every group tackling it will conclude matters in different ways. Sometimes with *Breed or Breathe?* it finishes with total world war and bleak nihilism, at other times with firm world government, at another with a benevolent worldwide dictatorship. The *Dream Game* is especially so open-ended that by some law of averages the same situation of a dream could never occur twice; so much so that it is possible to feel that not even the same game is being played. *Who Cares?* is tighter but participants always play the characters very differently even though the role is seemingly specific. As in all imaginative games we exercise all our latent ingenuity or creativity to wriggle out of situations, to persuade, to examine a problem differently. Problem-solving is creative endeavour. It is calling on our unique response. Even if the resultant behaviour may be similar the inner processes can be most different. Who is to know when we listen to a Bach recording what the seraphic glazed expression may mean? To each his own. So with simulation. We play it our way. We break the rules, we cheat, we misinterpret, we get muddled up; we are altruistic, we are amused, we are bored. We go about every encounter differently. We make, fashion, mould the role to our own perceptions. All good personal interaction is an exercise in creative living and simulation is no exception.

Just as the playing of a game can only be validly assessed in terms of creative engagement, so essentially is the making of it. Any teacher devising a simulation is in creative play. Although there is a noble educational theory that one must start with an aim, just as a new scientific theory is supposed to start with detailed observation, like all creative experience the idea is usually the point of beginning. Simulation is an art form, though like novel writing there are only a handful of basic archetypal plots, and there are short stories as well as three-volume epics.

Simulation making can become an obsession, as does all art, when one minor success leads to another. The enormous time consumed in devising them is justified if they work in practice, as much for the encores of later participants. Any committed simulator has a drawer full of unsuccessful simulations and he turns to these on rainy days with new determination. Others which have been finished in great haste and played successfully once, lie unused in large envelopes waiting to be adequately completed for a second airing.

Games open new possibilities for creativity to the teacher. Although they are now based on every possible subject at all levels, they must exist only as models and stimulus to the teacher to make her own. Each playing situation is different and games must be remade and adapted, plagiarised and refurbished so that they fit a particular group. They call for creative reassessment, not slavish following through. They call on ingenuity and insight in their construction. They evoke eureka experiences as well as diligent perseverence to get the structures right, so that some kind of success is more or less guaranteed in its being played. The form and the content, as with any art, are enmeshed as one.

Facts: Cognitive and Affective

The person who factually learns most from a simulation is the teacher. At the end of devising a game or stylised reconstruction of reality, it is the teacher who will be brimful of the most minute detail of the subject matter. In order to be simple, clear and effective, he will have had to refine and refine; otherwise he will confuse. With a less good simulation

27 the rules can be more difficult to learn than the content; the medium can too easily become the message.

It is best for the simulation to draw upon existing knowledge, whether of human experience or of a subject content, for there soon comes a limit to what can be taken in before the game can be started. Sometimes additional knowledge needs to be fed into the game later to save decisions becoming too naive. In *Breed or Breathe?* there was very little previous knowledge called for and only a superficial knowledge of the world required—though the game works much better when knowledge is richer. No specific information was given during the game, only assumptions and conjectures. But pupils will find themselves dredging up from their experience a great deal of latent knowledge, and at the end of the experience this shared reservoir of knowing will have been sustaining for everyone. There is then a stimulus to find out more.

The two original devisers of that game spent one way and another almost a year working on it. They read a great deal of the Doomsday literature and much else, turned to United Nations prognostications, consulted national agencies and tried it out with several thousands of young people, changing, adding and restructuring it after many of these trials. They became minor experts for a while. Theirs was task-orientated learning in an area that was not their specialism. Once bitten with the bug they could not let the game alone until it really worked.

Simulation is more an agent of revision or induction than it is of detailed instruction. It would aim to give motivation and cannot be a substitute for diligent study. It is not magic, nor a panacea for all ills. But it can teach things that cannot be learned in any other way. The moon landings were simulated in the hangars of Houston, Texas. Army operations still simulate war after all the textbook instruction and filmed playback. Being within the experience is totally different from reading about it—but before we are put within the situation we need to be secure that there is a possibility that we can succeed.

The most unlikely areas of knowledge can be structured into a game—thus the world of dreams is given form and spaceship earth a symbolic embodiment. As all knowledge has its structures there cannot be anything that given enough ingenuity and perseverence could not be given a shape or framework for exploration. It is the finding of the right model sufficiently simplified that is the main problem. The experience often speaks in metaphors—witness the excellence of *Starpower* and *Outsider*. An evaluation of a simulation in terms of factual content would only be achieved through an examination of the deviser not the participant—his learning is in other directions.

Evaluation

(Although the whole question of evaluation is discussed at some length in chapter 8, a preliminary word is needed here.)

Possibly the greatest learning in simulation comes from a reflection-in-action during the playing. This is why histrionic emotion is of little value, for pupils are then too busy attempting to cope at a primary level of feeling. Because the player always knows that the experience is a pretence, the self-examining mechanism is already in play.

Post-play discussion is vital. Sometimes it is better done after a coffee or lunch break, sometimes immediately afterwards. It is important to catch the emotion while it is warm: it is a different exercise again to reintroduce it a week later for further reflection. A third of the length of the entire initial session is usually recommended for this activity. Evaluation is best achieved with players seated in a circle and the leader is most effective as a good (neutral) chairman. There is evidence in action to be assessed. In *Who Cares?* there was just too much and it went on being discussed informally several days later.

There is the question of the real feelings experienced by the participants in the process of the game. There is the description of what actually happened, which is invariably perceived very differently by the various players. This is the simulated achievement of what resulted and why, from the situation. There are new areas of learning that need to be made explicit. *Breed or Breathe?* is very biased towards one viewpoint. The evaluation did actually bring this out and it was hotly debated. Many simulations in the humanities are in controversial areas and are prepared by various liberal agencies which all have their special concerns. It is richly educational to explore this bias and let the group make suggestions as to how it could be righted, if it should. Certainly the metaphor of the simulation will be designed to leave a strong impression in the player's consciousness and which may be explored more fully later. Neutrality can rarely achieve this—nor does it in poetry, fiction or drama, and simulation is only a living fiction. Evaluation is not easy, it is likely to ramble and disintegrate. The teacher/leader needs to be well prepared for this, with notes to hand so that the right questions are asked to help in the understanding of what actually happened.

However enthusiastically one might make claims for simulation, the telescope needs reversing at times. For gaming is only one weapon in any competent teacher's armoury of enactive processes. It is important to see the work in its context and then to examine more deeply its central concern with empathy and human relationships.

References

Bruner J. S., *The process of Education*, Vintage Books New York, 1963
Bullock A., *A language for life*, Her Majesty's Stationery Office, 1975
Jeffreys M. V. C., *Personal Values in the Modern World*, Penguin Books, 1962
Jones T. P., *Creative Learning in Perspective*, University of London Press, 1972
Martin W. et al *Understanding Children Talking*, Penguin Books 1976
Schaffer H. R., *The growth of Sociability*, Penguin Books, 1971

3

The Classroom as Workshop

The Ground of Action

Perhaps our generation will be fortunate to see in the secondary school the evolution of the classroom into a workshop. There are encouraging signs that matters are changing in this direction. There is an entirely different sense of willing purpose in those secondary schools where first and second forms have workshop bases which house ability groupings disposed in physical units and teachers who cover a broader range of curriculum content.

This is especially so when third formers and their seniors move between specialist subject workshops in the humanities, languages and English as well as science and the arts, each laid out as an enactive approach to the specialism. Longer period groupings, which are increasingly essential, call for interclass movement only during break times, when pupils collect books from bases in cloakroom and wall lockers and not form rooms. This will allow the subject teacher richer opportunity to determine in her working space the right conditions for active learning.

Each school has to solve this central problem of creating the conditions for learning in its own way. But its credibility as an institution that professes concern for the socialization of all sorts and conditions of young people into our culture can no longer be upheld if this challenge is not seen to be tackled. Our senior pupils as well as their parents have been made aware by the media of new curriculum developments as well as educational research.

There are a number of excellent teachers who have advanced our understanding of the learning process, as well as shown the possibility of different patterns of teaching. From them we can see that many so-called

30 informal approaches are merely excuses for bad teaching; that a creative classroom, with scope for real motivation and understanding of the pupils' needs, requires most careful and subtle structuring and completely new ways of classroom management. The teacher herself has to understand the way learning and thinking processes develop with the growing child, how concepts can be deepened, how language determines all and how little is learned if relationships and feelings are not acknowledged. Such teachers discover intuitively and then make explicit their experience.

At the same time both pupils and public have been made well aware of the areas of failure in an education system for which the ratepayer has never contributed so much. Whether increasing or not, the large numbers of secondary pupils still unable to read is an appalling statement. The alienation and apathy of so many senior pupils speaks volumes about the depersonalized and to them seemingly irrelevant curriculum which is offered. There is a groundswell of feeling for more structure and more framework, smaller schools as well as a rigorous expectation of commitment to learning and understanding.

These new sets of features are not as mutually exclusive as those who would mythologize education into the opposing heroes and villains of progressives and formalists would allow. Instead we need a profession of educators who are up-to-date in their subject area, and seek a rich first-hand experience of the active processes of learning. One of the main hopes in changing education from within lies in the development of professional centres and the spontaneous generation within schools of teachers' workshops, whole-staff courses and the machinery for local curriculum development supported and informed by advisory staff. Throughout the country there is evidence of this change.

The real centre of gravity of teacher education may yet become that of in-service teacher training; learning and sharing more with colleagues and tutors, attending courses, holding staff conferences and subject departments devising materials together.

In all these processes and on such courses learning in action at the teachers' own level is the strong distinguishing feature. Formal lecture sessions feature less than group-created tasks, or individual and pair projects, and there is a greater use of technological resources. The socialization of the group and its understanding of the battery of learning resources will feature more prominently than knowledge to be handed on. There is a conscious aim to make the environment stimulating, a place where the learner is an active agent, making meaning from a new enthusiasm. There is an attempt to explore the dimension of play involved, of working from a personal motivation that engages curiosity. Subject barriers have often to be transcended once the disciplines are learned.

As the teacher experiences again, or for the first time, these new modes, she is constantly asking herself how such a new technique or experience could be applied to her classroom with thirty pupils. Classroom management and teacher confidence then become crucial. She looks to structures to contain both her inexperience and the pupils' apprehensions: that will give scope for socialization and better personal relationships within the group, as well as ways of sparking motivation. Here the world of simulation and role play find their right context, so that they can emerge quite naturally for the pupil and teacher as an everyday tool, as normal as those other equally strange but accepted practices of writing on a blackboard or completing exercises in

31 rough-work books. For we are making models of reality and that has always been common to the experience of man.

There have always been pioneers in enactive processes throughout the history of education, exceptional men who believed in the experience of encouraging a self-learning process, but perhaps the explosion in curriculum development in the 1960s and 70s has thrown a new light on the way we learn and at what age. It may be that in looking at processes rather than products we can first perceive how the ground is being newly tilled.

The Active Agent

Learning is an individual act. Teaching has traditionally been a communal one. There's the rub. Knowledge needs to be made personal. The teacher or lecturer can inspire, motivate or explain. We can listen and perhaps remember a fraction but until we have talked it over and rehearsed it in action, then it is chaff to the wind. The active learner starts with experience. From a sense of wonder he is provoked to wondering, he becomes interested, curious. The experience is now toyed with, chewed over, played with. Questions have to be asked and sifted, a probing begins and at length the problem emerges. The defining of the problem is the most critical step. This will then call for skills, knowledge and techniques to explore it; it may need research, resources, specialist help. Then comes the difficulty, the moment when it will not work out. This is the moment of greatest potential learning. Somewhere here the creative moment of insight comes, a new piecing together of the fragments. The answer may still take much more hard work but the way has been shown.

Something of this process happens to us all—child and adult, whether grappling with a five-minute mathematical problem as a pupil in class or engaged on a five-year scientific piece of research. The solutions and methods are personal. They are often highly satisfying and pleasurable, giving a taste for more. But though private, there are points when in school the teacher can step in to enter the experience, especially in helping to ask the questions towards the definition of the problem and in making new associations and posing topsy-turvy dilemmas when the block comes. The more the teacher is aware of this process, the more he will trust the stumbling attempts of his pupils while not wanting to wrest the moments of insight from them. Encouragement to perseverance and to the acquisition of new skills is an essential role.

None of this is to recommend the classroom as a constant ants' nest of seething activity. Of itself frenetic busyness means nothing: making and doing are of little worth without thinking. Though there may or may not be physical activity throughout this process, the insight and active learning that we are most concerned with here are those of an inner activity—the growth of thinking, insight and active learning—the tools to make better tools. Only good interpersonal relationships generate the motivation that leads to active learning, never fear or boredom. To start from an outer world of learning and leave the relationships to look after themselves courts the disaster that has already hit many of our inner city schools. Pastoral and educational matters are both the responsibility of every individual teacher; there will be no learning without their elements being present. Whether in terms of intellectual or moral growth, mathematical or linguistic, there would seem to be a continuum, a series of stages which we mount, each in turn, that are quite independent of our physical and chronological growth, and where we may well remain. This again is highly individual and as various as our heights or complexions. Many of us remain at the stage of the concrete, where things must be seen in terms of specifics, when issues cannot be generalized or brought into the abstract. The teacher must contend with just such a spectrum of individual conceptual stages; each will determine different learning experiences apart from any stimulus the teacher initiates.

Simulation and gaming make a minor but useful contribution in just this crucial territory of new relationships. Being enjoyable and open-ended, they seem more than many other classroom methods, when rightly handled, to untap a little of the ambrosian motivation.

Activity and Enaction

Recognizing the need for a more individual active-agent learning process to be a common feature of every subject discipline, current British curriculum development schemes have pursued a policy of discovery and activity methods in their subject materials. Whether science for 13 year olds or geography for 18 year olds, the major objectives of such materials read much the same: interpreting findings critically, developing interests, attitudes and aesthetic awareness, exploring and ordering observations, developing basic concepts and logical thinking, posing questions and devising experiments or investigations to answer them, acquiring knowledge and learning skills, communicating. Objectives as these call for experiments, for the handling of apparatus and materials, for field work, for individual enquiry as well as small group or pair problem-solving. There is bound to be talk, questioning, the asking of help from the teacher, movement between work benches as more resources are called for and put into use, greater responsibility for a pupil's own learning. Such activity has always been the distinguishing feature of subjects such as physics, chemistry, biology, home economics and technology. The workshop aspect of these subjects has always been real to some extent and a source of their popularity. The new syllabuses and published materials make the content more relevant and immediate, calling for a greater personal investment in pursuing an individual enquiry rather than requiring that all the class attempts the same work together.

But increasingly a new dimension is being called for and this was rarely so prominent a feature of such materials before Schools Council and Nuffield days. This is the dimension of enaction, as well as action—an acting out of the issues involved, not only of individual discovery or enquiry. It has nothing overtly to do with theatre or drama, as traditionally conceived, although inevitably it borders on those worlds because its concerns are similar. It is primarily focused in simulating a human situation, discovering the social expectation of roles and their conflicts, trying to understand human interaction and the way human personality functions. The use of enactive ways is sought to look again at the moral and political implications of the world we are creating. *Breed or Breathe?* attempts just that.

What is beginning to happen in mathematics, science and engineering, the examination of the human communication system that lies behind all their endeavours, is now in full spate in many areas of the humanities. Most areas of the curriculum are now devoted to a greater or lesser extent to some means of examining man-in-action in his relationships, groups and social processes. All of them call for the classroom to become

The classroom as workshop: a place of talk and interaction, where knowledge is process

33 a human workshop. The processes of enaction, (often very new to teachers both young and experienced), not of instruction, are called for to facilitate this and these seem to fall into four kinds of activities.

1 *The Handling of Resources*

Tape recorders, cameras of all kinds, cine and still, record players and slide carousels are now a feature of all classes of homes as well as of classrooms. Eventually there will also be cheaper videos and synthesisers. Many of these technical gadgets are now literally child's play and the enthusiastic primary school pupil can soon become more of an expert than his teacher: certainly resource-based learning for secondary pupils is now no novelty. The eternal school anxiety is keeping equipment secure, easily available and in working order. This is why the demand for lockable specialist rooms grows, so that the individual teacher knows that he has the resources available just when required, for this is the heart of the workshop method.

    Young people rise to the challenge of utilising machinery efficiently and creatively when the project to hand gives scope and seems adult. In pairs, fours or small groups, a range of options around a stimulating theme can be self-chosen. Consumable materials can be simple. On an agreed theme one group may be making a newspaper, which involves

34 interviews, the use of a polaroid camera, drawing, typing, laying out graphics; another group may be making a tape and slides, photo-play, where either slides in abstract colours can be complementing a record of music or taped sounds, or a documentary involving real photography and interviews. Others may have an epidiascope for making a cartoon strip by way of instruction to illuminate an aspect of the theme, adding taped sounds. Models and mock-ups could be built by another group to illustrate new systems in a given area. A short cine-film or video programme may provide a term's work for other groups, perhaps exploring fantasy, or a simulated historical reconstruction, or a documentary about a local or national problem. Puppets, animation, or a duofade involving two carousels, that almost creates animation, can be used to look at such issues in different ways. All involve tape recordings that include music, sounds, poetry and quotations, as well as interviews and observations.

The learner as an active agent   Interviews are either genuine with the actual people involved, or as in the case of historical reconstructions are clearly simulated. When visuals are used, either in video or slides, there will be the need to impersonate and make convincing. In order to obtain many of the effects or create more authentic situations, other people around the school and the neighbourhood become involved. It is much better to interview real old people than to simulate. Also in the handling of materials and resources new ideas arise. Confidence grows in handling the apparatus or materials and a personal desire to do it better next time will develop.

The use of materials as well as books is common in most subject areas now as stimulus to thinking. Supplying documentary evidence in history for pupils to deduce the circumstances that gave rise to this evidence is essentially a way of entering into the feelings and needs of men from the past, and to relate them to our own emotions and behaviour. Presenting problems in geography, such as where to build new industries or towns, how to farm or what priorities to give alternative commodities equally brings home the specific and human element of the situation and removes it from generalities which are so often boring and un-

35 illuminating. More abstract materials can initiate new kinds of spatial and linguistic thinking as the work of Edward de Bono shows. Thinking is about selecting priorities, taking a broader view, being able to decide, to show judgement, understanding other points of view, working out the consequences. Using materials and resources in novel and skilful ways is essential to survival in our world, as is the sensitivity to understand how others feel.

2 *Small Group Discussions*

There have now evolved a host of ways of small group learning without using resources or apparatus and based on talk. Studies have shown the futility of whole class discussions if the fluency of every pupil is the aim. For in whole class discussions the teacher and most confident pupils talk a great deal, the hesitant say only a sentence or two and those in greatest need to begin to articulate their fumbling thoughts continue to say nothing, even if asked. For most of us do not know what we think or know until we have spoken about it. Often we discover that 'we did not know that we knew that'; frequently we discover that what we thought we knew we don't—it has never become part of our action knowledge.

In the small group there is opportunity for everyone to make a major contribution; if the range of problems and techniques vary then the range of spoken registers and responses, and so vocabulary and constructs, will be enriched. We slowly learn the need to listen, to understand more about the person opposite and to gain confidence in our own views and opinions.

It was the Schools Council Humanities Curriculum Project (1970) which first systematically attempted to make teachers more aware of group discussion processes. It is urged that all teachers attempting to use these materials should be adequately trained through an experience of the materials. Discussions can only take place in half classes, sixteen being the optimum size for effectiveness. The group will sit in a circle and evidence or stimulus is presented to them on themes chosen from a range of controversial topics, all concerning problems of our society today. But the important factor is that the teacher shall be a good chairman, should facilitate learning but not formally teach. Here is a course without instruction but with rich inputs of 'evidence' of all kinds, whether through film, outside visits, speakers or printed materials. The teacher, as a teacher must remain 'neutral'. He is not to do the pupils' thinking for them but to define the questions that they are beginning to ask. There is inevitably a long period while the pupils have to learn how to discuss, to listen, respond, begin to weigh evidence and to challenge views and accept other viewpoints.

There are other methods that the teacher can use. There is the *task group* where each group is given a small practical task and asked to problem-solve it within a time limit. It involves purposeful talk and some management. In the *brain-storming group* a theme or word, idea or problem is taken and very quickly through word association, turning the issue on its head, humour and quick-fire response, the group tries to make the decision or solve the problem in as many ways as possible, however unusual. Often in evaluation when groups pool their results the unlikely solutions may contain a grain of useful new thinking. A scribe is helpful to catch some of the ideas as they flash by in the group. In *case discussion groups* a problem about a human predicament from a newspaper, book or duplicated source is given to each group, to work out

Observation of non-verbal communication in a dialogue by two volunteers

the different possible lines of approach, ways of dealing with the issue and what the consequences of such decisions would be. Sometimes each member of the group can take on the role of individuals in the case and explore it. A development of this is the *committee group* which may be set up to determine some priorities or make a decision or report for a club, organization, or local council. In a *critical appreciation* group, experiences of poetry, listening to schools radio, music, watching a film, seeing an exhibition or assessing a visit can be discussed and appreciated by the group much more easily than by the whole class.

In all of these the students can realize from the process of pooling ideas that a wide range of responses can be valid. One may be better than another, but it will depend on the person's way of tackling the problem. Here is a ready use of language right across the entire curriculum. For there is not one subject that could not benefit from the involvement of small group work somewhere in its activities. This would be central to the instruments of policy that the Bullock Report (1975) called for in a school's concern for developing 'a language for life'.

3 The Arts as Emblematic Communications

In essence the activities of music, drama, dance, art, film, poetry and storymaking are symbolic means of giving form to our feelings. In the field of enactive education the processes of the arts are making an increasingly significant contribution. They are excellent servants in embodying an experience of any aspect of the curriculum when there is a need for it to be communicated. To sum up a body of learning in some shape, presentation, exhibition or performance and have it explained simply and imaginatively is one of the finest ways of 'testing' a group's assimilation of concepts. For in doing so it demands an act of accommodation, it pushes the learning a step further. The finding of the

37 right metaphor or form to tell others needs an embodiment of the issue's essence and a paring away of superfluous detail; this means selection. It needs symbolic action that will tell more than it says, it needs parallel forms for putting over ideas in new ways so that there is hidden illumination, it needs a framework which will be more rich than the sum of its parts. The ultimate experience of the sharing yokes the group together in ways that little else can in the classroom. Just as one of the vital roles of an English department is to make the entire school staff aware of the relationship of language and learning, so a major task of drama, art and music teachers is to help colleagues use these other media in their own specialisms when the situation is appropriate.

4 Role Play, Gaming and Simulation

So to the heart of our matter. No educational tool has developed so rapidly in the last ten years as the uses of these techniques. These are important new ways of examining human behaviour; they transcend any subject barrier because every curriculum subject in the end must have a human dimension. These are techniques also which provide a structure to which the insecure teacher and the inexperienced pupil can steady themselves while gaining confidence in enactive processes. Having set them in their broad context of active learning, we need now to examine them at work in their exploration of human relationships.

References

Barnes, D., *From Communication to Curriculum*, Penguin Education 1976
Bono, E. de, *Teaching Thinking*, Maurice Temple Smith, 1976
Britton, J., *Language and Learning*, Penguin Education 1970
Bruner, J. S., Jolly, A., & Sylva, K. (eds.), *Play: its role in development and evolution*, Penguin 1976
Department of Education and Science, *A Language for Life: Report of the Committee of Inquiry*, H.M.S.O. 1975
Fines, J. & Verrier, R., *The Drama of History*, New University Education, 1974
Gibson, T., *Resources and the teacher*, Pitman Educational Library 1975
Holt, J., *How Children Learn*, Penguin Education 1970
Hunt, A., *Hopes for Great Happenings: Alternatives in Education and Theatre*, Eyre Methuen 1976
Leeds University Institute of Education, *The Objectives of Teacher Education*, National Foundation for Educational Research 1973
Rogers, C. R., *Freedom to Learn*, Charles E. Merrill, U.S.A. 1969
Stenhouse, L., *The Humanities Project—an introduction*, Heinemann Educational 1970
Storr, A., *The Dynamics of Creation*, Secker & Warburg 1972

4

Beginnings

Warm-ups and Ice-breakers

The leader always needs to keep in mind the function of warm-up activities. These exercises can provide an excellent means of breaking the ice, of shaking away the immediate previous experiences the group has been subjected to, of generating some fun and energy and claiming involvement from the whole class. They are simple, demand no factual learning and give a good opportunity for developing talk and spontaneity. But they can be self-defeating. Some pupils may find them alienating and purposeless, especially when over-used. This may be in part because they themselves are threatened or insecure in the new activity, but partly also because the leader has not been able to move easily from the exercise directly into the main matter of his theme or materials: the ice may be well broken and the leader has missed all opportunities to take the plunge. The class not only want to feel the relevance of the warm-up but somewhere along the line its purpose needs to be made explicit. It is this second function which is often neglected. Each of these exercises has deeper possibilities than only warm-up; they are often microcosms of broader issues. The group needs to understand the meaning of the activity and then relax more fully into it for the warm-up to become more effective.

Λ further danger is that although some groups may at first need to spend quite a time on such acclimatization activities, they need increasingly to graduate to more substantial fare, otherwise the work becomes pointless. The lesson or session may be all preparation and promise and no fulfilment. Five minutes spent on one or two such exercises will soon prove sufficient for many groups. What follows here is just a taster of a whole range of such materials; books of games are now

39 legion. However, these are our favourites which we use most regularly and they have survived most classroom situations. They come from a wide variety of sources and only one or two are original; their common feature is that they can all be undertaken simply with chairs and desks and are focused in talk. They require no moving about and aim to be supportive to the teacher of any subject discipline as distinct from those exercises involving a great deal of movement as in drama or English. They should be adapted to the leader's style.

1 Talking him down

Everybody has a partner, who is both close to and facing him or her. Holding eye contact the whole time, both are asked to talk to each other at the same time about a given topic for a given period, initially of thirty seconds, then a minute. The aim is to keep on talking at all costs and to make the other person dry up. No physical contact must be made, only talk used. A player should not hear a word that the other person is saying but must concentrate on his own story. A good starting topic is 'Everything that happened to you from the time you woke up this morning.' Other suggestions are: 'Tell your favourite fairy story, with as much expression and animation as possible'; 'Be a travelling salesman

Learning
through
communication

trying to sell some kind of product'; 'Persuade the other person to adopt a belief you hold most dear—soapbox style.' The topic should be an easy one that can be done immediately out of the top of the pupils' heads.

This is an excellent starter and needs vigorous setting-up. It is brief—one thirty second and one minute examples are enough. It makes a lot of noise, generates laughter; people can overcome their initial apprehensions in the racket and soon get tired of the shouting. It can lead quite naturally into something quieter. Neither player hears the other; there is no interaction, no dialogue, so no relationship. The leap can be made to real life situations where without a give and take of attitude and position in an argument, without listening and response, there can be no useful contact.

2. Colour clash

Players work in pairs, each partner choosing a different colour which he might regard as his favourite. Given a time limit of several minutes, each has to listen to the other and try to persuade him that his own colour is far better and is one that should be adopted. Any arguments or means of persuasion can be used.

This sounds straightforward but many groups find that as they try to persuade the other person, they become more convinced of the validity of their own colour; then more complex arguments are generated. Colour is most personal and there can often be rich material to be used. In examining what happened in the pair we often find that by taking a fixed line of argument and knowing that the other's attitude is unchangeable we only reinforce our stand: this results in a deadlock. Other pairs, however, may use flattery, bribery and more subtle means of persuasion than confrontation, which can all be further explored and illustrated.

3. Gentle persuasion

Work in pairs and decide who is A and who is B.

(a) A sits on a chair and B has to stand up. Within two minutes B has to use any means whatsoever, except physical violence, to persuade A to give up his chair so that B can sit on it. Pool back results and the ways it was tackled.

(b) Now A has to do the persuading. He has to imagine that he has some unusual attribute or quality and has to persuade B, who will be full of doubt and questions, of its truthfulness. A could choose a magic toe nail which tingled when it detected lies, or glasses that allowed him to see what others were thinking.

(c) First A and then B could make an attempt to use some of this battery of persuasive means to tackle something more real.

    (i) persuade your parent to turn the TV over to a programme that you want to watch

    (ii) persuade your brother/sister to lend you the thing he/she treasures most

    (iii) persuade your busy friend to stand for the job of secretary of your youth club

    (iv) persuade your father to increase your pocket money to cope with inflation

    (v) persuade the dinner lady to give you a second helping of the pudding you like most

41 (vi) persuade your grandmother/grandfather who lives with you to go away for the weekend at the same time as your parents are away, so that you can have a party

(vii) persuade your form teacher to sponsor you generously at the Charity School Walk

(viii) persuade the bus conductor to let you travel home even though you have no money.

These exercises call for more ingenuity and invention. They aim within the pressure of limited time to cause the persuader to push his ideas through, to embellish them and if they are not convincing to try another tack. All the different means of persuasion need to be explored here in pooling back, and new ones tried. The doubters in both cases have to respond appropriately and parry the proposals because they will know the aim of the persuader. The group can decide which ways of persuasion they found most effective and which were the most inappropriate. Clearly, listening is involved.

4 *Quarrels*

Work in pairs, decide who is A and who is B. The first situation starts with A saying 'No you didn't', B replying 'Oh, yes I did' and quickly leading into an argument about an obvious cause for disagreement. The situation must develop and not continue at a 'No you didn't' 'Yes I did' level. On the second time round, B starts off with 'No you didn't' and so on reversing quickly. No time is given for preparation; the players must start immediately the situation is given, picking up clues and cues as to whom they are imagining that they are. Situations can be anywhere; on top of a bus, in a shop, in a school corridor, in the street, at breakfast table, in a fairground. After several attempts of a minute or so each, try some handicaps:

'Advocates' calls for quick thinking as a warm-up to looking at a case study in roles

(a) Clasp each other's wrists or hold hands during the encounter.
(b) Argue without words, only in mime.
(c) Argue with eyes closed.
(d) Sit on your hands during the confrontation.
(e) Stand or sit as straight as a board.

> The aim here is to generate easy talk and to encourage a quick appraisal of the situation where no information is given. The aggressive framework helps the scenario to develop very quickly, especially after the first attempt. All the handicaps are to concentrate on making pupils aware of our total involvement in interaction and not just talk; by isolating faculties their contribution can be reflected on.

5 Communications

A series of short pair exercises to explore our means of communicating.

(a) A and B sit facing each other. A is explaining the working of an imagined machine in front of him when the leader calls 'change' or makes an agreed noise, like sounding a bell or cymbal; both players then continue in gobbledegook/gibberish nonsense patter, as if nothing had happened. They revert to English when the bell sounds again, back to gobbledegook when it sounds once more and so forth.

(b) A and B sit back to back, heads are not to be twisted around but must remain looking in opposite directions. They talk together either discussing the machine and how it was invented or more personally, perhaps what they did over the weekend.

(c) A and B sit face to face, with eyes closed and continue a conversation.

(d) A and B sit face to face but cannot speak or hear. B has a problem and tries to convey it to A by mime and A attempts to help.

(e) A and B sit facing each other. A is a rather deaf young person in a busy post office with a long queue; he wants to send a parcel to America but does not know about the customs declaration form. What happens?

(f) A and B sit face to face and hold hands. Without using any words B tries to express a need and A responds to it.

> As with the handicaps in 'Quarrels', the aim here is to help the players become aware of the contribution of non-verbal dimensions of communication, as well as those of intonation in talk as well as its content. After each exercise they could talk together in pairs about their feelings during it, how each differs from the last, what was most difficult, where communication broke down. When A was the deaf young person was he treated as if he were old or foolish? At the end the leader could ask which of the senses or means of communication they would most hate to lose. The objective here is not to gain consensus but to see how interrelated and important they all are.

6. Touch code

A and B face each other. Both imagine that they are deaf and dumb and close their eyes as if they were blind too. The situation is that they meet in a street and A has a need which he attempts to communicate with B through the sense of touch. B responds with advice through touch. Perhaps the issue was where to find a library, a bus to a certain place or wanting to know the time. Whether these work or not, the same exploration can be made about our own and society's codes and taboos

43 with regard to touch. Many people dislike touching; why? This may well lead on to a discussion of different national customs, the French with their kissing, Arabs with close standing, or how children are treated and when one ceases to be a child.

7. *Listening*

The group works in pairs, A and B.

(a) The leader calls all the As to him and tells them, so that the Bs cannot overhear, that they are feeling worried that nobody likes them. They feel depressed and want to talk with someone. All the Bs are then called to the leader who tells them that they have had a most dreadful morning; they have had a row with their parents, were held up on the bus or tube, were late for school or work. A is B's friend and he needs to tell her all about it. The two of them now meet. What happens?

(b) Now the leader calls the Bs to him and tells them that they each have a problem that is weighing them down and that they *must* talk about it. While they work it out, As are called to the leader and told that this time, without in any way making the other person aware of it, they are to try to say as little as humanly possible, after some initial greeting like, 'Hello John, you look very glum; what's up?' They can nod, smile, look sad, say 'hmmmm' and phrases like 'go on' or 'why was that?' but nothing else. They must see if in non-verbal ways they can urge A to continue without saying anything at all.

> The objective here is to illustrate the value of creative listening. The evaluation should be made after the second exercise to see the difference and talk about feelings. In forcing A to be silent he can also focus more on B's non-verbal signs of distress as well as what he says. This model of using a negative approach to highlight a positive also demonstrates that briefing players secretly and differently has infinite uses and adaptations.

(c) A further dimension can be added by briefing A with a problem that needs a great deal of listening and support; this can be done by producing a duplicated slip with brief details. The Bs are all now privately briefed to give an initial strong response of concern and interest. But after three or four minutes they are slowly to disengage their interest and without making it too obvious 'switch off'—not listen or pay attention to the other—even if looking directly at the As. They are to lose themselves in their own thoughts and see what happens.

> The intention here is to see what stratagems the enactor with the problem uses, if any, to try to regain the other's attention; and to explore the feelings of the person with the problem of his rejection and the lack of concern by others. Young people frequently detect this switching off in adults talking with them and some techniques worked out by the group to regain involvement might be helpful.

8. *Word Games*

Groups of four and more sit in a circle.

(a) *Story Telling* Each person speaks one word only, passing round the circle, the next immediately following with another single word to carry on the sense, building what will most probably turn out to be a most unlikely story. Speed makes for fun here. Try setting up a rhythm beat on a cymbal which beats for each new word. Stories can also be told by giving a sentence or so leaving the narrative suspended half way through a sentence for the next to continue.

(b) *Word Associations* First person starts with a noun, say 'desk', second person quickly says the first association he makes with that, say 'books', a third adds, say, 'stories' and so on. A variant here is for the player to add a rhythm after the last word and the new word, with clapping—twice on knees, twice in the air, then two silent beats. So—desk—tap-tap, clap-clap, rest-rest—desk—books; tap-tap, clap-clap, rest-rest; books—stories, tap-tap, etc.

(c) *Word Dissociations* Same pattern with rhythms or not but within reason the word following must have no immediate associations with the last word at all—more difficult than it sounds.

(d) *Reversibles* Players spell their first name backwards. Then they try to make up a dictionary definition of the new word.

These can help for quickness of thinking and spontaneity but also lead into looking at different associations which words have for us. Players can react to some of the words and how some are associated with significant moments of experience which always remain with them.

9 Babel

In pairs using only nonsense words, gibberish/gobbledegook (not foreign ones), using consecutive letters of the alphabet, or consecutive numbers, take it in turns, with interruptions and interaction, to—(a) have a quarrel (b) tell a funny story (c) break bad news (d) propose (e) try to borrow money (f) confess you've done something wrong (g) pass on some scandal (h) demonstrate a new gadget or machine you have just made. This can be enjoyable and exhausting. Groups then might want to talk about intonation and context, about understanding foreign language, about non-verbal communications. The gibberish can help some hesitant talkers but it can inhibit others further.

10 Commentaries

These can all be single person activities. Players pretend they have a microphone or a telephone and give a running commentary into it like a radio sports commentator.

(a) one-sided telephone conversations—infinite variety here—including crossed lines.

(b) driving a car, giving commentary of what the driver is doing, with all the sounds of the car's operations, and what he can see out of the window.

(c) commentary of working at a bench, making noise of all the tools and the mechanical gadget you are making.

(d) giving a running commentary as if you were present at some imagined and well-documented event, like the Fire of London, or San Francisco earthquake, or an air raid in the last war.

(e) giving a running commentary of the teacher or leader who mimes a game of tennis for the class, as if the player is a foreign radio correspondent with a strong accent.

(f) giving a suave, polished commentary of one of the girls of the group walking up and down as if modelling for a House of Fashion.

(g) giving a commentary while washing a car or an elephant or a baby, or making pastry.

Some of these the leader might ask to hear individually, but generally they are private events to try to generate a speech flow, some spontaneity and clear strong diction. Many pupils enjoy this as their contribution gets lost in the general hubbub; others tend to mutter into their hands and opt out as there is no interaction.

11 *Starters*
The work is in pairs. In turn each is given a one line starter and perhaps the situation for it. The second person must pick up the situation immediately the first has spoken. By changing the situation the starter line can be used in various ways:
(a) 'Is he still breathing?' On the pavement: emergency ward 10: in the jungle.
(b) 'Sorry no foreigners'.
(c) 'Why don't you get your hair cut?'
(d) 'Has it got two heads or is that three?'
(e) 'They're a menace; it's time they did something about it'.
(f) 'Now we're done for, I forgot to bring it with me'.
(g) 'Where on earth has my wooden leg gone?'

> Each situation need only be followed for a minute or two but it gives a good opportunity to improvise and back up the other person to make it work. Sometimes amazingly detailed plotting comes out of this.

12 *Alibis*
Groups of six or more. One person elects to be the detective who stands in the middle of the group. He thinks up a crime and states where and when it was committed. He is now going to cross question one of the suspects. The whole group acts corporately as that one suspect, remembering anything that any one of its representatives says. The detective turns to a member and begins his cross examination; then he quickly switches to another and another, as if they were one person, so continuity is important. The detective aims to catch out the suspect and break his alibi when he contradicts himself or forgets what he has said. Then that person becomes the detective and the situation starts again: '. . . . where were you on the night of the murder?'. . .

> This is as much a testing of the detective as the suspect to keep the questioning quick-fire. It demands memory work and invention to keep the situation plausible and not to become ludicrous. It can easily lead into any law and justice issue.

13 *Advocates*
Again groups of six or more. It is another catching-out game. In the middle is a prosecutor who is trying to elicit facts from the accused. But the accused, the person the prosecutor is looking at and talking to at any time, never speaks. Instead, his advocate always talks and this is the person standing on the accused's left, who of course will be different every time the prosecutor faces a different accused. When anyone makes a mistake he substitutes and becomes the new prosecutor.

> Again this depends on the prosecutors keeping the questioning at a brisk pace. It is fun when done quickly and is a test of reactions and concentration.

A problem at work reflects a 'real concern' in a youth club situation

14 *Magic Shop*

In pairs, A is the shopkeeper, B wants to buy some personal qualities like 'beauty' or 'wisdom' or 'good health'. He has to exchange them for some other quality like wealth or good looks or laughter. The shopkeeper will want to haggle and barter. Perhaps 'wealth' is not enough for 'wisdom', maybe 'hearing' will have to go. B must decide if he could tolerate that and if not, make alternative proposals.

> Some groups take this in a very happy-go-lucky way and it becomes just a simple shop exercise. Other groups take it much more earnestly and weigh up what qualities they genuinely would be prepared to bargain for and what they would be prepared to give up. It can give rise to some very profound discussion if followed through. It can also be usefully revealing of attitudes and values and provides a base for further work.

15 *In others' shoes*

Groups sit in fours, A B C D. Ideally players should not know each other, so this is very suitable for a training course or residential experience with new members. There are no allocated roles to start with.

(a) A now interviews B and C interviews D. They do this in some depth and spend at least 10 minutes over it, asking about background, biography, beliefs, interests etc. The second part is more difficult. A is now going to imagine that, having interviewed B he now actually is B and that C actually now is D—even though members may be of both sexes. Now D is going to interview A and B is going to interview C in their new roles. Everything A and C say must be either what they have been told or what they imagine that B and D would do or say if they were still there. Not only are the attitudes and information important but all the non-verbal communication too; how they would sit, or use their hands or the facial expressions they would use. They must do their best really to climb inside the other person using whatever cues and clues they have gleaned. When the leader declares time up, A and C should go back to their original partners to see how close some of their invented replies were to the truth. Now the whole exercise could be reversed with B and D undertaking the initial interviewing.

(b) A variation on this is to play it only in pairs. After A has interviewed B he becomes B and then B interviews 'himself' (i.e. A). Clearly B can use this not only to see what A made of him but also, because he knows all the areas that A did not ask about, to see what assumptions A will make when he asks him. This can be very revealing for B. It can also be hurtful if A is not sensitive for there is a double action going on in all this for the Bs often probe As to explore their own self image and how it is communicated. It can lead to some very real expression of feeling afterwards and can be very reassuring.

(c) A different approach is for the leader to choose several topics in the area he is wanting the group to explore and pose these to everyone in pairs. The aim is to see if there is any genuine point of disagreement. It may be as simple as seeing what different football teams or pop stars the other supports, or more importantly finding attitudes about a range of current national issues. The two should explore any points of difference. Then the leader will ask everyone to reverse roles and discuss the opposite point of view as convincingly as possible, picking holes in their partner's (i.e. their own) attitude.

These are all more probing exercises where there is less pretence and more genuine empathetic response from a 'real' stimulus. They are usually enjoyable because most people like the undivided attention that any interviewer usually gives. This needs to be well discussed afterwards in the pairs or fours to give an opportunity for the real feelings that will have been involved during the exercise to be explored.

16 *Broken roles*

These situations can be taken at a fun level or can lead into interactions that can become quite serious. In pairs or small groups a problem is posed where the role of one of the players is different from what we and society would expect.

(a) A father/mother needs to borrow money from a teenage son/daughter.

(b) A sea captain who is sea sick.

(c) A judge caught stealing in a supermarket.

(d) A soldier who refuses to fight.

(e) the doctor who is always complaining that something is wrong with him.

In discussion afterwards the valuable issue to explore is why such situations seem especially comic or alarming, whether it is right that this should be so and what burdens of guilt or special temptation certain roles have implicitly built into them.

17 *Viewpoints*

To prepare for a deeper exploration or more detailed simulation it is often helpful to take five to ten different aspects of the problem and let everybody sample them for 30 seconds to a minute each in a quick range of roles. Then when they take the one role that might be allocated to them their responses will have been alerted to the wider issues. It does not matter how stereotyped or superficial the responses are initially; it is the cumulative effect and the wakening of interest that is important in the wider social context.

(a) A motorway is to be built: how might the following react—two farmers, two shopkeepers, two unemployed navvies, two conservationists, two garage mechanics, two councillors, two to-be evicted tenants, two charladies, two senior citizens?

(b) Civil war is to be declared in 1642: how might the following react—two young sons of a parliamentarian, two elderly king's men, two beggars, two shopkeepers, two courtiers, two puritans, two of the landed gentry, two Scotsmen, two scholars?

(c) King Duncan has just been murdered in Macbeth's castle: how might these react—two of Duncan's servants, two ambitious warrior lords, two of Lady Macbeth's maids, two newspaper reporters of the *Dunsinane Echo,* Hecate and her mother, Macbeth's sons (with L. C. Knights' pardon), the porter and his crony?

(d) Trouble at mill: what happens between the following—boss sacking old workman, employee asking for more money, new employee being shown around, employee being offered promotion, planning initiation ceremony for new apprentices, workers trying to draw up list of improvements, disagreement with shop steward?

The aim here is quickness of response and a preliminary overview

49 which draws upon unrealised existing vague knowledge before new information is fed in. If some of the situations are comic this is all to the good in generating enjoyment before the topic buries everyone in over-earnestness.

18 *We are many*
This can be played in pairs or in small groups. Rather like the last exercise it aims to move quickly over a range of situations but each might run for a slightly longer period, perhaps two minutes. The intention is to give evidence of how we react during a day to the range of roles we come into contact with and to show that there is a consistency behind all those contacts if there is to be integrity and authenticity. It could be that each group or pair has an observer to write down examples of our adaptability and our consistency. One player in the pair or group must take the central role throughout e.g.
(a) school pupil
   (i) with parent at breakfast time
   (ii) with brother or sister who wants to borrow some of your clothes
   (iii) with your form teacher who wants to see you about your work
   (iv) with your friend to plan what you will do tonight
   (v) with the head teacher who has called you into his office because of poor reports of lateness and inattentiveness
   (vi) with the youth leader who wants you to represent the club in an activity you are keen on
(b) mother
   (i) with son/daughter at breakfast time
   (ii) with tradesman who overcharges
   (iii) with a workmate whilst doing your part-time job
   (iv) with a rare visitor (husband's boss, vicar, prim aunt) you are entertaining to tea
   (v) with your husband over the evening meal
   (vi) with your closest friend who calls in to see you.
(c) father
   (i) with wife at breakfast time
   (ii) with a workmate while working
   (iii) with your boss of whom you are asking a favour
   (iv) with your best friend who is sharing your hobby
   (v) with your child's form teacher on parents' day at school
   (vi) with your son/daughter coming home late

This always produces a very rich discussion and evaluation. The leader can ask, is it right to adapt to different company? Should we always be ourselves, come what may? What is 'ourselves'? How do we make people different from ourselves feel at home or comfortable with us? What were the differences both observed and felt within that range of situations? When were you most yourselves and when least? Why and does it matter?

19 *Animal crackers*
This may come after one or two other pair exercises and when there is some trust in the group. A is asked now to imagine that B is going to have a film made about his life. But it is to be a Walt Disney film and B will be personified as either an animal, fish or bird though B's own voice will be used. Decide on the animal or whatever and then introduce B in this new

50 guise to other members of the group, accounting for some of his typical animal antics and foibles. Reverse roles and try again.

This can be fun and quite revealing, but could raise difficulties if done with an unsympathetic group. With some groups perhaps a stipulation could be that only an attractive animal can be chosen to 'sell' the film.

20 *Mixed doubles*
Groups of four are needed. A and B each have an inner voice who sits to one side behind them and speaks their thoughts, often after the person opposite has spoken. Attitudes expressed can be very different from these thoughts, especially if the two people playing the same role share similar views and tastes. After each exercise the speaker and inner thoughts should reverse roles. Situations can be superficial or fun: for example, two women meet to show off new hats to each other, or one visits the other to admire new home decorations, or two men boast to each other in a pub. Alternatively the situations can aim to probe more sensitively how we interact with others: a teenager trying to express a problem to a parent; a teacher trying to encourage and reassure a pupil; two acquaintances trying to develop a friendship; a disagreement with an angry opponent who has done something foolish and is trying to justify himself.

In each case the outer voices A and B have to take their interaction slower than usual and wait to listen to their inner voices, having already listened to the outer voice of the other. It is a much more conscious process and needs both concentration and practice but can be rewarding when it moves on from caricature.

21 *Circular role play* This requires six to sixteen participants playing in pairs. Half the group sit on chairs in a circle and their partners stand behind them. The chair is identified with a certain clear role. Whoever sits in that particular chair takes on that role. To help in remembering this, an appropriate hat can mark the chair—cloth cap, bowler, policeman's helmet, flowery hat, peaked cap etc.—or newspapers folded up into sailor-boat style hat with the role written boldly in felt tip pen across the front. A situation is then given to a group. If the numbers are large perhaps it is a committee meeting to plan, say a village garden fete, a youth club fund-raising scheme, a finance committee making cuts in local spending. If it is just three roles then perhaps parent, teenager and grandparent meet to plan a family holiday, or teacher and parent together help a teenager make decisions about the future. In each case the person standing behind the chair is the 'thought man' and can advise the chair-sitter on what to say by whispering to him and putting forward points of view. The person in the chair has to carry out these actions as if they were his own wishes. However, the leader can make three alterations to the enaction, perhaps by using a whistle or some mode of calling; the changes must then be made speedily and with no obvious interruption to the flow of the situation.
(i) one blast or 'change': all people standing up change places with their partners sitting down, hats changing heads
(ii) two blasts or 'left': all those sitting on chairs move round one chair to their left, leaving their hats behind them
(iii) three blasts or 'special': two chair-sitters only, whom the leader points to, change position leaving hats behind. These will often be the main protagonists at that moment but it could be that a speaker in a lively role exchanges with a role that has not been opened up.

51   This game is usually good fun, often hilarious, and helps to develop a responsive group feeling; it is also a way of involving the quieter, less forthcoming members. Clearly it seems superficial with all the chopping and changing, yet groups can gain an understanding of how different players in the same role can transform the nature and direction of decision-making. It gives hope to those who feel that personality transcends role and that we are not all socially determined.

22 Waiting room

This works in groups of four or five. Each player has to imagine a strong role, like a tramp, city gent, charlady or bluestocking and work out some reason why that person should be waiting somewhere. But he must not make that explicit at all—such as waiting for a dentist, for a train to arrive, a dog or cat to be vetted, car to be cleaned or repaired, the result of an interview, at the gates of heaven, for a bus, or a food queue during the war. The players must assume that each person is there for the same reason as they are. The aim is to keep a straight face and make the others laugh without disclosing the reason for being there. Each can ask questions of the others in their mistaken assumptions and react feelingly to the opening news that 'It won't be long now—only three minutes to go' as the starter.

 This is mainly an entertainment but can be seen as a test of ingenuity to keep up the differing roles and confuse the situation without breaking into laughter. The tension of the waiting helps to make it work.

23 Interview

(a) Of all enactive processes, preparing young school leavers for interviews is the one most commonly undertaken and most clearly relevant, with the need for rehearsal obvious. The skill lies in the interviewer. At first the teacher might set up the situation in the centre of the room with the whole class as observers, asked to look at particular aspects of the interviewing situation. The interviewer (the teacher) certainly needs to prepare, especially if it is to be a young person in the role. Sometimes panels of two, three or four interviewers are best, as in real life, with a chairman appointed, to work out beforehand how they should question and what they are looking for. An outside school visit of any kind is bound to involve seeing people in work situations beforehand; the class can be asked to look at certain workers in action, observe the range of skills necessary, and prepare to select a suitable candidate. When observers involved in the selection report back, they should be trained to be constructive rather than the opposite. The candidate or interviewee could have an opportunity to try the situation again to see if certain social skills can be improved, perhaps after the teacher has given some training to the entire class: certain speech mannerisms, ways of sitting, lack of eye contact, gestures, knowledge of what to wear, can all be easily improved without undermining self-esteem.

(b) A development of this, after initial training, is to set up a number of panels consisting of three or four interviewers who are looking for an employee; each panel is from a different firm. There would be the same number of interviewees as panels, say four with a class group of twenty and four pupils to a panel. Over a double period each panel would pool the preparation which had been done for their homework, then in turn interview each of the four applicants who could move from panel to panel every fifteen minutes. The panel would finally select one of the four applicants for its job. In the meantime the applicants can decide which of the four firms impressed them most, remembering that an interview is a two way selection process. If the jobs are very diverse the hope is that the same person would not be chosen by each panel.

In this way all the class gain useful experience and both interviewer and interviewee have increased awareness from comparing the situations.

(c) A kind of interviewing at a different level is that of the media man who interviews members of the public for 'man in the street' responses to issues or for some reason such as winning the pools, success at sport or examination, or sudden fame. These are easier for the players initially if everybody plays himself. A interviews B on what he thinks about school, sport, parents, homework and may need to report back briefly. B could then interview A who might be in a role like headmaster, parent, policeman, schoolkeeper on these or other topics.

(d) Authority interviews are easily set up and enable the teacher to see how naively the pupils perceive authority figures. Again there is scope here for some facts being fed in. Some examples are: teacher/pupil, parent/child, employer/employee, shopkeeper/buyer, doctor/patient.

(e) Another kind of interviewing again is the sudden arrival of an intelligent and English-speaking space man from another galaxy who wants to have certain points explained to him which he has discovered since landing. This can be about any aspect of society, jobs, roles, how things work, institutions, customs and so on. It is an excellent way of probing assumptions and questioning attitudes.

24 *Mood swings*

These are all worked in pairs.

(a) The As are privately briefed to take up a certain mood quite strongly, imagining what had been the cause of it—cheerful, sad, angry, friendly. Bs are privately briefed to be neutral, pick up A's mood and then to echo it, so they also become sad, cheerful and so on.

(b) Bs are now briefed to take up a mood strongly. As are detailed to go in, discover the mood and take on the opposite mood through interaction and see what happens.

Both these need to be talked about and feelings examined. If this works at all, it is worth examining what is happening here as it may throw some light on the processes by which our self-opinions are formed.

(c) A is privately briefed to think of a strong feeling like fear, courage, loyalty, hate, or joy and to imagine a problem situation that might give rise to this. In setting up the problem with B, A does everything in his power to push the feeling on to B so that he becomes fearful, courageous, loyal or whatever.

(d) B is now privately briefed to have some kind of minor practical problem, such as that he cannot do his homework, has broken, or lost something important, or cut his hand. but he is also briefed to praise, flatter and boost A for his help in discreet but positive ways, not forgetting A's physical, intellectual or social skills. A is separately informed that B has some kind of problem and needs help, but that A does so only reluctantly.

These can be useful exercises to explore how we are in part made by other people's needs and how far we are prepared to go along with them bearing in mind our own needs.

Such situations lie behind much great drama and fiction. In these simpler forms here they can be enacted in pairs or in threes. If in threes, then the two conflicting roles need to embody the different demands that are pulling the central enactor in different directions. What resolution can there be?

(a) conflicts between work and public roles with domestic and private roles:
> (i) The father/husband's work is taking up too much time. His wife/ children need the money but now see far too little of him. Similar situations with a working mother.
> (ii) A shop steward's family cannot cope with financial problems while his firm/factory is out on unofficial strike.
> (iii) A teacher's son/daughter is a pupil in the school where he/she is having great discipline problems.

(b) conflicts between work roles and belief roles:
> (i) The scientist who can no longer reconcile his knowledge with the doctrines of his religious faith.
> (ii) The factory worker who is a convinced pacifist and discovers his firm's insecticides are now being used in weapons for germ warfare.
> (iii) The social worker who feels she cannot desert her clients and strike yet is called to do so by her union of which she is a loyal member.

(c) conflicts between work roles and friendship roles:
> (i) The factory worker foreman who has to discipline and dismiss an employee who is a great friend.
> (ii) The political leader who persuades his best friend to join his party for the votes it will bring but which will be hurtful to the best interests of his friend's reputation.

(d) conflicts between social roles and work roles:
> (i) The councillor who is also the leading local builder and is responsible for placing tenders for civic work.
> (ii) The magistrate who is also the local banker and has access to confidential information which contradicts statements made in evidence.
> (iii) The voluntary director of a major charity which depends primarily for its funds on the profits of the sale of spa water which as Health Inspector he has just found to be contaminated.

There is rich material here, highly dramatic, beyond just a warming-up exercise, though they do make stimulating starters for a thoughtful group. Many could be elaborated, more carefully set up and with a whole detailed scenario. They rightly lead us into the whole arena of the making of simulation and games. It is to those processes that we now turn.

Sources of further practical openings and starters:
Krupar K. R. *Communication Games,* Free Press, New York, Collier Macmillan, London, 1973.
Casciani J. W. *Speak for Yourselves,* George Harrap, 1966.
Burton E. J. *Teaching English Through Self-Expression,* Evans, 1949.
Way B. *Development through Drama,* Longman, 1967.
Day C. *Drama for Middle and Upper Schools,* Batsford, 1975.
Self D. *Talk: a practical guide to oral work in the secondary school,* Ward Lock, 1976.

5

The Making of Games and Simulations

There is no structure which, once discovered, cannot be represented by a model of some kind which shows its mode of being. From galaxies to atoms and genes, from soil erosion and gas formation to the workings of the human brain, a symbolic representation can be made that approximates to these processes in action. Before us on the workbench, aspects of astronomy, chemistry, physics, biology, geography can be understood in metaphor or simulation and their mysteries retreat while their marvels remain. Human processes are no exception. However multiple and open-ended are the choices and pressures, the only way to fulfil the needs of our inner selves is through interaction with other people; each society embodies these in different forms of cooperation and social agreement. To understand these patterns in action we need not only to have them explained but to experience them in rehearsal. The urgency and pleasureableness of children's dramatic games have their pulse from the need to come to terms with experiences, fantasies and feelings that are still bewildering and only understood in part, and to prepare for what is known to be coming. As adults we rehearse, in the theatre of our minds if not in fact, the interview or meeting we are about to attend, the dispute we anticipate, the party we are going to. In more concrete terms, we go over the wedding ceremony the night before, market our soap powders in country mansions on weekend training schemes, groom hostesses, waiters and politicians, train mechanics, surgeons, chefs and firemen all in mock-ups of the real thing. Who can deny the world's a stage?

It is important that we discover ways in our classrooms and clubs to engage young people's feelings in an attempt to understand that the whole world is at stake in the quality of human interaction; and that to

55 help improve this we must be involved in social change. To these ends the structures of simulation and human gaming provide a positive and helpful tool and technique.

Playing the Game

Definitions and differences: In their pristine form *games* are often highly structured, self-contained metaphors with little or no role playing and where chance predominates. Their overt content will usually not be the source of educational activity. *Monopoly* is a classic board game; after years of play, especially without any knowledgeable post-play discussion, it may teach little explicitly about property development and high finance but more about competition, counting and arbitrary chance. *Starpower*, devised by Dr. Gary Shirts in America, is a most popular example of human gaming. Players are each given a number of coloured counters, each colour having a different value. They are traded over a series of rounds of play in order to obtain the highest possible score. Soon the players become divided into three groups: the circles with the upper scores, the squares with the middle scores and the triangles with the lower scores. They are then allowed to trade as groups or individuals and find increasing difficulty in moving out of groups without breaking the rules; during the process, strong feelings are often generated. The overt aim, the acquisition of counters and winning the game, becomes immaterial, especially when in post-play discussion players learn that despite what they were told the counters were rigged and the upper, middle and lower groups already determined. It is the experience of the feelings of the players in action that becomes important. The implications of the game extend beyond that of social class attitudes to any disparate distribution of resources, whether in personal terms of intelligence or national terms of world power. *Breed or Breathe?* described earlier, is in essence a complicated game structure but there the overt content is also educational.

Simulations are simplified patterns of human interactions or social processes where the players participate in roles. They are usually more open-ended than games, less bedevilled by chance, more concerned with the quality of human encounter. A classic model is Shelter's *Tenement*, which deals with the problem of inadequate housing. Half the group of players are tenants of a multi-let old house living in rooms or small flats inadequately maintained; most tenants also have family or individual problems. The other half of the group are professional workers in a range of social agencies who, seated at desks around the room, represent the Department of Social Security, the landlord, the Voluntary Housing Aid Association and so forth. Everybody is supplied with a simply expressed factual sheet of background information about his needs or his agency. The aim of the simulation is for the tenants to try to gain help and the agencies to assist them in as far as their resources and professional limits allow. There is no further structure, except for some chance cards; what happens depends on the way the players take their roles. They all interact as in any normal situation and may have to queue to get into a busy agency. *Who Cares?* described earlier is a simulation with a similar structure but a different content.

However, in practice, the difference between games and simulations is not worth a further thought. Often they are indistinguishable and some people use the words interchangeably. Some simulations use a game format like *The Dream Game* described earlier and some games use a simulation format like many of those exercises in *Beginnings*. In common they are concerned with revealing systems and interactions as analogues which focus on some simplified aspect of behaviour, cutting out the complexity but engaging emotions as well as powers of thinking.

Relevance: There are now hundreds of simulations and games available for purchase in Britain and America, touching every possible area of the curriculum and catering for all age groups. But none was designed to fit a particular class or group. These published materials provide excellent models or starters but in the end one needs to devise one's own, however simple, if they are to serve particular needs. If the pupils do not feel that this is an integral part of normal activity then they dismiss it as an activity for an occasional rainy day or Friday afternoon pastimes. The simulation needs to grow out of ongoing work, either encapsulating what has been learned so far, as a kind of revision or even assessment of understanding, or preparing for what is to come. The objectives of the leader in wanting to use it at this stage and at a particular time must be clear.

Plausibility: Simulations and games are time-consuming activities. There are enormous decisions of priorities to be made under curriculum pressures. The leader new to such processes, having felt that he can justify the time thus spent, wants to know if a particular simulation or game works. He will need to do some preliminary investigation. This can be done in several ways.

(a) It is always recommended that a beginner tries out the simulation first, perhaps having played it on a teachers' course or with colleagues. It may be a disastrous failure. If he can recall the feelings he had when playing it and those that others may have expressed afterwards, then he might anticipate some of the potential stumbling blocks with the pupils.

(b) He will also have evaluated the rules to see if they are confusing or can be quickly assimilated and if there is scope for pupils to play about and lose interest. It is axiomatic that games and simulations must involve every pupil most of the time. It may be that they are very differently involved; the 'banker' in a resource area is essentially using counting and mathematical processes while the bulk of players are concerned with interactions, some as facilitators, some in need; but at least everyone has a task.

(c) He will also have assessed if there is sufficient reality behind the simplification or whether, despite the framework, it is misleading, inaccurate, biased or too fantastic.

(d) He must have concluded that he has the confidence and skill to carry it off and whether both he and the group are ready for it. If the group are not accustomed to any enactive processes, it is suggested that earlier preparation is required before something as substantial as this can be sustained. The class must have experience of group work and talk before any simulation will take off.

(e) Now in relooking at the simulation and thinking of Form 3D or 5B he or she may feel the need to simplify, omit parts or rewrite bits to make it fit the personality of the group. The leader may feel she is being disloyal to the devisers of some well-known game. It is not sacrosanct and should be altered at will. But clearly these amendments should be done with care and examined to see what effect they will have on subsequent stages of

57 the work. Sometimes the less successful parts of games are concerned with overcoming a difficult structural problem in the playing, to stop cheating, or keep some other group of players in action.

Having a go: No simulation is teacher-proof. There is still much to be done although the materials are all complete.

(a) First he *needs to check* that he has all the accessories that are necessary for the work. These are usually, but not always, listed at the beginning of the materials. Sometimes it is assumed that everyone has paper and pen, is English and literate or will have a handkerchief and so on. These requirements are worth pasting on the inside of the box or whatever, for other colleagues are bound to want to borrow materials after hearing how well the activity went. It is embarrassing if items are missing when played again. Postcards are often required as well as counters of different colours, some form of name label, dice or string: they all take time to collect and should be gathered in at the end for future use, however battered.

(b) Ideally the *working space* should be laid out in the pattern required for the group prior to starting. This suggests to the players that something different is going to happen and that the leader has taken time and trouble to prepare for it. For the leader it saves a tumultuous start to the session, free from the clamour of moving furniture. It also allows her time to concentrate on the activity in hand.

(c) When the class or group comes into the working space they may need some *warm up activities* to prepare them for the problems or issues at hand. These can set the tone and are important. Through them the leader can start introducing the theme. All simulation work that involves role play at some depth needs some preparatory activity. There may also be a need for some release of tension arising from apprehension in the group.

(d) Only a small number of *rules or instructions* can be absorbed at once by a group of players. The main ones may need to be written on the blackboard. Certainly any lists that involve the values of counters, as in *Starpower,* will have to be. It is better if the instructions are not read out but told like a story; a handwritten postcard may help as a prompt here. Playing a simplified trial round can be useful, then later feeding in more rules, if necessary. Silence, concentration and full attention are necessary for the rule giving, with no-one asking questions until the end. Sometimes the questions confuse pupils who thought they understood the instructions.

(e) *The way we give out roles* is vitally important in simulation. In a game structure, if roles are more arbitrary, then—

   (i) Where players are to be in X groups, as they come into the working space they can be numbered 1, 2, 3–X. A piece of paper stating one of those numbers can mark a different area of the room to which that numbered person now goes, or

  (ii) Chairs can have a card on them or a coloured disc; whoever sits on them does what the card says or the disc indicates, or

 (iii) All the role or job or instruction cards can be held face downwards by the leader. Everybody randomly chooses them, and, on looking, keeps that information secret if needs be. The tendency is for pupils to want to see other pupils' cards; in many simulations this may spoil things if they do, for different information may be given to individuals within the group.

58 In some simulations it is important that players play roles of their own sex but this is not always possible. In that case it is better if the older aged roles are played by the wrong sex than the younger. While girls in a single-sex school will usually tolerate playing the opposite sex, boys rarely will. When devising simulations it is helpful to keep to general roles like parent, grandparent or teenager rather than be specific. Where possible sub-groups can choose their own leader or spokesman.

(f) Once the action begins there will be *noise and movement* which must be expected. The leader needs to mingle with groups and players to see who is confused, does not understand, or is cheating: he may want to enlighten or help as himself or in an appropriate role. Some of the problems of 'contracting out' have already been explored. But in simulation a quick way of involving those who say they are not interested is to let them act as a 'banker' or 'resource man' at the control desk, if there is one; or with some apparently more objective task that does not initially seem like a role—though if involvement does come he may often develop into a media man or evaluator.

(g) Gaming calls for ingenuity and there will be frequent occasions when players want to *challenge the rules* or suggest an improvement. In a game this may be more difficult, though it need not be, but in simulations these are often worth taking into account. Split-second decisions have to be made but the question to ask the players is 'What would we do in that situation in real life? Would the person have that information you are proposing or be able to take that line of action? What would be the constraints or openings?' If the proposal can just about satisfy such tests of actuality then it could be allowed and things would follow accordingly. Alternatively the leader could quickly throw the matter open to discussion to the group and get their decision, so maintaining a feeling of participation. When the leader has played a game several times such dynamic changes bring it alive again for him if new rules can be incorporated and fresh ideas have been assimilated. After all, we claim that it is a creative activity and so we need to be flexible in our approach.

(h) The leader has to keep his eye on *the time,* especially in a single period. Playing time is often very limited. In a forty minute period the pattern may go like this: 10 minutes—settling down, warm-up, setting up; 15 minutes—playing time; 10 minutes—pooling-in, debriefing and discussion; 5 minutes—evaluation of experience.

In a double session of say 90 minutes with a more involved topic, the pattern may be: 15 minutes—preparation, warm-up and instructions; 40 minutes—playing time; 25 minutes—reporting back, debriefing and discussion; 10 minutes—evaluation.

This would be roughly the scheme for *Tenement* and *Starpower.* The tendency is for playing time to over-run its allocation, especially if it is proving enjoyable, and the opportunity of drawing conclusions and furthering of understanding is diminished. This is a great loss. It means we have to be more selective in what we put into our playing time.

(i) It is during this last part of pooling-in and post-play discussion, described more fully in the previous chapter, that the leader has to *privately assess* what he feels the group has gained from the experience, whether he would use the materials again and whether it fulfilled his objectives. Some verbatim response, from the players are always worth jotting down and used as discussion points in later lessons. It is also useful to incorporate new proposals and amendments in the instruction sheet with the materials, as a reminder for next time.

59 (j) Once is not enough. As the beginner grows into the activity, wants to use more materials, and tries to devise his own, he needs to *work with other colleagues.* Many teachers' centres over the country have set up monthly or irregular simulation workshops to bring like-minded colleagues together, to try out new publications, pass on experiences and to create something of their own for children of known background and need. There is always scope for more such groups.

Devising Something New

Working together: Simulations and games are best devised in pairs. Threes or fours are possible though more cumbersome; any greater number is not profitable in terms of limited time, except occasionally on courses. Too many people have conflicting interests or ideas which they would like to see incorporated, but sounding out ideas with individual colleagues is invaluable. So often in the work one gets stuck and no end of pacing up and down a study will seem to solve it; half an hour with a sympathetic colleague who can turn the problem on its head or look at it from a new direction may be just the stimulus for a new solution.

Allocating time: They now have to decide how long they can both afford to spend on preparation together or even at home. If it is only several lunch hours or just one evening, then short cuts or just adaptation are going to be necessary. Some games, especially like *Breed or Breathe?,* take weeks of work to make the final materials ready for wider use.

Defining constraints: The list is long and varied.
(a) How much time is available for play—single period or double, half day or all day?
(b) How many players will be involved, just a small group, a whole class, a large conference or a year group?
(c) What is the ability and experience of the players, their age and sex?
(d) What mode of learning are we aiming for? Is it to be task-orientated and individual, or in pairs, each pair working at the same time, in small groups, or with the whole class together as a unit? Whatever the mode we must ensure that there are learning possibilities for everyone.
(e) How many leaders or helpers will be available to assist, or will the deviser be on his own?
(f) How many rooms are allocated? If only one, is it small with everyone practically on top of each other; or is it a large hall where 'agencies' or sub-groups could be fairly remote and private?
(g) Who will be teaching next door and how well do your neighbours take to such activities and noise?
(h) Have you money available to buy materials like badges, labels, counters etc?
(i) Are there reprographic facilities for producing items that the players will use? Or will you have to do everything by hand? If so what time have you available?

Objectives: Probably the simulation's curriculum area, say social studies or personal relationships, first brought the devisers together. It is not usually difficult quickly to narrow it down further into a particular topic, such as the problems of unemployment for a large group of students or an exploration of friendship for small groups of fourth formers. Now

60 more detailed objectives must be outlined. What social skills are to be involved, what factual information needs to be imparted, where does it lead to, what can this method achieve which is more productive than more conventional methods of tackling the particular topic, what is to be the overriding image that we want to leave with the players? What are the new concepts we wish to introduce?

Think tank: Whether the objectives have been written clearly or not, the devisers will want to forget all practicalities and enjoy a quick 'think tank', jotting down words, phrases, references, quotations, associations and expressions of their feelings about the core issues. Ideas may be allusive, intuitive, free ranging, perhaps comic and irreverent. Eventually they will run out of steam.

Reflection: As the writers look over the scrawled pages and lists, a theme may emerge. Alternatively, one quotation or incident seems to be significant and will naturally lead into discussion and exchanges.

The idea: Eventually, out of this may come a central agreement or an image; maybe it is the title for the game. If this idea is a fruitful one, it will now take on a life of its own and push the devisers to look again at their objectives and the topic itself. A good idea often has fairly immediate implications for a model that might be used to achieve it. Sometimes an idea is worth sleeping on—next day it can seem either brighter than ever or not worth pursuing.

The structure: Looking over the great number of games and simulations available it is possible to detect about eight archetypal models. These follow in outline later in this chapter. This typology may be an arbitrary one and others will make their own divisions differently; but we have found the code helpful to beginners. As in any classification there are overlappings and every manner of combinations. There are very few genuinely new ideas. Published material in being intended for widespread use often loses some of its vital spirit and the beginner can adapt his material to his needs.

The form embodied: With the structure tentatively chosen then the fun is over and the hard work begins. If it is a simulation, all players have to have roles and attitudes. These should keep everyone involved and give both a stimulus for action and scope for creation. The players may need to be given some information as well, either on an individual or a common basis. This must be concise, accurate and easily grasped. Illustrations and diagrams are often more readily absorbed. Writing roles can be hard work. This is the kind of task to be shared. A range of attitudes needs to be embodied in the variety of roles. It is always worth keeping the continuum in mind and literally drawing it out with the extremes at both ends and then every gradation in between for the particular problem.

It is the number of people in the central areas who are more likely to be swayed one way or another and who often determine the excitement and interest of the work. It has earlier been explained that because of over identification in enactive processes it may be wiser to avoid the extremes. They may be more dramatic for an actor but less educational for a young person.

19 seriously. The groups were divided by the conflicting attitudes and experiences but both minuted some proposals. Then finally for nearly an hour the group assembled as a whole and came out of role.

There was an immediate gasp of relief and a great hubbub of talk. Every person was called on in turn to say what had happened to him while in role and whether he or she was in any way helped by anyone. Those who should have helped and did not justified why in role they thought they could not have done so. Many were just not aware of the problems quite close to them or had misinterpreted signals. 'It sounds as if I was in a different room—I didn't know that.' 'I've never felt so raw about anything—I'd hate to have been in his place.' 'Everything was pressing in; I just couldn't have done anything. I pity her.' Various helping agencies like Samaritans were clearly new to many players.

The discovery dawned on several who voiced it clearly about how interwoven our relationships are and how if we don't help our nearest and dearest 'who else will? No one else has got the time.' The urgent need for parents who can be talked with and friends who can be trusted was the common theme. The debriefing became more general and personal. A great deal of loneliness and anxiety was admitted to; the awareness of having been made vulnerable was acknowledged.

The group broke late for lunch but the talk went on. It was the turning point of the week. It showed in various individual ways how the leaders could attend more closely to some members' personal needs. After that it was felt possible to talk about anything openly because permission had been granted to speak the unspeakable. At the end of the week one girl said, 'It's the first time that I realised that things could be other than they are.'

References

Davison A., *The Dream Machine,* from *The Making of Myth,* Cockpit Arts Workshop, Inner London Education Authority, 1976

Davison A., *Who Cares?*—our network of relationships, Cockpit Arts Workshop, Inner London Education Authority, 1976

Faraday A., *The Dream Game,* Penguin Books, 1976

Ward B. & Dubos R., *Only One Earth,* the care and maintenance of a small planet, Penguin Books, 1972

The Ecologist, A Blueprint for Survival, Penguin Books, 1972

McGoun S. & Hedley D., *Breed or Breathe?* Media Resources Centre, Inner London Education Authority, 1974

Ed. Richardson R., *Learning for Change in World Society* World Studies Project, One World Trust, 1976

Schofield M., *The Sexual Behaviour of Young People,* Penguin Books, 1968

2
Reflections

From out of those experiences described in the previous chapter it is possible to map certain features in common to most gaming and simulation situations. These features might also be claimed as sources of justification for such activities. It would need an analysis of transcripts to reveal the details of the terrain; this can only be an initial sketch.

The Context

In different ways each experience comes within a context of planned learning. They were no fill-in activities for a wet Friday afternoon. The teacher's aim in *Breed or Breathe?* was to bring together a group of sixth formers from different schools for the first time. He had also chosen a complicated, ambiguous game which opened the door to a whole variety of different explorations: yet a game that did not demand the kind of detailed role-playing which needed a stronger context of trust and experience. He wanted to create interest in a term's work with students from a range of subject backgrounds.

The religious education teacher in the *Dream Game* had already inducted her class into a range of enactive processes over the year, so that there was by then some degree of confidence and understanding in the pupils that these activities were indeed 'work' and had a validity. She could never have started a year's programme with an uninitiated group in such open-ended and demanding activity. In some ways she was using the occasion as a form of informal assessment to see if the class was ready to move on to new concepts. She was certainly at a stage when she could expect a personal response and rely on group activities being naturally accepted. Like the sixth form teacher, she was not a drama specialist

21 and both had learned their skills piecemeal from workshops, in-service courses, trial and error and the slow growth of personal confidence.

In each of these cases, the school was sympathetic to enactive processes within the classroom. In both schools the rapid curriculum revolution of the last five years has enabled staff of diverse discipline areas to use methods that previously were rare, except where brought in by the occasional brave student in training. Pupils may not have had regular sessions in these methods by other departments but they would have had some: and it was the experience of some teachers first playing the *Breed or Breathe?* game in previous years with the sixth form that gave sufficient spur and courage to try out something new in their own specialisms.

The *Who Cares?* simulation was the most risky of all but it was deftly calculated and fortunately worked well. The group was more than awkward at the beginning of the course; everyone felt threatened because each was a total stranger to the other. To have started with such a simulation would have courted disaster and probably roused fierce aggression. But the work in role play and improvisation over the previous days had helped to accelerate the processes of group assimilation. It was thus possible to capitalize on the experience and enrich such processes handsomely in return. The context here was within the leadership of a group of friendly open young adults who had already shown that they cared and had expectations.

Enjoyment

It seems impossible to please everyone all the time but the atmosphere in each of those situations was of distinct involvement and pleasure. There was a great deal of laughter at times with participants moving in and out of role, both in commenting on the action by being able to stand outside it and at other moments being absorbed with the issues. For sections of all three experiences the groups were genuinely 'at play', caught up in the game structure. At different times practically everyone coasted for a while and was prepared to watch others in action, while at other moments there was quiet and intense negotiation or urgent encounter, sometimes with anger and strong words. Feelings had been engaged in the pretence and emotion was the motor of the action. Both the experience of the game as well as the concluding evaluation probably gave rise to the most significant area of learning—an examination of human interaction.

Fun was permitted; it was an allowed element in the learning process. Nevertheless it is only honest to add that several of the sixth formers admitted that they would have preferred a lecture and discussion as stimulus, and that some of the residential course members felt the strain of keeping the activity going was considerable. It is admitted that though seemingly on the fringe of the activity they did not discover anything which could not have been gleaned using more traditional approaches. They were perhaps looking for the wrong results. For the rest there was great enthusiasm; their appetites had been whetted for more, both of content and process.

Social Education

One such gain often hidden to youngsters who have been conditioned to see education only in terms of facts is the real human interaction that

22 occurs even in the midst of the pretence. Reality is always operating at this double level, for whatever the guise or role, members of the group are seeing each other in a new light and learning more about different aspects of others as well as themselves. No matter what the model of the game, the learning invariably takes place in small or large circles, in face-to-face encounters.

In *Breed or Breathe?* it would have been possible for the pupils to have worked in pairs or small groups or with everyone else in the whole class group, sorting out problems and making negotiations. Then again in the regular press conferences and international councils, different attitudes of friends and colleagues would have been witnessed or encountered—perhaps in opposition or conflict, perhaps in plotting and double-dealing. The situations draw something spontaneous and improvisatory from the participants who can find themselves describing new thoughts and behaving in new ways. They give an opportunity for different skills and social interactions to be experienced. More of the player's individuality is drawn on and this can be appreciated by others. 'I never knew John had it in him.' 'I never knew Shirley was like that' are common enough comments.

In the *Dream Game* the groups of four or five took the brunt of the encounter but everyone shared each other's dreams. Not only were these quite considerably different, with the participant sometimes surprising himself by what he had brought out, but the watchers were aware of in-jokes and in-relationships, which were given a new twist however seemingly tight the structure of the sequence. The fact that movement and physical expression were called for, especially to compensate for lack of props, stretched the imagination of player and observer.

Who Cares? called for different qualities of sensitivity and understanding. The issues were intimate, touching areas where all the group were deeply and individually involved. All the players 'risked it' together and shared situations where they had either to show care and sympathy, or express a lack of it. As in any such experience the camaraderie at the end of it was appreciable. One is never quite the same, nor the interrelationships quite so impersonal or distanced.

Those who use enactive processes with any regularity will vouch for the better social relationships within the class. It may be a slow process to help cohere a fractious group, but the learning in all subjects is likely to improve.

Another telling factor is the different pupil-teacher relationships that occur in simulation. Frequently the teacher is working alongside the pupil shoulder to shoulder, often in role, not as 'teacher'. There is less likelihood of didactic stances being taken. With the teacher willing in this way and able to share in the enjoyment there is much greater chance of this spilling over into other areas of work and extra-curricular relationships. Social aspects of education seem to activate greater motivation and there lies the key to all learning.

Whole Self Involvement

In all these three experiences the intellect was called into play—either at the game level, the problem-solving level or the personal interaction level. Reason, logic and argument and a seeking after understanding were involved. But this was only part of the experience. The most obvious outward feature to anyone observing these groups was their animation.

61 *Role cards:* There is a great problem of giving too much or too little information. If too little then there may be either caricature or insufficient motivation; if too much the enactor will get bogged down. Of the many personal attributes that could be written down some devisers argue that all personality characteristics should be left out and just five or six factual features be included that are crucial to the situation and can be easily absorbed. It is always worth having a mental check list of characteristics such as age, sex, nationality, family and social status, leisure activities and recent history from which to choose.

An excellent training exercise is to take a situation and devise a series of cards on which the roles only are written—say social worker, councillor, grandparent. The enactors are introduced to the background of the situation and given any one of the cards. They are then asked within a time limit to construct the personality and life history of an individual, making up a name and giving five other facts. When this is completed, all the cards are redistributed less arbitrarily, and the simulation played. During the post-play discussion an assessment of the success or failure of the role-briefing cards will be made. For new devisers this shows some of the problems of role description in an active and practical way.

Chance cards: A good handful of chance cards can be prepared by the deviser to keep the action moving, especially if a player looks lost or bored. These cards must reflect possible problems within that particular context. They can be conceived as letters in envelopes or messages from others in role. In some simulations the cooperation of the players can be obtained, especially those who are experienced in such matters; within their role they can devise and distribute such chance elements as considered appropriate. When players can become involved in such improvements of the game they are at the start of being able to devise their own, however simple.

Feeding in information: There may be a need for additional material to be absorbed for a full understanding of the issues. One way is to divide the simulation into rounds and give either verbally or in written form new information to start off the next round; another way is to build problems into situations that need some reference to books or resources. Some leaders have introduced a film or television programme, slides or cassette, sometimes after play has begun; in this way enactors may identify with roles that might be close to those they have been allocated. Others use the introductory role-play warm-ups to keep feeding in new information; some have staged an incident or argument in role with a colleague that will focus in on a new aspect or open up the situation. Leaders can also start the whole briefing, giving basic information in a strong role to make a more snappy beginning.

Rules for action: In gaming it is not roles that are the problem but ways of devising rules that work. They should not give rise to widespread cheating, involve either too much clutter of counters and bric-a-brac or detailed instructions that cannot be taken in at a first or even a second playing. Existing patterns like *Snakes and Ladders, Ludo* and *Bingo* where the squares in each case are to represent something more related to content and might even necessitate some role play (which could be encouraged) are well worth using as a model—lock, stock and dice-box. Many devisers, including ourselves, are not happy about the total

62 arbitrariness of the dice when it comes to areas of social interaction. Only the utter cynic would claim that real life is merely a game of absolute chance and that we have no power at all to operate on our own between the 'throws' when fate intervenes. Much more natural are chance cards which are introduced in simulations to keep the pot boiling. Letters in the post, accidents and disasters shock us all in the tenor of our life but there are also areas of freedom to treat others in ways that are special to ourselves. Dice give scope for none of this unless we build in functions that are untypical of most commercial board games. The medium is the message and it may be that board games are never any more than board games whatever the content.

Simulations, however, also need rules though these are usually simpler; they are simply developments of the structure and are determined more by the normal pattern of the social processes they echo. A round of the game or a period of action usually represent an agreed time span, say a session or a day or five years, as in *Breed or Breathe?* Many simulations require the leader to step in at certain times when she sees the moment is ripe to move the action on to the next stage. Often the leader can adopt a role here to quicken up the end of the last section—perhaps going in as the caretaker, jangling keys and saying 'Can't wait round here all night for you lot. You've got three minutes and if you're not out you'll be locked in in the dark,'; or as the convenor of a meeting or its chairman introduce the next stage, perhaps when all sub-groups meet as a final whole group. Other constraints may have to be built in, either to make it work as a game or to keep it closer to a simulation of reality. Neither should inhibit the players too greatly but must be aimed to keep them in play.

Synthesis: Now the developing project must be looked at as a whole and worked through chronologically, to see what happens to everybody in it and how the action is kept flowing. Is there enough for everyone to do and does it relate to the original objectives? Often the idea has taken it several steps away or it has now developed in a slightly different direction. However, it still may be a valid piece of work and the new direction is just as valuable as the old. All that is needed from time to time is to change the objectives and let them define the new function which the simulation fulfills. It is never possible to determine exactly what will happen, otherwise exploration is predetermined and blinkered. This will be exactly the case also with playing it in action; a good simulation is ultimately taken over by the group and is transformed to meet their needs. Exact goals cannot be determined, nor could it be guaranteed that they would be reached if they were: we are educating at risk and not aiming to indoctrinate. Issues must be managed so that the players draw their own conclusions in an informed and thoughtful way after reflection and post-play discussion.

Topping and tailing: It is important, when the first trial takes place, that the instructions for the game are simple and clear. Then the devisers need to list all the items necessary for its action. Relevant warm-up activities or preliminary role induction exercises also need preparation and a list of the major ideas or concepts that are to be explored in the discussion and evaluation period has to be drawn up. These should now relate directly to the leader's overall aims and to the specific newly-defined objectives. The devisers will find it has all taken much longer than they planned, but they will also find great satisfaction from the completion of something new and creative.

Presentation: The final stage is now to prepare all the materials in a durable and reusable form. *Role Cards* should, if possible, be typed for clarity, especially if there is a reasonable amount of detail. If there are only a few words then clear handwriting in felt-tip pen is usually satisfactory. Postcards are helpful but do not last long if players have to keep them in their hands. The thicker mounting card used for picture framing is better; it is more expensive and durable and comes in different colours. As it is white on the back, this is useful for distinguishing different families or sub-groups or agencies. Another way of distinguishing groups is to rule the edge of white card in different colours with felt-tip pens. If necessary the transparent plastafoil can be used to cover cards for preservation.

Again, if it is possible, the sheets of *information* should be typed; double spacing helps assimilation. Drawings, cartoons or diagrams are helpful and speak far more than words. The Shelter *Tenement* game is a model of clarity and presentation in this respect, though its financial information cannot keep up with inflation. This is the fate of all information about contemporary issues; leaders have to be aware of new legislation and social change. *Source banks* of further information can be kept at the controller's desk for a simulation that takes a half or whole day. Players can have time to inform themselves about new areas or procedures, just as we need to do in real life. Knowing that we have to put that information into action in half an hour is good motivation. The leader's helpers can man this resource bank by giving further oral information or discussing questions of fact, process or background. It is when we come to translate knowledge into action that we realize how unclearly understood the process really is. Unless it is a game of instant hilarity, *names* of the enactors should be completely neutral and not comical; so Mrs. Golightly and Officer Plod, Councillor Hardbottom and Miss Hap have to be buried along with Paradise Villas and Chez Nous. The busy deviser should sit with a telephone directory, open it at random and take the first ordinary and boring name that he sees, otherwise time is wasted. In some simulations players can use their own surnames or whole names; this helps to make for easy reference by other members of the group.

Many games or simulations need the players to have *lapel labels* with name and role conspicuously printed on them for identification. The pin-on conference badges are useful but expensive and rather small. However with the stick-over labels that most stationers now produce they can be used many times for a range of other games. Larger pull-off-cellophane-and-stick-on circular labels are now available in a range of colours and these can tie in with the colours of the role cards. They can only be used once which is a disadvantage. It is not easy to find a local shop that sells cheap *counters* in materials other than cardboard about the size of a large coin. Some manufacturers of materials for primary school numeracy activities can be helpful but one may buy tubes of tiddlywinks which are small, and in four colours. If a simulation takes place over several rooms a *map* of room distribution in the building could be drawn on the blackboard at the resource and controller's area; the rooms themselves need to be clearly labelled. On a recent course a group of simulators appeared half way through lunch. The label had come off

64 their door during the morning, so they had had no clients and no one had informed them of the post-play discussion, evaluation or lunch!

If *board games* are to be made and used in the classroom then they really need to be larger than normal size if more than four people are to gather round them. Hardboard is best for durability but not for portability. Our Trade Union game on two sheets of 8' × 4' grew too cumbersome in the end. The painting of the board in emulsion really becomes a project in itself and might require the cooperation of the art department. If simple outline sketches cannot be drawn, pictures from the colour supplements and other glossies, with text cut away, can always be used to illustrate squares, and large size letraset employed for any wording. Everything needs to be varnished over to save it from becoming worn away in use. Again transparent plastafoil can be used on a reasonably-sized board. A cube of wood can be painted for a large die, if necessary, and counters or tokens may be painted wooden shapes. If all this sounds rather daunting, then unless one is devising the small boards for two players, it is best to ask if all this effort is really worthwhile. It needs evaluation.

Evaluation: With presentation complete, the game will be tried. After play, pooling back and post-play discussion, the group can be called on to make its own evaluation of the project while the leader is mentally making his own and perhaps taking notes. Our aim must be to make the players self-aware of all that they have just undergone. The danger is for the group to focus only on content and not on its own real interaction. In a supportive atmosphere we must ask what the relevance of the experience is to their own lives—can this new knowledge be put into action? The values implicit in the simulation and its processes need examining. Where was there bias? Was that inevitable? How could it have been avoided? It is important that bias should regularly be perceived and discussed. Simulations are rarely neutral in being intensely human and idiosyncratic. Was the game too unreal or the simulation too stuffy and well-controlled? Did the method match the material? Was the enaction too long for inadequate post-play discussion and its learning possibilities stunted, even after all that hard work? Does it need to be made simpler? As the leader encourages the group's self-awareness then his own perceptions may be sharpened. For his own evaluation is only likely to be a very subjective one. Did it work? Did they enjoy it? Did they seem to get a lot out of it? If so, then it's as good as any other teaching device he uses and assessed just as subjectively, as only one technique in a universe of discourse.

Participants' projects: Players themselves need to be caught up in the making process too. More and more self-programming can be built into the process from fairly early days. Practice in preparing role cards, rules and background information can soon lead into devising a complete game. Some will be fascinated by the possibilities. Making games may be a richer mode of cognitive learning than playing them, where affective skills may come into use. In many curriculum areas a simulation may make a valuable C.S.E. mode 3 project and be kept for later school use. An evaluation of the experience may be part of the project.

Keeping in touch: There are two especially valuable organizations in Britain for the novice would-be deviser of simulations. One is the *Central Index of Games and Simulations* (C.I.G.S.) manned by Peter Stopp at

65 Bishop Groseteste College, Lincoln, LN1 3DY. This welcomes all information about new projects and will send details of any game or simulation about a particular subject area upon request, upon receipt of a stamped addressed envelope.

The other organization is the *Society for Academic Gaming and Simulation in Education and Training* (S.A.G.S.E.T.) set up in 1970 and now administered from The Centre for Extension Studies, University of Technology, Loughborough, Leicester LE11 3TU. Besides running workshop courses, helping, advising and acting as a clearing house of ideas, it publishes a quarterly journal which is a most thorough review coverage of everything new in gaming and simulation, and contains as well articles of practical information. Two articles in vol. 5, 1975, are especially relevant to the new deviser.

Legal aspects: A barrister, Nicholas Merriman, explained in the July 1975 edition about the problems of copyright and plagiarism in simulation. He described how ideas once expressed or discussed by their originator are not protected by law; that ideas once aired are public property. Only if the listener has been taken into a confidence is he morally obliged to retain that secret. The law of confidence is strong and there is a 'duty to be of good faith'. Once the project has been given physical form then the property is protected, for copyright extends to 'every original literary and artistic work . . . drawing . . . photograph' as soon as committed to paper and no registration is needed. Internationally this works by the Universal Copyright Convention of 1952 and items must bear the symbol © with the name of the copyright owner and first year of publication. An infringement of copyright is 'reproducing the actual work in any material form' or 'publishing it'. But the idea is not copyright, only the original work in its exact form i.e. the way it is expressed. So the actual drawing and rubric are protected but not the symbols, rules of games etc. if they are expressed in other words or redrawn. The patent law does not apply to games, but it is still not possible to 'pass off' as your own another maker's game. Trade marks (not symbols) can be protected by the Trade Marks Act of 1938 initially for 7 years then a further 14, if properly registered.

Obtaining materials from abroad: Jacquetta Megarry, editor of the *SAGSET Journal,* mentioned (October 1975 issue) some of the problems of obtaining games and simulation from abroad, especially from America. They are often quite expensive and can be infinitely delayed if care is not taken. She advises that air mail and not surface mail should always be used in both directions, with AIR marked in large red letters and that the sender stamps it personally, not leaving it to the school or college office. Surface mail can take up to four months. Cash, including postage and package, should be sent with the order to save delay, and a dollar draft asked for. She recommends that authorization is obtained from the applicant's institution before sending money, and an order form or letter to show to the bank. A fully inclusive receipt from the supplier should be secured for reclaiming expenses from one's institution. The materials when sent should be described on the wrapping as 'printed matter' or 'educational aids' not 'games', otherwise they will be commercial and not educational and attract a heavy duty.

Board Games: a large-scale board in action for the Cockpit Theatre-in-Education Team's 'Trade Union' simulation

66   *Models and Structures:* Details of different types of published games and simulations that are easily available are given in chapter 9. A good novelist can transcend his chosen genre of western, crime, romance, science fiction, and create experiences that we feel to be 'truthful'. A portmanteau writer, like Dickens, can interweave a medley of genres. Even with lesser writers the reader is willing to suspend disbelief in looking at reality. There will be certain techniques and stylistic devices that he will expect, acting as short cuts and metaphors, for his delight and instruction.

Any game or simulation is also a symbolic short cut, a distorted view through only one facet of reality; it can never attempt to be the whole truth, even in the highly sophisticated portmanteau variations. Like the novel, many have distinctive modes of operation which call on certain skills of participation rather than others. Eight reasonably easily defined genres can be detected. Some it could be argued are more 'realistic' than others but in a world of multiple realities such as the novelist knows, who is to say that *Middlemarch* is more realistic than *Lord of the Rings?* Both may enable the reader to come to an equally profound understanding of man's humanity in totally different ways. At a slightly lower level *Tenement* and *Starpower* use contrary modes to explore concepts of underprivilege and to create an awareness of what it feels like to be a 'have not'. Who is to say that one is more real than the other? In gaming and the more imaginative aspects of simulation the intuitive and

67 symbolical are as much in play as the rational and the logical. So hunting for realism, which many publications advocate as the test of worthiness of a simulation, may be as fruitless as defining objectives. These eight archetypal patterns can be set in past, present or future time and are often in practice a mixture of the three.

1 Board and panel games

Like card games, board games can be most difficult to devise if they are to be kept simple and quickly picked up. Initially it is better to use existing models as a pattern. *Ludo, Snakes and Ladders, Bingo* and *Monopoly* are useful models. Instead of the squares always being blank they will usually have tasks or role play situations, or call for decisions to be made, or qualities and characteristics to be taken into account. For example, one of the mathematics games in chapter 7 uses *Bingo* as a model. Some games use dice and rely totally on chance as the stimulus; others use cards with instructions, which can be arbitrarily fed in. Our apprehensions about this total reliance on chance have been expressed earlier. However, for some less able children board games can help with motivation. A simple framework may help both reading and numeracy skills. *Cluedo* and *Master Mind* are excellent models for deductive processes.

Some board games are less symmetrical than those mentioned and are set out as an action maze. These can have a more complicated design, still using squares and with symbols or counters. At certain points decisions have to be made. The choice may lead down one of three alternative routes, which in turn means more decisions with new alternatives and so forth. Some ways may lead to dead ends, as in life, and the player has to retreat. Often the games are geared so that certain decisions lead to greater success while others force the player into underprivileged or deprived alternatives. The winner is the one to arrive at the goal first. Action mazes have been devised in many areas including career opportunities, leisure activities and mountaineering. They are hard to devise, need infinite patience to make all the variable alternatives valid and call for a good graphic designer.

Chance cards or community chest are also time consuming, but for a small team this is good fun to work out. They aim to show the effects of choice and the consequences of action taken; but unless some of the problems lead into role play the board can be the dominating feature. The effort demanded hardly justifies itself when the alternatives of setting up simple role plays in pairs is so much easier. Nevertheless, even if board games are restricted for use in exploring human relationships in a very meaningful way, they can be excellent for use in mathematics and for exploring concepts in science. Some of the professionally published board games in mathematics have proved most stimulating with reluctant pupils.

Panel games from television, radio and party games books can often be adapted. If they are well known then the pupils will often imitate the current television stars and it can become a glorious pastiche and great fun. Because such games are so well liked they can be excellent motivators and hold interest, but their very structures and their popularity can often intrude into subject content. The *Whodunnit* structure is an exception to this. The class in sub-groups can take a character and examine some crucial incident in which he is involved; they will need to improvise a whole range of situations in the person's life. The sub-groups in turn present these to the class, first of all enacting the central incident to which they ask the question, Whodunnit?—who was

68 responsible, who is to blame? Members of the audience can decide on three or four different aspects of the individual's life they want to see and the sub-group enact these from improvisation. The audience individually make decisions and vote once only for one of the three, four or five causes that they feel are responsible for the incident, the range of causes having been previously determined by the sub-group. The class are now in a position to discuss the final decision. After this, another sub-group presents its incident. This obviously needs a group with confidence, who may have some experience of educational drama; but it is an entertaining way of exploring moral issues and makes young people more aware that many factors are involved in behaviour.

2 Task-orientated

Within a given period of time a physical task involving a great deal of making and doing has to be completed. This could be undertaken singly, in pairs, in small groups or with the whole class. It may be in role or out of it; if outside it will be implicitly very close to a role situation and the player could slip into it. However all task-orientated games involve paper and pen if not the actual handling of materials, as well as decision-making and talk. For those not too familiar with enactive processes this may be a safe way of starting, for the goal is concrete and easily understood. Some examples will help.

(a) *Singly:* In desks by themselves the pupils imagine they are archaeologists. They might be given pictures and detailed descriptions of findings that have been unearthed from an archaeological dig, as well as background information and dating charts. In the role of an archaeologist, each person has to prepare a report based on his findings. This will take into account the kind of people they were investigating and when they lived. Clearly this would arise out of a course of study dealing with such work. After reports have been completed the 'archaeologists' could meet in small groups and discuss their findings.

(b) *Pairs:* Pupils in pairs work as town planners with a large sheet of paper between them. On it a river has been drawn winding its way through one part of it and a main road cuts across another. They also have a series of red coloured squares for council houses and blue coloured squares for privately-owned houses. Twenty other differently coloured and shaped pieces each labelled school, fire station, town hall, etc. are given to the players. They are told that their council can afford to build only ten of these public amenities. The pair have to lay out all the houses and buildings and be prepared to justify their choices. Again this may easily edge into role, especially in group interactions.

(c) *Small groups:* Each group is the editorial team for one page of the newspaper—sports, news, entertainment, features, foreign, advertisements. They are given some stimulus material for copy and materials for a mock-up page. A time limit is set by which the whole class has to have produced its newspaper. Or in a game structure the sub-groups may be different nineteenth century American railroad companies aiming to forge routes from the west to east coast; this may be set in a competitive framework with given geographical restrictions. The task is to create the first new route. This may involve planning and decision-making but not necessarily role playing. Some tasks or projects can be broken into *components* and these fed into the groups on a series of cards which are arbitrarily given to each group. The group then has to put all these components together in a new structure and present them to other groups. *The Dream Machine* in chapter 1 uses that technique. Dreams and fairy stories have been analysed to discover their structures and the structure broken into a series of components. These then have to be re-enacted in a new form. Any literary genre could be explored in this way from Jacobean tragedy to melodrama.

(d) *Whole classes, large groups:* Here the group could be a marooned crew of a spacecraft whose task is to work on the urgent problem of getting back to earth. The group could alternatively be survivors on an island who have to create anew the means of organization, government and welfare. This whole area of setting up situations where groups or society have to start again from scratch has infinite variations at all levels: it is essentially a political activity.

In many of these activities the task will be sufficient to set the action going. Rules and procedures often follow spontaneously from the way the participants set about tackling the problem. The focus is on the task, not the interaction and there may not be much conflict built into the structuring. But from such experience it may be an easy step into role taking.

3 *Pair and small group simulations*

A great deal of enaction in personal relationships such as counselling training is set in pair and small group situations. Their focus will often be on interpersonal behaviour and a little material might be explored in depth. These processes were discussed in chapter 4. Participants may be:

(i) verbally briefed by the leader, either a) publicly so that all participants know what everyone else is aiming at, or b) privately by the leader who takes the different participants aside;

(ii) briefed by role card or written case history;

(iii) invited to devise roles and brief themselves from a given situation, documentary report or article.

Enactors can work:

(a) in pairs, dyads, with the possibility of role reversal;

(b) in threes, triads, with the possibility of an observer who is briefed to study an aspect of the other pair's interaction, especially if the other roles are of an authority and a client. If there is time, this triad can be reversed three times for all to experience the three roles:
First time: A = authority, B = client, C = observer;
Second time: A = observer, B = authority, C = client;
Third time: A = client, B = observer, C = authority.
A training exercise is given in chapter 6 as an example of this.

(c) in fours, either interacting as one unit, or alternatively interacting three times within pairs and then finally together. This is an excellent way of initially building up roles for the final successful coming together. With this pattern, one simple situation needs at least a whole lesson.
First round: A works with B; C works with D;
Second round: A works with C; B works with D;
Third round: A works with D; B works with C;
Fourth round: All work together, then decisions, resolution and evaluation.

70

An excellent model
of role information
—Shelter's
'Tenement'
materials

Although such structures may be multiplied throughout the group, say eight groups of four, it may be possible to cross-mix them differently and plausibly in role. So all the eight A's can meet together, the eight B's and so on, perhaps in venues suitable to the role: thus if A's were school-teachers, in a staff room, if B's were teenagers, in a youth club. Finally it might even be plausible for everyone to meet in role as a whole group faced with the central problem. In this way the leader can assess whether anything of interest has been taking place in the sub-groups. This is part of the pattern of *Who Cares?*

Four basic roles for these might be (i) those committed to a cause or social action; (ii) those out to destroy it, basically anti-social; (iii) those uncommitted such as passers-by; (iv) those who stand for the status quo.

Feelings as well as facts

4 *In-tray exercises*

The social microscope is now focused only on one or two participants in this type. The remainder of the group are either visitors or callers, appropriately briefed, or observers sitting around the circle with the enactors in the centre. The enactors will be fulfilling any task that the group wants to explore and the enaction follows the decision-making and its consequences over a part of a day. For convenience the worker is often placed at a desk, even though this may not be typical of all the duties involved in the role. The desk may have a telephone, or an agreed system of telephoning as a substitute if this is not available; perhaps one of the outer circle players in role could ring a hand-bell. In-tray exercises have been devised for headteachers, youth leaders, secretary-receptionists, social workers and managers. The preparation comes in having materials ready to feed into the situation. The morning mail may see the start of the problems; phone calls, memos from the boss, visitors to the office follow. Decisions have to be made within time limits; other problems will arise as a consequence of those decisions in rapid succession. The worker is under pressure and the simulation is a valuable way of examining how we manage to keep several balls still in the air at the same time. It is instructive for the observers to see how other people handle human affairs and the consequences of decision-making under minor duress. It is an excellent careers training pattern with widespread applicability.

5 *Committee structures and case studies*

All social organizations operate through some kind of committee structure. Members of the committee may be there in their own right or as a representative, elected or co-opted. Procedures are usually simple, with a chairman, who should have information laid before him of how to conduct the meeting, and a secretary who may later report back. Every

72 player will be separately briefed: information will be given as to his role, where he stands on certain issues and what he wants to gain from the committee's resources or functions. Most committees operate within strict time limits and often have to come to a decision for their organization to operate until they convene again. Committee members have to strike a balance between their own personal feelings, beliefs and attitudes and those of the people whom they represent.

Committees are set up to make plans for events, to allocate limited resources, determine priorities and put forward a consistent policy. They must resolve differences, advise larger groups and select staff among many other tasks. A committee will have its agenda and can use early items to enable enactors to get into role, saving the meaty or crucial ones until later. The background information to issues can be studies for homework. For many young people an understanding of committee procedure can be most helpful to their involvement in youth activities, extra curricular clubs and groups and House affairs. They can also see that having good ideas is not enough, but that human interaction is going to determine whether they are put into practice or not.

Case studies can often develop into committee-like situations. Out of an incident or description in a book, journal or newspaper which the group has begun to discuss, a decision can be made to see how a group of professionals would try to resolve that issue. All players can embody some of the professional roles that would be involved in the situation, others can be called in to give evidence or advice and so the discussion moves into a case study conference or a committee. A *planning exercise* can be based on similar procedures. A sub-group meets either in or out of role to prepare a report about an incident or a problem. The information will have been given to the whole group in a variety of ways—slides, film, written evidence, talk, demonstration. Even though the sub-group may undertake the task out of role, when it reports back to the whole group there is a panel of players who are in role and react according to how the report affects them. The latter might have visited each sub-group in turn beforehand while they were drafting the report, either to put their own point of view or to put some pressure on the sub-group. In some circumstances it may be possible for the sub-groups to report back to the people who are to be informed, especially if it is a topic which affects that particular community.

6 *Trading game structures*
This most useful model echoes the pattern of playing shops. A series of stations or agencies are set up, either using half the group, as in *Tenement,* or the whole of the group, as in *Breed or Breathe?* or *Starpower.* These can be distributed around separate rooms for verisimilitude. Then in a series of rounds, half the group, in the role of clients or buyers or representatives, come to shop or seek information from these agencies. Alternatively members of each group go to bargain with those of other groups, leaving behind some members to represent their own group. The variations on this are enormous as the pattern is relatively close to most social interaction, whether families or firms. The rounds can represent agreed time divisions, for example where clients have to go back home. A *training variation* is the 'flying circus', which is rather like the pattern of lessons in a school day. In a group of 30 enactors, five sub-groups of five players are constituted with five unattached clients. There are five rounds to the simulation. In each round one member from each sub-group acts as a counsellor or social

73 agent to one of the floating clients, watched by the other four. After *x* minutes of enaction, there is an agreed *y* minutes of evaluation to see how the counsellor operates, with observations coming from the other four. Then all the floating clients move on clockwise to the next group, so that they receive a different client and he is dealt with by a different counsellor. The clients all need sound briefing and some rehearsals but they will see how they are differently treated and will discuss this at the end. It needs a period of at least two hours for any satisfactory outcome. With 40 players, six groups could be set up, with 20 players four groups and with 12 players three groups.

'Star Power', the archetypal analogue

7 Whole class meetings, confrontation and enquiries

Many teachers working with classes of up to 30 pupils or leaders of a youth course with perhaps 40 participants want to achieve a final coming together situation of some dramatic possibility. Everybody should still be involved in role and yet have good opportunities for wide interaction. These tend to be public meetings of all kinds set up to resolve a problem, or bring it to light; there is often a measure of confrontation which helps the drama but can become too polarised if not treated carefully. Such meetings are frequently set in church halls or town halls, with an appropriate chairman, who may well be the leader in role, several representatives of the major parties or factions involved in the problem and the bulk of enactors in role as members of the public. Roles should be worked out to cover the widest range of attitudes; care must be taken to use extremes only if they will not turn the issue into a clash which may merely reinforce prejudice. A great deal of preparation for this public meeting is necessary to establish roles in pairs, small groups and then intergroups. The public meeting is a useful model because it does not involve confusing procedures. It is very suitable for looking at most local issues that might occur in a social studies programme.

Other simply set up meetings for large groups could be staff meetings or councils in a school, a trade union meeting (though niceties of

74 debating procedure may be necessary here), a clan pow-wow or palaver, a general meeting of a club, society, firm or organization, a political or religious meeting, or a local council meeting. In some of these, especially the last, a knowledge of procedure and role is most vital. They must be correctly researched by the devisers and built into the roles, without too many instructions. It is the best way of demonstrating social processes in action, especially if the group can see beforehand a real meeting in progress. To maintain the momentum and to avoid a great deal of irrelevancy, it is advisable to have the leader in the chair, preferably in a role that is clearly quite different from his own. Both *Raftonbury,* and *Who's to Blame?* in chapter 6, show this model in action. *Enquiries or Tribunals* are more formal. Society is frequently anxious to blame and sets up processes for examining why a disturbance or accident occurred. Evidence is also weighed for and against a process of change—a new motorway or airport. This is usually a cooler procedure than the public meeting, less dramatic and vociferous but it is an excellent way into such issues. There needs to be a chairman and two, three or four other assessors, magistrates or judges; a clerk of court who should be briefed on procedures, with an assistant; a presenter of the case or prosecutor or advocate, with an assistant; an opposer to the issue or defendant with an assistant; and several members of the press. This leaves a group of twelve or so witnesses for one side of the case or the other in a class or group of 24. The leader could be either the chairman or clerk of proceedings. The room is best arranged as follows:

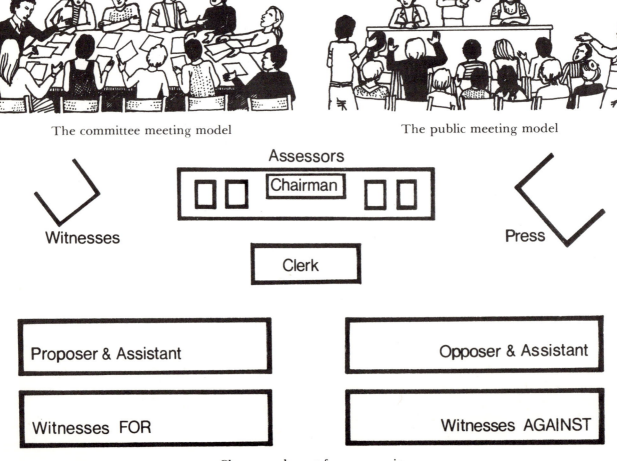

The committee meeting model

The public meeting model

Classroom layout for an enquiry

75 This is a much freer procedure than a formal court of law. Again a great deal of preliminary work in pairs and groups is needed. The inquiry itself may take up to a double period of school time. Preparation for the session should have been carried out in the previous week. Setting up a mock court case is often beyond the skills of many groups. The legal procedures constantly get in the way of the content. Even if the group has previously enacted the case and obtained witnesses, it is difficult for the prosecution and defence to keep in role. It is much more interesting for a group from the class to act out a prepared court case from a published script. The 'audience' this time can be divided into groups of twelve and sworn in appropriately as the jury; then no previous knowledge whatsoever is required by the class. When the case is completed, they elect a foreman and come to a unanimous decision with no further evidence presented. This is a fascinating process, especially as groups come up with different verdicts.

8 *More complex simulations*
Many organizations and colleges have created highly sophisticated materials for a training session or weekend workshop lasting a day or more. Consequently they need to be much more meaty and content laden. Inevitably these employ a mixture of many of the previous modes, including meetings, confrontations, committees, tasks, and trading stations, small group work, in-tray elements, parliaments and enquiries. National and world issues are often expressed in complicated structures so as to reflect the different dimensions of the issues: they are rarely published because of their very limited usage and usually have to be borrowed. Such complex situations will inevitably need a full bank of resources and a central *control area* which may involve more help than just the leader/controller. These helpers should, if possible, be professionals, from the particular sphere being explored, so that advice is authentic. The controller may need access to a public address system throughout the enaction areas to give information of decisions being made or input of new stimulus and pressures in the form of news bulletins. A useful stimulus group on such occasions will be the *media men*—both press and radio or television. Access to duplicating or lithographic facilities will be vital, as well as tape recording and video. Not only can the mass media document and reflect news with half-daily programmes but they can also comment on and provoke new directions, perhaps supplying new revelations and information—either on their own initiative or with the controller's connivance. This device, used in *Raftonbury v Fibreasbo* in chapter 6, can be one of many techniques for keeping the simulation open-ended. The final decisions and directions will be determined by the group of enactors and every group will react differently. It is the process and its evaluation in post-play discussion that is all-important, not the final verdict or conclusion, if one has to be made.

Political Education
The more simulation and gaming activities move away from examining human interaction between small groups of people in families, friends and significant others, the more they will inevitably lead into an exploration of social and political institutions and procedures, the central concern of any programme of political education.

If, as leaders, we are fully to appreciate the implications of our work in simulation and aim to educate rather than merely entertain or project

One of a series of juries at work during the project 'Judge for Yourselves'

our own biases and worthy causes, then an understanding of the political dimension to our work is absolutely fundamental. In recent years this area has helpfully been clarified in educational terms. The Hansard Society in association with the Politics Association, funded by the Nuffield Association and the Schools Council, has developed a programme of curriculum development aimed at enhancing 'political literacy' among students in secondary schools and further and higher education; for the evidence now is that young people at 18 and 20, let alone young school leavers at 16 are basically politically illiterate.

Bernard Crick and Ian Lister prepared much of the groundwork to the materials of the project. By political literacy they mean the knowledge, skills and attitudes that are necessary to make a person politically literate and able to apply that literacy. This is different from traditional British (or American) Constitution or Civics in that it starts with the actual political conflicts of the day and attempts to develop some language or system of concepts to give critical expression about such conflicts and to develop a capacity for realistic action. They argue that skills are gained from processes of role play and simulation as well as action research; that attitudes are to be found in the values of civilized procedures, such as the freedom to choose between alternatives, toleration, fairness, respect for truth and for reasoning rather than in substantive doctrines, and that knowledge involves an awareness of differing value systems and interpretations of concepts like democracy or equality. Only from a knowledge of how the present system of government works, and from developing that knowledge with skills and attitudes for active participation can we consider the possibility of change.

Politics, being concerned with groups in action not with individuals, implies a relationship of rulers to the ruled, of the access to power. So primary concepts would be explored: government, power, authority and

77 order, justice, representation, natural rights, freedom and welfare. The aim is to recognize the political dimensions of any human situation and consider what conflicts of interests and values are at stake and see how they are conciliated. This knowledge of the context and its constraints, the choices of action for operation within those and the likely consequences of such actions and their justification would help build up a consistency of approach, not to influence students' basic substantive values directly but rather their procedural values, especially of reason and tolerance.

These prime values of reason (understanding) and tolerance (empathy) lie at the heart of all curriculum development in moral education and also in religious education, where those values and ideals concerned with ultimate meanings and beliefs in right relationships, will be given expression. It is the primary concern of all gaming and simulation to educate for understanding. The leader cannot but help therefore having to prepare himself with a basic grounding in the concepts of moral, religious and political education. To opt out of a systematic understanding of these three focal dimensions of all human intercourse is to make it into an excuse for mere chatter rather than for rigorous structured learning in action.

Sources of inspiration
Gaming, role play and simulation have their own gallery of heroes, whose writings can all be eminently recommended. Anything of value in this current book is only an echo of what they have said far more distinctly and our indebtedness to them is legion. We look especially in terms of simulation to Pat Tansey, of Berkshire College of Education, the elder statesman of the movement, one of its leading pioneers; to Rex Walford of Cambridge University Department of Education and his prodigious energies in promoting gaming in geography; to Diane Brace of South East Derbyshire College of Further Education and her lively materials for political education; to Peter McPhail at Oxford University Department of Education and Don Feasey at Chorley College of Education for their probing work in moral education and role play; to Dorothy Heathcote of Newcastle University Institute of Education and to Gavin Bolton at Durham University Institute of Education for their challenges to a new understanding of dramatic improvisation; to John Fines of Bishop Otter College of Education for putting that into practice in history; and to D. H. Hamblin and Leslie Button at University College Swansea Faculty of Education for their important work in group counselling. Together in the decade from 1967 they have created a whole new world of possibilities for active learning.

References

Brennan, T. & Brown, J. (eds.), *Teaching Politics: problems & perspectives:* B.B.C. Publications, 1975
Longley, C. (ed.), *Games and Simulations,* B.B.C. Publications, 1972
Megarry, J. (ed.), *S.A.G.S.E.T. Journal,* University of Loughborough, quarterly
Taylor, J. & Walford, R., *Simulation in the Classroom,* Penguin Education, 1972

6
Some Games and Simulations in Practice

Our concern is now to give flesh to most of the eight models and structures already described and to embody them in a context. To see them dance, however, would need an experience of them in action. Many games play much better than they read, but at least a quick reading can indicate the scope and adaptability of the models. They are certainly not models of excellence but indicate work in progress and might perhaps spark an idea that will help enrich a particular group project in a particular situation. Everyone in this field works by adapting other people's ideas, there is little that is really new under the sun.

All of the following games and simulations arose out of particular needs and were often made in the face of nearly impossible deadlines. They are the output of one aspect of the work of the Inner London Education Authority's first purpose-built theatre and youth arts workshop, the Cockpit. Conceived and managed by the Inner London Youth Service, this unique provision comprises a flexible theatre workshop arena, studios and workshops for music, art and drama and its own small printing and design unit. But most importantly it houses a staff of full-time musicians, composers, artists, actor-teachers, writers, drama teachers, designers and community workers, who work in five departments but with the ready possibility of interaction. The three teams concerned with the stimulation and support of the arts in secondary education are the Theatre-in-Education Team, the Art Department and the Music Team; the two teams bridging those concerns into the youth and community service and the world of leisure are the Outreach Team and the Theatre Events department. So the Cockpit is in part a youth centre for arts activities, a complementary education centre for senior pupils and students' projects during the day-time; and a public theatre giving performances for and by young people. It is a springboard into the community for arts activities catering for all ages in Westminster, and has a teachers' centre, running workshop courses, preparing materials for and with teachers and youth leaders.

The Cockpit's teachers' centre responds to all kinds of requests from individual teachers, advisers and inspectors running teachers' courses, organisations trying new techniques and youth leaders planning residential projects. Some of these requests involve the making of new games and simulations—for the Cockpit is an appropriate symbol of a gaming den in the past or a space-craft simulator in the present.

Most of the following simulations are *iconic* in that they attempt to reflect in a simplified way some aspect of reality but a few are *analogues* like the *Quest, Gronks and Friends* and the *People G.R.I.D.* where a further leap must be taken to see how they correspond with the everyday. Some *symbolic* games follow in the science and mathematics games of Chapter 7. The material in this chapter is partly chosen also to reflect a wide curriculum area in English, social studies, history, geography, religious, moral and health education.

1 Task-oriented
The Quest (any subject content—any age)
This is an exercise in problem-creating for others to solve. It can be played singly in pairs or in small groups. The use of role playing in these games is optional.

2 Pair and Small Group Work, Moral Education and Personal Relationships
THREES *Triad Training Exercise:* adults.
FIVES *Gronks and Friends:* over 14s.

This type indicates the wide use of small groups, either to examine some aspects of interpersonal behaviour in single situations which are then reported back to the whole group or alternatively to build cumulatively on a series of small encounters into a whole group situation where everyone stays in role. In the *Triad Training Exercise* a number of situations are given for 'I–thou' exploration with the addition of an observer in the Triad: there is no intention of a group experience. *Gronks and Friends* develops this pattern in fives but the different sets of fives eventually interact in role until finally the whole group is called on to become a unit—with deliberately disastrous results if the earlier identification is sustained.

3 Whole Class meetings, Confrontations and Enquiries
Raftonbury and Fibreasbo (Social and Political Studies)
Over 16s.
This simulation shows one of the ways of preparing for a whole class event. A range of information and attitudes richly filled with different viewpoints have to be examined as a basis for action. In *Raftonbury and Fibreasbo* the social macrocosm is here exemplified by a series of public meetings for up to 100 players, deliberately structured to involve a whole society first threatened with growing unemployment and then with a possible death dust. Raftonbury is a useful model for any whole community simulation, especially for use in a residential course, where one may be dealing with an island or simulations about survival.

In this project, a series of sub-groups, committees or cases give ample scope for the players to establish a role and to explore where responsibility begins—but it is only at the final whole group meeting that the implications and desirability of these decisions will be seen. The built-in dramas of each situation should ensure some questioning as well as the commitment of the players; such confrontations are often highly entertaining.

4 Trading Game Structures *(English, History, Geography, Social Studies)* 8–12 yrs.
The People G.R.I.D.—growth, relationships, interaction, development
 (i) *The Growing Up Game*
 (ii) *Our Word House*
(iii) *The Global Cake*

The aim of putting these three similarly structured games in together is to show how the concept of 'development' is deepened by devising games which employ a symbolic mode of exploration; they are designed to be used successively in a term's work. Each game is basically a series of 'shops' round the edge of the class from which players have to buy and sell, starting with an image of the self, then extending to our immediate community of the street and so to the whole earth. It is one of the easiest models of all to operate with an enjoyment of bartering acting as a metaphor for reciprocity in relationships.

5 Committees And Case Studies *(Personal relationships, moral education)*
These straightforward examples can be used either as straight discussion material with the group, or group members can take on roles of those who have the 'subject' within their care. Alternatively, the players can go right into the situation role and enact an attempt of putting that 'care' into action. The earlier example of *Raftonbury and Fibreasbo* is also an illustration of a committee structure in operation.

6 Board and Panel Games *(Moral education and personal relationships)*
One of the best known types of games. See Chapter 9 for examples.

7 More complex Situations (*History*)
 This Howse to Let: Over 15s.
Space prohibits the full text of this quite specific historical simulation set in the January of 1649 on the day that the news was made public that Charles 1. was to be tried for treason. By using the Cockpit plaie howse in Drury Lane as a central image of the body politic, a historical microcosm of a 'world turned upside down' in political, religious and social beliefs is able to be explored unusually in action. Actual historical material is presented, along with a range of contemporary documentation about beliefs and attitudes; the public meetings range from households and shops, to prison and church. It clearly must come in the context of a course of study dealing with the period but it gives rich opportunity to put such study to the test.

The PEOPLE G.R.I.D.

The PEOPLE G.R.I.D.

(Growth, Relationships, Inter-Action, Development)

Three games and activities for ages 8–12 years

THE GLOBAL CAKE

Recipe for Cherry Cake

The Growing-Up Game

THE PEOPLE G.R.I.D.
(GROWTH-RELATIONSHIP-INTERACTION-DEVELOPMENT)

Three games and activities for ages 8 - 12 years, relevant to English, History, Geography, Social Studies and Health Education.

These materials, though able to be used as separate items, were designed as an entity. They symbolically explore the key concept of development. Its embodiment ripples outwards, starting from the self (the Growing-up Game), then moving into the street (our Word House) and finally is expressed in our spaceship earth (the Global Cake).

The aim of the materials is to create opportunities for a possible understanding of the need for tolerance. As individuals the pupils are all at different stages of personal growth; different facets of themselves are growing differently. This is not good or bad, praiseworthy or blameworthy; it is just a matter of relativity. There is need for their acceptance of those differences. In our street and the immediate community there are social groups who are less integrated into the common fabric than others. But, as the history of our language shows, they will ultimately become absorbed into the pattern of things and seen as an integral part. Society develops, the body politic changes. Not only groups but countries too are at different stages of development. Empires decline, the third World grows; new directions are taken, differences have to be accepted. Conversion or co-ersion are less and less tolerable.

Development implies growth, but endings and decay as well as beginnings and fruition. This has implications for the People G.R.I.D. For a further theme to be teased out of the materials is that all individual, social or national development can only occur through interaction and relationships. We have no meaning or ground for being if left alone, as an individual and cultures are less enriched when isolated.

Ideally the activities should be used as part of a whole term's thematic project on development. This was the case in Beckford Junior School, London, where the materials were first tried out, with pupils relating together the Merry-go-round Sex Education T.V. programmes, with the historical growth of West Hampstead and many local visits, to the development of Monarchy for Jubilee year and trips to the Commonwealth Institute and Kew Gardens. Each game helped to prepare for the use of the symbols-in-action of the next . The children began to draw links between the disparate elements; they began to see the GRID.

*   *   *   *   *

One different aim of the materials is to interest Primary School teachers in the use of simulation and gaming techniques for exploring curriculum learning. Such techniques have so far been more evident in secondary education across the curriculum and there are few materials available for younger pupils. These activities are easy starters in this area for the inexperienced teacher and the games almost lead to the brink of simulation which would naturally follow. Some suggestions for this will be found in:-

1. Schools Council Health Education Project 5 - 13:
   (All About Me (5-8s), Think Well (9-13s)) Nelson Education 1977;
2. Learning for Change in World Society - reflections, activities and resources World Studies Project, c/o One World Trust, 24 Palace Chambers, Bridge, St., SW1.
3. For developing the language aspects of the Word House game:-
   The Books of Girls and Boys Names; Sleigh and Johnson, Harrap.
   Your Book of Surnames: P. Hughes, Faber.
   How Surnames Began: C.M. Matthews, Butterworth.
   Story of Surnames: L. Devereux, Blackwell.
   For teachers:
   Bozzimacoo: Mary Marshall. To coin a phrase: Edwin Radford
   Slang Yesterday and Today: Eric Partridge.
   Language of the British Isles Past and Present: W.B. Lockwood.
   Keywords: Raymond Williams. Our Language: Simeon Potter, Penguin.

*   *   *   *   *

STARTER ACTIVITIES FOR THE GROWING UP GAME

One or two of these might be helpful in directing the class's attention to the areas about to be explored and in creating a sense of action before the game. Everybody plays them at the same time.

1(a) <u>Think Tank</u>. Work in pairs. Each pair write down the word DEVELOPMENT and see if they can make a list of any words that can explain what it means, or that they associate with the word, or mean the opposite of it, or that they might connect with it in any way. Some pairs read out their lists and the teacher tries to sift out the meaning of the concept and some ways in which it is used.

(b) <u>Word Making</u>. Now each pair is asked to take the word DEVELOPMENT and see how many words can be made out of it without using any letters more than they occur in the word – ie. envelop, men, mop, lemon, pen, novel, vote etc. Now each pair has to take one of these words and imagine a situation which starts off normally but in which the object chosen starts growing larger and larger in a most unusual way. The growth happens slowly but the players must react in the way that the people who were using the object really might. Pairs can tell the class at the end what happened.

2. <u>Inter-action</u>. Work in threes. Players call themselves A, B and C. Teacher asks all As to raise their hands (to check), Bs, and Cs. Then she says that quickly she is going to give A, B and C a different person or thing to be and they must inter-act in the way that they think best – with just a minute allowed to see how the three get on together.
   (a) A is a spider, B is a web and C is a fly.
   (b) A is the victim, B is the crook, C is Bionic Girl or Boy.
   (c) A is a soap-box speaker, B is a heckler, C is the policeman.
   (d) A is asleep in bed, B is a burglar, C is a ghost.
   (e) A is a rose, B is the greenfly, C is the insect spray.
   (f) A is a caretaker, B is the pupil, C is the teacher. etc. etc.

3. <u>The All-Change Wardrobe</u>. Work in threes. One of you owns a bedroom wardrobe which has an odd habit. When you put anything into it that object changes back into what it was in an earlier state. So your woollen socks might become a sheep, your feather hat a pheasant, your hand-bag a crocodile, china ornament a mass of clay, pencils or paper a tree etc. If you take an object out and put it back in again then it goes one stage further back again – tree into acorn, clay into rocks, sheep into lamb etc. Imagine an incident when you are entertaining your friend, showing him or her something to do with your hobby in your bedroom. You go to collect something from your wardrobe and the object has changed backwards very dramatically. What do you do? Eventually your mother or father comes into the room. How do you explain the disturbance? Are you believed? What if one of the three of you got inside the wardrobe to investigate? Work it out in action. Let some of the trios tell the class what happened.
   (this idea comes from Penelope Farmer's book 'Castle of Bone' Penguin)

4. <u>Growing</u>. Pair situations.
   (a) A is growing so fast that you can be clumsy at times and you have knocked over and broken your aunt's favourite vase. Go and confess what you have done to her.
   (b) B is always growing out of clothes. It is an important occasion and you are standing talking with a rather posh visitor, A. He or she drops a handkerchief and in bending to pick it up your trousers or dress rips in a most awkward place. You are too embarrassed to let the visitor know. What does B do? Work it out in action.
   (c) A is a grandfather or grandmother and is telling B, who is your age, for the hundredth time what is was like when he/she was a child: B cannot get a word in.
   Now B is the same child but he/she is most talkative and is telling Grandpa or Grandma (who cannot hear very well) for the hundredth time some of the antics you used to get up to when just a toddler or so: A cannot get a word in.
   (d) It is a strange kind of party, like something from Alice in Wonderland. Some of the cakes and sandwiches make you suddenly grow hugely tall, others make you very small; some of the drinks and jellies make you very fat or extremely thin. Everyone in the class is at the party and you are all helping to pass the food round for everyone to try. Enact what happens.

THE GROWING UP GAME

For 18 - 30 players; playing time 60-75 mins.

The aim of the game is to show in a symbolic way how each of us grows up very differently from each other, and also how different aspects of ourselves grow at different rates. The hope is to encourage more understanding and so tolerance of our differences. There is also a concern to show that all growth results from inter-action.

The teacher will need the following items:-

1. *One picture of the Growing-up Figure for each group of six children.
2. *One Noises Chart for each group. This must be displayed for all the group to see and the teacher must colour-in before-hand each of the five squares in the colours indicated on the chart - animals to be red etc.
3. 10 unifix blocks for each player, 2 x red, 2 x blue, 2 x green, 2 x orange and 2 x yellow. The colours correspond with the noises and the pencils.
4. 6 red coloured pencils in a beaker, 6 blue pencils in a separate beaker, and similarly with 6 x green, 6 x orange and 6 x yellow pencils.
   *These can be photo copied from the originals, as each playing will consume a set.

Preparation

1. The teacher needs to set out groups each with a table surrounded by six chairs. There can be no more than five groups, so only 30 children can play at once.
2. On each table the teacher places a beaker of six same-coloured pencils.
3. By each chair the teacher places a stick of 10 unifix blocks. Each stick must comprise 2 or 3 blocks of each of the four colours that are different from the colour of the pencils in the beaker. So if the group has red pencils then each player must have 2 or 3 blue, green, orange and yellow unifix blocks. The point of each round of the game is to barter to get blocks of the colour that you need - that is the colour of the pencils.
4. The Noises Chart, fully coloured-in, should be displayed prominently near each group.
N.B. If there are only three or four groups playing, then all the coloured pencils will still be needed but one or two different sets will be out of use at any one time.

Introduction

1. The children come into the room and the teacher allows the players to work in social units, sitting in the chairs which have been pre-arranged in groups.

2. Ideally the game needs to have arisen at a ripe time when the teacher is wanting to explore some concepts and aspects of Growth. Perhaps she could remind the class of how this arose before and that now they are going to develop some new ideas in this area. As it is to be a lesson with some inter-action, there may be a need for preparation and warming up. This would be the time to introduce some of the Starter Games.

3. Once there is interest and expectation in the idea of growth, the teacher can explain that the class is now going to explore five years in their own growth, perhaps from 6 to 11 years, or 7 to 12 if more relevant. First of all they must try to think of all the different aspects of themselves that grow. This may start from the body, skin and bone etc. but needs to be extended to the idea of our brain and intelligence growing, our skills in doing jobs and making things, our ability to get on with other people by making friends and mixing, the growing awareness of our feelings, that we must no longer be so childish in our temper but think of others and be prepared to stick at a job or interest with some keenness and enthusiasm, also how we grow to understand what good and bad is, how we can be fair and honest, keep our word and be kind, and finally our ability to keep alert, caring for our body and appearance with confidence and grace. This will take some time to tease out. During it, the idea that all these different aspects of ourselves develop at different rates and in different ways is important to pursue. Many will understand the 'growth spurt' in terms of the body; it may be necessary to seek out experiences and examples of how the other aspects of our selves boom and slump at times.

4. Now the teachercan hold up one of the Growing-Up Figures and explain that the class is going to play a game in which we are going to explore how one person grows up. Those six different aspects of growth that have been talked about are to be represented by a division of six different parts of the body. Each player in the group is going to take charge of one of those aspects. So someone will look after the head and watch the growth of intelligence, someone will look after the right arm of fellowship, or the left arm of

skills, or another will keep track of the body of feelings, or how our person puts his right foot forward in doing right, or develops alertness and keeps fit which is represented by the left leg. The Growing-up Figures can now be given one to each group. The Group must then decide a name for the figure, boy or girl, and write this boldly under the word 'Game' on the card.

5. Now the rules of the game are explained.
   (i)   The figure grows by having the squares filled in with a coloured pencil of the part of the body for which each player is responsible.
   (ii) How many squares the player can fill up is decided by how many unifix blocks the player can barter in the course of a round, each round representing a year of life.
   (iii) The unifix blocks the player needs in each round are those that are the same colour as the coloured pencils in the beaker. So if the group has red pencils in its beaker, then it must try to barter red blocks.
   (iv) If at the end of the round the player has four red blocks, then he is able to fill in four squares with his red pencil. Next round the colour will be different.

6. Barter, however, is not easy. Normal language is not possible. If you want a red block you have to make an animal noise, or a blue block a noise of some kind of transport, or green will be a musical instrument, and so on according to the coloured Noise Charts around the room. Players can only exchange one block for one block with any other player; then they both have to move on. They cannot exchange two blocks with the same player in the same round. Players can use any animal or bird or instrument, not just those in the pictures. For the first round, or even the first two rounds, the teacher can encourage the children to make a wide variety of noises and ensure that no-one is using English. But then she could suggest variations:-
   (a) For one round mime the animal, bird, instrument etc.; no noise.
   (b) For one round be a person in a job associated with animals, birds, weather etc. using words and actions, e.g. a pet shop salesman etc.
   (c) For one round use any words associated with instruments, or transport eg. "conductor, fiddle, notes, bandstand, march, bow-string etc."
   (d) For the last round ask the players for any ideas.
   The time for the first round might be five minutes. Then the teacher can see if the group needs longer or shorter for each round; ideally it should not be longer.

7. At the end of each barter round the players go back to their groups, count up the number of the coloured blocks they have been trying to gain and then each player fills up that number of squares in his part of the body. They then talk together in the group about the different amounts that the different parts have grown and try to imagine what has happened in the life of their Figure to explain why that is so. They may have gained a lot of Head/Brain squares and very few Right Arm/Friendship squares. They could explain this by saying that their Figure has been so busy reading, thinking and studying that he has had no time to go out to play and make friends.

8. Now the teacher asks each group to give an end of year report on their Figure. Either this can be done by asking a representative of the group to speak, taking a different player at the end of each year, or they all can have contributed to a written report which is now read out by one of the group. This is good for having a record to look back on and see how growth has fluctuated; some years were good for Intelligence Growth etc. others were poor. As the years go on, the report should account not only for that new year's growth but also for the cumulative position of the Figure's growth.

9. When the reports are over, the teacher moves the different coloured sets of pencils on in a random pattern across the groups. No group must ever have the same colour twice. Then the teacher tells the new barter rules, "Mime this time, not sound etc." and the players are off looking for a new colour. One or two of these they may have in their unifix block to start with, that does not matter and the bartering can be shorter.

10. After the fifth round, the players may feel that their Figure has developed a personality and can give him a nick name, as well as his real name. They should give a final school - leaving report on him, assessing growth and any character.

11. Now the class will need to talk about what their coloured Figures finally show. Is this close to their real experience? What does the inter-action and barter represent - food, relationships..? Ample time is needed for this, so that some understanding can be gleaned and the purpose of the game seen. The Figures can be left on display with other project work on the theme.

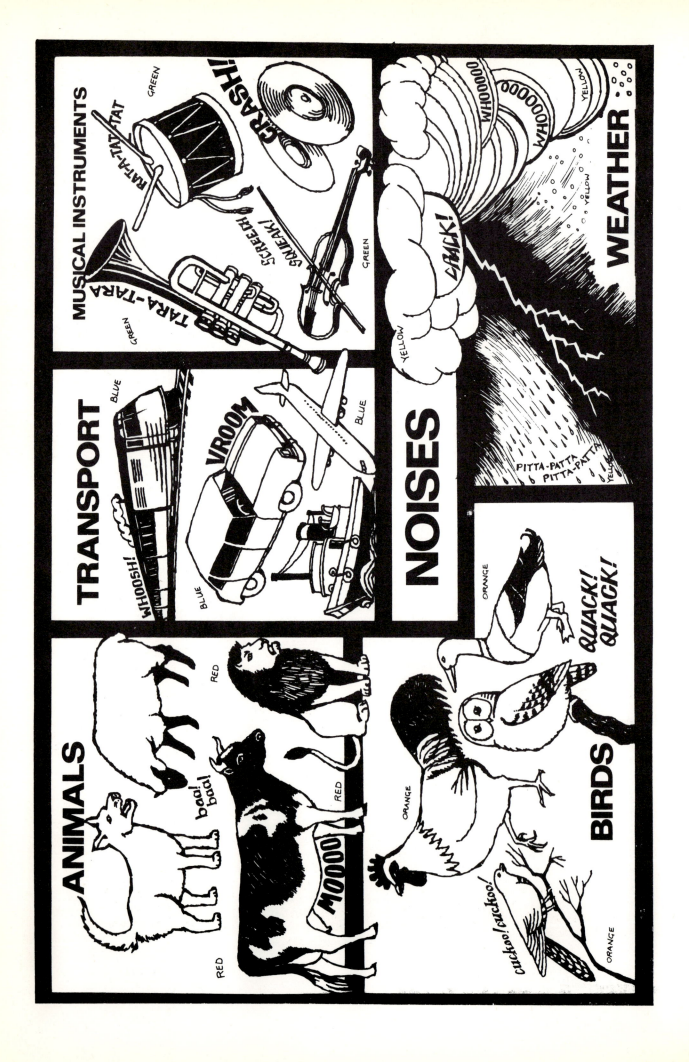

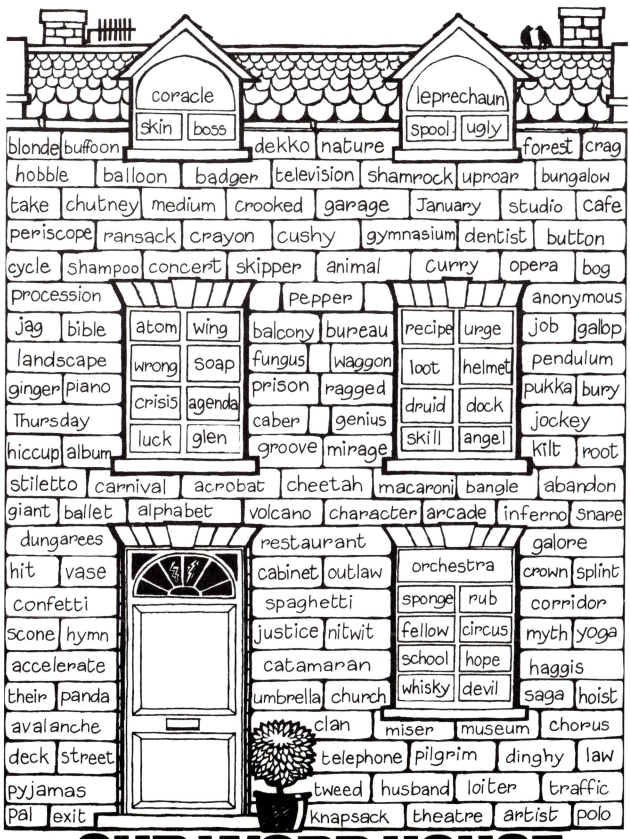

OUR WORD HOUSE

OUR WORD HOUSE

A game for 16 - 32 players, lasting 60 - 75 minutes.

The game must be played in a context that has shown how English, as well as being spoken or read by the largest number of people in the world, is the most adaptive and receptive of all languages to words coming from other countries. With the word comes the concept, the idea, another more exact way of pinning down experience.

The aim of the game, then, is to show that through the inter-action of all the peoples who have ever come to Britain or with whom the British people have ever been in contact, something valuable and lasting has been gained. It is clearly a plea for many of the new immigrants to Britain to be seen in a more welcoming and positive light. It is also an attempt to make children interested in their own language.

The teacher will need the following items:-

1. A Word House card for every two players;
2. A national family card for every two players; (these must be cut in half)
3. A coloured pencil for every family that could be the colour of its family card;
4. Many 1" - 2" strips of paper for sentence making;
5. A sheet of white paper per family to make a National shop sign;
6. Quantities of newspaper, sellotape, scissors and tissue paper for hat making.

PREPARING THE CONTEXT

Three themes here are A: sounds of language; B: structure of language; C: its origins.

A1 Commentaries In groups of three: one is a radio/T.V. commentator who speaks only gobbledygook, the other two are international competitors in an "It's a Knockout" football match, tennis tournament, Come Dancing, Crazy Golf etc. Try it three times round. What new words did commentators make up?

A2 Draw a Sound Take some interesting words like plunge, boom, jibber, gossip and using the letters of the word shape them into a drawing of the word's action.

A3 Origins Take your friend's surname and see (a) what job it might suggest he/she does (b) what country his family originally came from. Repeat with place names or neighbour's names.

B1 Home-made. All players imagine they are building something special with either toy or real bricks. They talk to themselves in gobbledygook, describing what they are doing, making sounds of all tools. Now in pairs each shows and describes his making to the other, answering questions, both in gobbledygook. Talk about words used.

B2 Bricks How many uses can each pair think of for a brick. Try to make a parallel with adaptability of words as bricks in a language.

C1 Eating out In small groups name (?) 5 things you might find in an Indian, Italian, Greek restaurant in your town. Report back. Are these words English now?

C2 'Pure' English? Ask how English came to be as it is. List all the different people that have come to England since earliest times. On blackboard sort these out into a chronology (teacher could use family cards in game to help her). How do words change, become Anglicised? Any examples, especially of slang becoming acceptable?

INTRODUCING THE GAME

The chairs and desks of the classroom need to be set out in pairs in a circle, with space between pairs for access and a central clear area. The game is played in pairs and players could work with their friends but in classes of mixed ability some of the linguistically more able could partner those who may be less able. Within the context of seeing the building bricks of the English language as being made in many different countries, the teacher now explains that the class is to experience this making of the Word House in action.
The class is to imagine that it is a series of families, all from the different countries of the world which have deeply influenced the English language, living next to each other in a row of terraced houses. The classroom is Our Street. There are to be eight different nationalities who have been the greatest influence - Celts, Romans, Greeks, Scandinavians, French, Dutch, Italians and Indians. Either the players can choose a nationality (which in many a multi-racial classroom could be their own) or the teacher could go round the class following the listed chronology. This can be repeated again for any number over 16, then each nationality will be doubled - though doubled nations must not be next to each other. If the group is over 32, then nations can be trebled but 48 players should be the maximum. Family cards are now given out.

BECOMING THE FAMILIES

The teacher will draw the families' attention to the fact that each family name has a meaning, which might indicate how it could behave! Each family card reminds players of when their ancestors first came to Britain and the card has twenty words in its word box from the many hundreds that it has contributed to the language. These are its bartering currency for inter-action.

Each family has now to do two things: to make a large sign telling its nationality i.e. <u>Celtic</u>, to display prominently on its desk shop counter, and to make a hat each to wear, similar perhaps to those in the pictures. Hats can be simply made with newspaper, sellotape, scissors and a limited tissue paper, either fully in a three dimensional way or with a head-band of paper and a cut out outline of the hat stuck on the front of this. Players could try out their national accents as they work and think of what they would eat at meal-times.

MOVING INTO THE STREET

When all the families are ready, with hats on, signs displayed and all making and doing stuff cleared away, they are given one copy of the <u>Word House</u> per family pair and one coloured pencil, which could be the same colour as their family card. To show that they have moved into the street they must write their family name and nationality on their front door and then with the coloured pencil colour in on the house the twenty bricks which are from their own word box. Word meanings can be explored. This will take quite a while and as they do it, they must try to think whether those words tell them something about the family - for instance the Dutch family will notice that many words are about the sea. Now the families are ready for action.

INTER-ACTION

Half an hour is enough for this. Families are now given a handful of 1" - 2" strips of paper for sentence making. In order to survive in their new land the families have to inter-act; they have to share what they have and give to others. The game is to see how much each family inter-acts. As they do so they will pick up and use the language of other families. This is shown by having more bricks on the Word House coloured in: Language is enriched and more colourful from more contact with more people. <u>So the aim of the game is to get as many bricks coloured in as possible within the time given.</u> To do this:

(a) Each family takes a 'foreign' (ie. uncoloured) word and on the strip of paper writes out an interesting sentence that shows what it means.

(b) Then one of the pair takes the sentence (ie. "I need an <u>umbrella</u> because it is <u>raining</u>") and the family Word House around the other house-shops trying to find out what country the word "umbrella" comes from. When one of the Italian family says "that's mine", then the player hands over the sentence. If the Italian accepts it as a good-enough sentence with the word properly used then the Italian colours in the word brick with his family colour pencil on the other person's Word House, who then takes it back home.

(c) Meanwhile the second member of the family will be sitting at home with his word box. When members of other families come around visiting, asking about different words, he must honestly say if such a word comes from his word box or not. If it does, then he will read the other's sentence and if he accepts it as correct then he will colour in that word with his coloured pencil on the other family's Word House.

(d) When the inter-acting member of the family returns, the two players make up another sentence and then the stay-at-home member this time goes out inter-acting. This alternation continues throughout the half-hour of play.

REFLECTION AND FOLLOW-UP

The teacher will want to talk with the class about the experience and what the players think they have learned. The aim is <u>not</u> for the children to remember what countries the words came from, just to realize that our language is highly international in origin and that this is what helps to make it so expressive and rich. All the Word Houses could be pinned up close together like a row of terraced houses. Later the class could provide a mural environment for Our Street with an inter-national flavour.

Just for fun the players could now be asked to try to put two of the sentences together that they have just been given in the exchange to make (a) the start of a funny story, or (b) another two to start an adventure story. They could try to put <u>all</u> the sentences together by adding links and additional sentences of their own. Or they could take the twenty words from their word box and make up a story to be set in the country of their origin. This would need some research into geography books. Another theme is to imagine that the players were one of the original families that came over or influenced England at the period of time on the family card. What happened to them and how did they cope in their new country? This would need some historical research.

Finally they could think of Britain since the second world war. What are some new words that have come into the language? What especially can they find that have come from Russia, Africa, the West Indies or America (that are not just corruptions)? Scientific, technological, food and youth-cult words are worth exploring.

The McCameron Family
CELTIC

McCameron = son of Crooked Nose (in Gaelic)
The CELTS came from Central Europe in the
6th - 4th centuries B.C. driving out the
Iberians who had populated England since
the ice age. The Gaelic Celts (the Picts)
were later driven into Ireland and the
Scottish Highlands and the Breton Celts
(the Britons) into Wales and Brittany.

druid	rub	badger	jag
clan	job	galore	haggis
crag	jockey	glen	button
shamrock	caber	kilt	tweed
whisky	coracle	bog	leprechaun

The Fitzroy Family
FRENCH

Fitzroy = son of the King (in French)
The FRENCH conquered Britain in 1066
and after that Norman French became the
language of the court, the law and the
church for the next 300 years, English
remaining only the language of the country. The French influence has continued
ever since through trade, war and travel.

ballet	balloon	gallop	garage
restaurant	blonde	mirage	crayon
abandon	bureau	nature	vase
artist	cabinet	prison	justice
avalanche	cafe	forest	procession

The Smith Family
SCANDINAVIAN

Smith = man (in Scand'navian)
The SCANDINAVIAN invasions of Britain
in the 8th-10th centuries A.D. followed
closely on the conquests of the Jutes,
Saxons and Angles (hence English) in the
5th and 6th centuries when the Celts were
driven north. The Vikings (Norwegians &
Danes) contributed richly to Old English.

Thursday	outlaw	snare	skill
their	urge	hit	wing
law	husband	take	ransack
fellow	skin	crooked	ugly
wrong	root	ragged	saga

The Prater Family
DUTCH

Prater = to chatter or boast (in Dutch)
The DUTCH traded wool and weaving with
us in the 14th century and we have long
shared a concern for fishing, ship-build-
ing and fen-draining. Many Dutch artists
worked in England in the 16th & 17th
centuries and in the 19th century both
countries colonized in South Africa.

skipper	luck	nitwit	uproar
deck	splint	hope	spool
hoist	dock	boss	groove
bury	landscape	hiccup	hobble
loiter	waggon	knapsack	scone

The Benedictus Family
LATIN

Benedictus = bless with sign of the Cross.
The ROMANS came from Gaul and Italy
conquering and occupying Britain from
43 A.D. to 418 A.D. Roman missionaries
brought Christianity in the 7th century
and scholars brought Roman learning in
the 10th century and the later Renaissance.
Our early schools taught mainly Latin.

Soap	sponge	recipe	fungus
helmet	album	january	miser
school	circus	giant	hymn
street	genius	exit	agenda
crown	medium	animal	pendulum

The Kallie Family
INDIAN

Kallie = a prickly saltwert (a weed)
The INDIAN contribution to English was
made mainly in the 19th century when
our colonial ambitions were at their
greatest and Queen Victoria became
Empress of India. This led to the
study of Sanskrit, the classical language of Hindu India, and its philosophy.

dungarees	loot	chutney	yoga
bungalow	pyjamas	polo	cheetah
bangle	curry	pal	dekko
shampoo	catamaran	pepper	cushy
dinghy	panda	ginger	pukka

The Theodore Family
GREEK

Theodore = gift of god (in Greek)
The GREEKS never directly came to Britain but from 800 - 100 B.C. their Empire was perhaps the richest in ideas and understanding that the world has ever known. The Greeks were conquered by the Romans who absorbed much of Greek into Latin and so it comes into English indirectly.

angel	telephone	bible	acrobat
devil	atom	theatre	periscope
church	character	alphabet	television
gymnasium	chorus	museum	anonymous
myth	cycle	orchestra	crisis

The Giovanni Family
ITALIAN

Giovanni = John (in Italian)
The ITALIAN influence of English began mainly with the Renaissance in the 16th century and came to a climax in the Elizabethan period when its fashions became all the rage and most English gentlemen made a Grand Italian Tour to enjoy its music, painting & architecture.

concert	volcano	balcony	dentist
confetti	arcade	umbrella	macaroni
opera	spaghetti	traffic	accelerate
piano	studio	buffoon	pilgrim
stiletto	inferno	carnival	corridor

THE GLOBAL CAKE

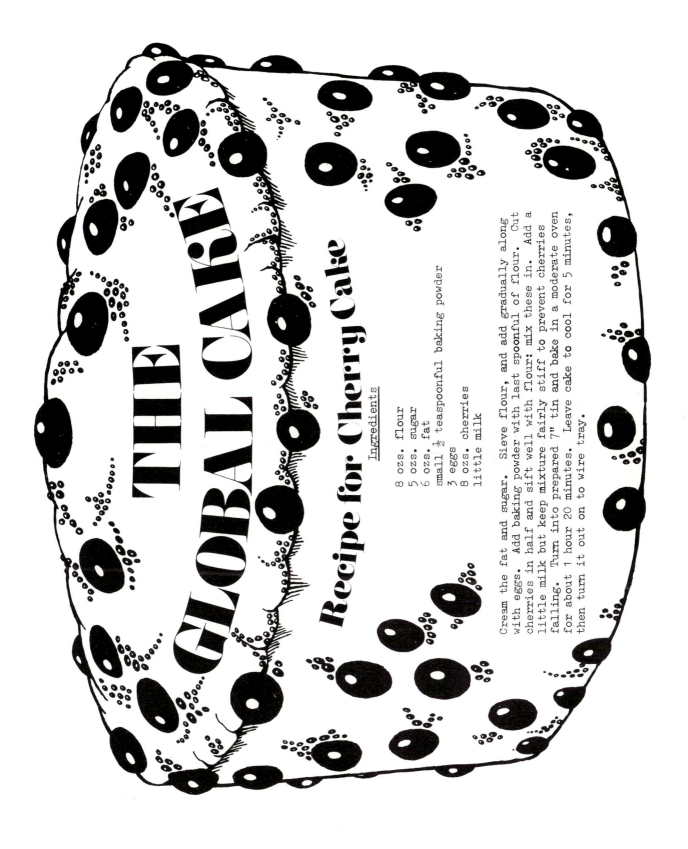

THE GLOBAL CAKE

Recipe for Cherry Cake

Ingredients

8 ozs. flour
5 ozs. sugar
6 ozs. fat
small ½ teaspoonful baking powder
3 eggs
8 ozs. cherries
little milk

Cream the fat and sugar. Sieve flour, and add gradually along with eggs. Add baking powder with last spoonful of flour. Cut cherries in half and sift well with flour: mix these in. Add a little milk but keep mixture fairly stiff to prevent cherries falling. Turn into prepared 7" tin and bake in a moderate oven for about 1 hour 20 minutes. Leave cake to cool for 5 minutes, then turn it out on to wire tray.

THE GLOBAL CAKE GAME

A game for 20 - 30 players, lasting 60 - 75 minutes.

The game needs to be played in the context of studies of the world and how its peoples are all inter-dependent on each other for a life of more than mere survival.

The aim of the game is to show by symbols how that inter-action actually changes us all and how it can enrich what life has to offer. It aims also to give an experience of what it may feel like being in a group of people at a different stage of development than other groups of people and having to work harder to receive less.

The teacher will need the following items:-
1. A large sheet of paper mounted on the wall for a proposed mural with the Global Cake illustration and recipe for Cherry Cake stuck in its centre;
2. An actual Cherry Cake (hidden away) already cut into 30 pieces (plus 30 paper plates)!
3. One of the seven card sheets of different ingredient templates with barter signs for each of the seven country groups;
4. A recipe of instructions for each of the seven groups;
5. 7 large signs with letters in the relevant group colours saying: CHINA, NORTH AMERICA, ASIA, AFRICA, EUROPE, SOUTH AMERICA and RUSSIA.
6. National Resources for each Country group as follows:
   (a) China: 10 or so sheets of A4 white light card; plus 2 thick card templates of arrows ½" wide, 2¾" broad, and the length of the width of this sheet of paper, so that 4 could be made from a sheet of A4;
   (b) Asia: 7 bottles of glue and some brushes;
   (c) Africa: 7 and more pictures of the blue Globe Map, with atlases available;
   (d) Russia: 7 blue pencils or blue crayons, 7 lead pencils;
   (e) Europe: One or several crayons or pencils of each of the following seven colours: yellow, red, green, brown, orange, black and white;
   (f) S.America: At least 40 sheets of grey A5 paper for making the 'products', (A5 is half the size of this sheet of paper);
   (g) N.America: 7 pairs of scissors.

It is possible to create a handicap in the game by not having seven bottles of glue or pairs of scissors or blue or lead pencils, so that groups have to barter and borrow more from each other.

Preparation
As well as having obtained all the above items, made the two 'arrow' templates, and mounted the empty mural on the wall, the teacher now needs to arrange the desks and chairs around the room in seven groups, with the relevant signs displayed on them.

CHINA	(yellow)	10 chairs, card for arrows and arrow templates on desk;
ASIA	(red)	7 chairs, glue and brushes on desk;
AFRICA	(green)	3 chairs, world pictures and atlases on desk;
RUSSIA	(brown)	3 chairs, blue and lead pencils or crayons on desk;
EUROPE	(orange)	3 chairs, coloured crayons or pencils on desk;
SOUTH AMERICA	(black)	2 chairs, sheets of 'product' paper on desk;
NORTH AMERICA	(white)	2 chairs, scissors on desk.

The children come into the room and teacher lets them work in social groups, sitting in the chairs as they have been prearranged. The figures given above are for a class of thirty children; fewer or greater numbers should be distributed between groups in those proportions.

Beginnings
1. The teacher explains that the class is now going to imagine that they are to make a special kind of cherry cake together.
   The class must tease out what is needed for making a cake, thinking not only of ingredients but also of the oven, utensils, implements etc. The teacher will want to ask what happens when the ingredients are cooked, how they fuse into something new, why it is then that they are eaten and what good does that do and so forth. The purpose here is to establish that a lot of some things and a little of others are equally necessary to make the cake, that great changes occur within the inter-action of the cooking; that something new is made from the creative act of cake-baking; that without food the cooks would not be able to live.

It may be that the class has actually made a cake in an earlier lesson and this may just be a remembering process (or it may be that after this 'symbolic' lesson a cake is made) but it is important that some of those concepts above have been well talked through.

2. Now the teacher explains that our special cherry cake today is going to represent a special kind of World or Global Cake, as if all the resources of the world are like the possible ingredients of some gigantic cake and that all the peoples of the world are like an army of cooks, who not only make the cake but then enjoy eating it. The cake represents in life not only food but all the things necessary to live by, shelter, clothing, toys, machines, facilities. This may need a lot of exampling and elucidation.

3. Finally the teacher explains that if we imagine that all the millions of people in the world, the cooks, were reduced to only 30, then roughly in the proportions that they would find themselves, 10 would be Chinese, 7 would be Asian (that is West Asia, Oceania, South Asia, including India), 3 would be African, 3 would be Russian (that is including all the Russian block and East Europe), 3 would be European (that is western Europe), 2 would be South American and 2 would be North American (that includes Canada and Greenland). Those seven country areas and the colour of the peoples are going to be represented in our cake by the seven ingredients for the cake, the largest amount of ingredients needed, 8oz. flour, being represented by the country with the largest population, China and so on down to the smallest amount, the small teaspoonful of baking powder, being represented by North America.

The Game

The aim of the game is to make a wall chart of the Global Cake within half an hour. Every country has a recipe and that recipe shows what contribution of ingredients the country has to contribute to the cake.

The resources that each country has, its industries, farming, oil, metals, knowledge, facilities and so forth are represented by the scissors, paper, glue, crayons etc.

Some are raw materials (like paper) others are industries (like scissors).

The teacher now needs to go through the Instructions (Recipe) slowly, so that everyone understands. Each country must appreciate what ingredient it is representing and how its symbol, barter units and colour represent this. Countries must keep to the International Trade Agreements for exchanging their commodities/resources for the number of units stated, but 'exchanges' can be set up within that value system. Once a group has sold any of its resources then it can use the money it has gained to buy other resources that it needs to make its ingredients. Countries must decide how they first cut up their barter units. Once the game starts all decisions must come from the Countries, the teacher is not to help, only in the mounting of the 'ingredients' on the mural.

Mounting the Mural

It is suggested that the seven Globe maps, with appropriate areas coloured in, will form an outer widely dispersed ring around the edge. A Country's first arrow will lead from that to the display of the various ingredient symbols as required, then a second arrow will lead from that inner ring into the actual Global Cake itself. The third arrow will lead back from the Cake to the ingredients (because that is how they are sustained) and a fourth arrow back to the Country (because that is how its peoples are fed).

Evaluation

Once the 30 minutes are up, (and the teacher will need to give warnings of this in the last 10 minutes), then all groups must stop, whatever state they are in, and gather round the Mural to see what it looks like. They must account for why some ingredients are better mounted than others, why some may not be complete yet, why others were complete a long while ago and what those people have been doing since.

It is here that the teacher should help the group to gain insights into the different stages of development that some countries are at and how this affects what they can contribute. What was it like having a large number in a group or a small number? How did they make decisions? What organisation or leadership did they set up? What were their feelings when some knew they were handicapped and others had life very easy? The fairness or unfairness of this can be explored and suggestions made why it is so. Leisure activities, the quality of life and tourism can be discussed - what does that all depend on?

Dividing the Cake

Finally, ideally with a real cake, alternatively with a cardboard circle or thirty pieces of chocolate, the cake is ceremoniously produced, already cut into thirty pieces, as if to give one to each child. However, instead the cake is divided between the thirty pupils in the way in which the world's cake of resources is currently distributed among its peoples. This will need to be talked through, explained and reflected upon.

China, 10 players, 4 pieces; Asia, 7 players, 1½ pieces; Africa, 3 players, ½ piece; Russia, 3 players, 5½ pieces; Europe, 3 players 8½ pieces; South America, 2 players, 1½ pieces; North America, 2 players, 8½ pieces.

RECIPE TO MAKE THE GLOBAL CAKE

COUNTRY	POPULATION NUMBERS	INGREDIENT REPRESENTING	PRODUCTS FOR CHART	COLOUR	NATIONAL RESOURCES	SELLING PRICE
CHINA	10 players	8 oz flour	8 sheaf of corn symbols	Yellow	Card for arrows & template	4 units each
ASIA	7 players	8 oz flour	8 cherry symbols	Red	Glue and brushes	2 units each
AFRICA	3 players	6 oz fat	6 grass/vegetation symbols	Green	World pictures	2 units each
RUSSIA	3 players	5 oz sugar	5 cane sugar symbols	Brown	Blue & lead pencils	6 units each
EUROPE	3 players	3 eggs	3 chicken symbols	Orange	Coloured crayons	4 units each
SOUTH AMERICA	2 players	little milk	1 cow symbol	Black	Paper for products	2 units each
NORTH AMERICA	2 players	baking powder	1 tin of baking powder symbol	White	Scissors	6 units each

THE MAKING OF THE CAKE = THE MURAL

All countries start with a sheet containing one large country symbol and 16 barter units, plus its National Resources within the time limit given, each Country has to:-

1. Obtain a Globe map and colour in your Country's area with the colour of the country;

2. Obtain sufficient card and using the template, make four arrows which must be coloured blue;

3. Obtain sufficient paper to make the required number of 'products' for the chart (see column 4 above).

    To make these products you must cut out your symbol to make a template of it, then with a pencil trace around it on the sheets of paper; these must then be cut out. Each 'product' must then be filled in with all the details of the symbol and coloured neatly the country colour. If you have time this should be most carefully undertaken.

4. When all is complete, obtain some glue and under the directions of the teacher all your items must now be stuck attractively onto the Mural. Your contribution to the cake is then complete.

5. Now you have time for leisure. By buying and selling different resources you can try to gain as many barter units (your wealth) as possible. Also, using your resources and buying and selling, you could make other, new products, either for your own use, or to sell to other countries who are enjoying their leisure. Be ingenious. You can also go visiting and watch other people at work, perhaps making appropriate comments as tourists.

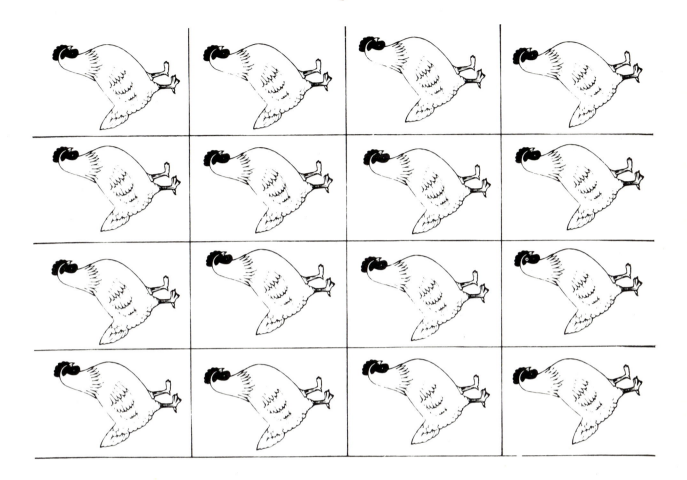

ORANGE

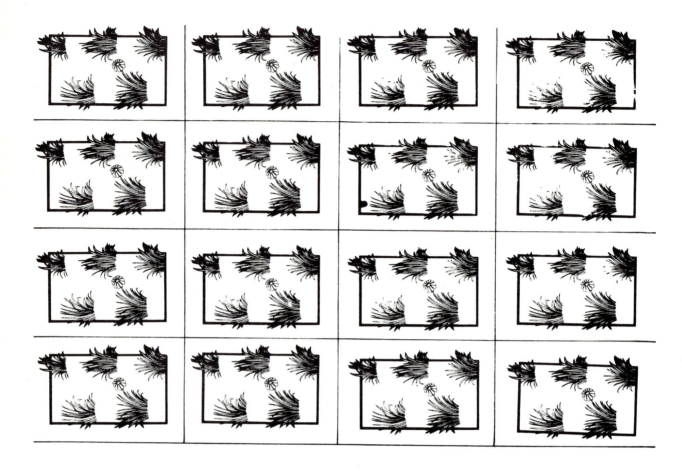

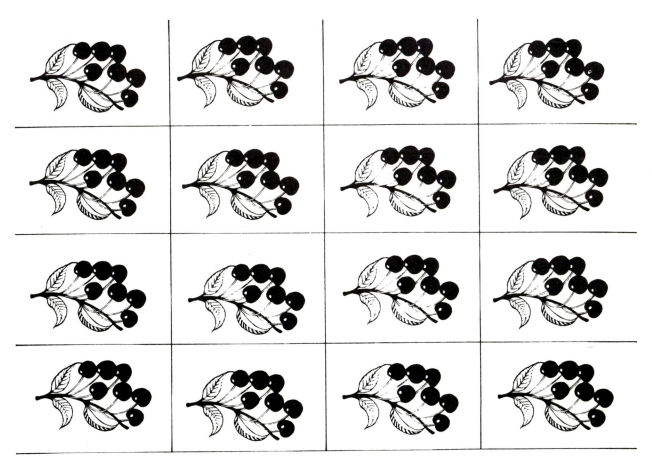

RED

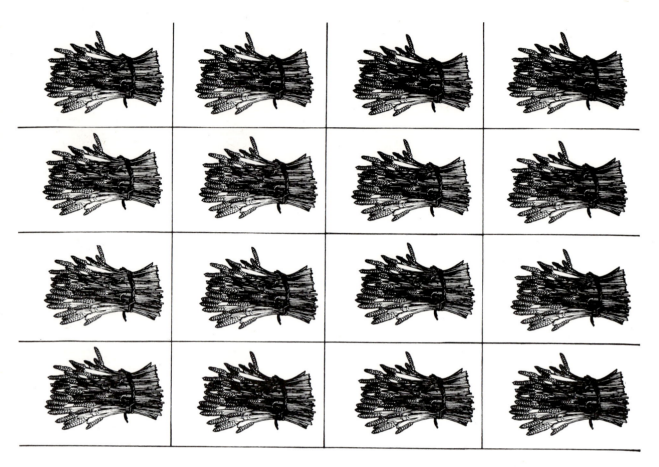

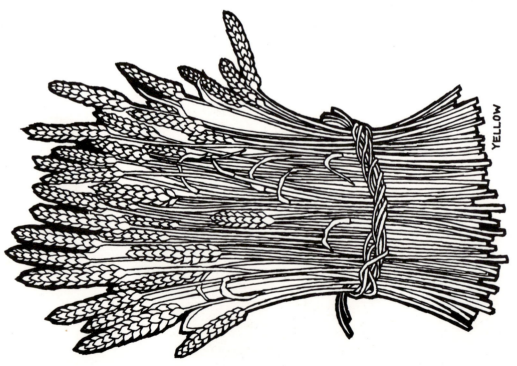

YELLOW

WHITE

BLACK

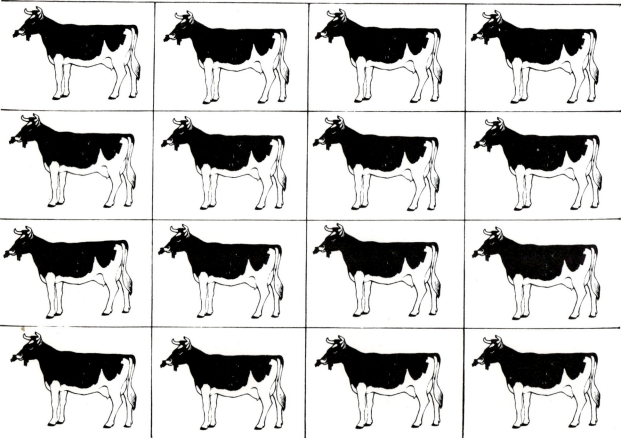

BROWN

GRONKS & FRIENDS

GRONKS & FRIENDS
KNYBE
TWERG
the social labelling
and
group identity game
SCRUD
SFINX
TWERG
PATCHES FOR EVER
SFINX
TWERG
KNYBE
HATS
HATS
HATS
HATS
HATS
Gronk
Gronk
What's that you said? Eh! What?
TWERG
SCRUD
KNYBE
UNITE
SFINX

GRONKS & FRIENDS

The Social labelling and group identity game

GRONKS AND FRIENDS is an analogue and is only relevant to the extent that any analogy can work. It aims to explore the interaction of social groups, to show how society shapes an individual's identity and what happens when the individual deviates from the group norm. The game tries to approach such controversial issues as prejudice, social labelling and stereotyping obliquely through a framework of fun.

Clearly it aims at greater tolerance, understanding and empathy through an experience of the opposite, the processes of alienation in action. The group can tease out from a 'safe' common experience how those processes were generated and carried through and how they might be echoed in their everyday existence. Any leader introducing the game must be fully aware of the dangers of negative reinforcement, as in all this kind of work, and each clan must be set up to have a cross section of the group of players within it. A clan must never be comprised of a natural social group of friends or ethnic sub-group of the whole group, or it will only exaggerate existing differences and actual alienation.

A leader needs to assess carefully his group beforehand to see if they could cope imaginatively with the nonsensical worlds of the Gronks and Twergs. Originally the game was devised for average and less than average pupils but we have found that unless the group can immediately enter into the spirit of its seeming ridiculousness and intuitively feel that it probably will have some purpose then the players will switch off and feel it is a complete waste of time. The game must be thoroughly entered into so that there will be emotional capital to be drawn on at the end during the post-play discussion.

The de-briefing session is the most crucial part of all. The group must explore for themselves what they thought the experience was getting at and discover what parallels could be made to their real life situations. They must examine how their emotions and feelings, including boredom and confusion, were involved in the game and how their feelings would have been much more deeply disturbed in reality, perhaps leading to certain behavioural responses.

The hope is that by pupils becoming increasingly aware of such social dynamics and conditioning of responses and expectations there may be a greater holding back from negative judgmental attitudes. The openness of childhood, they might discover, has to be relearned through experience and not innocence.

*   *   *   *

The game was devised by a group of teachers on the 1976 four day annual Cockpit "MAN IN ACTION" Course - examining role play and simulation.

It has since been replayed many times, altered and rejigged, with every variety of response. Some teachers have had to adapt it radically with their own groups, to make it work, which is as it should be. All agreed it is full of ideas and have requested a more prepared copy. Some have played only parts of it at any one time. Most agree it is too full and that "there are four simulations in there trying to get out". Perhaps it is best seen as 'work in progress'. It is not guaranteed.

Final revised form: Alec Davison; illustrations: Sue Henry; graphics, printing and collating Kevin Flett.

GRONKS & FRIENDS *HOW TO PLAY*

A game for 20 - 30 players needing at least 80 minutes playing time.
Equipment necessary for 30 players:

1. Coloured stickers, one for every player; 6 colours, 5 of each colour, if possible the same colour as the Clan's instruction cards.
2. Six large coloured signs boldly stating the six clan names, ideally the same colour as the Clan's instruction cards.
3. Six hats, of all kinds, one for each clan;
4. Six eye-patches, one for each clan;
5. Six walking sticks, one for each clan;
6. Five rolls of sellotape, one for each Scrud;
7. Lots of bits of string for the Twergs;
8. Masses of newspapers for the Sfinx;
9. Scissors, glue and paper clips for the Gronks.

<u>Cut each of the six A4 coloured cards in the kit into five individual cards.</u>
The game is intended for 30 players. It will work with 20 (but no less) and then the SCRUDS and the KNYBES should be left out; in that case the GRONKS could also handle the sellotape and the PLARMS could handle any furniture as well as chairs.

a. Set the room up beforehand in a series of six sub-group circles, five chairs each, each group away from the other, if possible.
b. Display by the Clan circle a large coloured card, the same colour as the relevant individual instruction cards and stickers, if possible, with the name of the Clan on, printed large.
c. Set the instruction cards on the chairs for each person, putting the hat, the eye-patch and the walking stick by the relevant card as it indicates. In the centre of each sub-group put the relevant coloured stickers and the relevant materials; sellotape for Scruds, string for Twergs, newspapers for Sfinx, scissors, glue & paper clips for Gronks.
d. Check everything.
e. Only now, let the players into the room. If you feel the need for some warm-up activity, then the players must stay in the centre of the area and not in any way yet go to the sub-groups or see the cards. When the warm-up is over then they can take a seat. In warm-up players could imagine what a Twerg, Gronk etc. etc. looks like, talks, walk etc. just from the sound of each word - quick 30 second exercises. Either way, warm-up or not, players are to be mixed up between Clans, so that there is a fair balance of sexes, so that friends do not work together, nor ethnic groups work together etc. etc.
f. Before everyone looks at the cards you welcome them, perhaps in a role yourself, to the Gathering of the Clans. You explain that we are all going to assume different roles in a new society to look at the way we make friends and get on with each other - it might be a foretaste of Britain after devolution! You urge everyone to stick faithfully to the instructions on the cards, which are all different, and to remember to be a loyal Clansman at all times.
g. Players should now be invited to read the top half only of the front of the card on their chairs. The front is the side that tells them they are Gronk 1 or 2 or whatever. Once they know this, they are to write their clan and their number onto the sticky label and put that on their forehead for all to see. On the card underneath where it tells them what clan number they are, it also tells them a private thing about themselves. They must now also put on any hat, eye-patch or hold a walking stick, as suggested by that private fact.
ALL CARDS ARE PRIVATE AND NO-ONE SHOULD SEE ANYONE ELSES OR SHOW THEIRS.
h. The time-scale of the activity now has to be judged by the controller. It cannot be less than <u>90 minutes</u> and could be much more, with a longer time given to most of the sections overleaf and other encounters added.
   Suggested pattern: 10 mins. Setting up (including warm-up)
                       55 mins. In play (outline indicated overleaf)
                       25 mins. De-briefing, evaluation, reflection.
                                 This could take place symbolically in the ruins of
                                 the shelter.

POSSIBLE PATTERN OF PLAY

The Controller moves all Clans on to the next encounter (1-8) at the same time.

A Read top half of front of card only (Front is side that says "You are Twerg 1")
   "Round pegs in round holes" (Clansmen must relate as the cards indicate.)
   Clan members 1 and 4 are going to interview members 2, 3 and 5 each in turn. Their
   aim is in finding out more about them to see what task they would be best suited to in
   serving their clan, being now of an age to start work.
   1. 2 mins: 1 & 4 prepare questions; 2,3 & 5 discuss what tasks they hope for.
   2. 4 mins: 1 & 4 interview 2;3 & 5 are asked to write a Clan anthem to a nursery-
                rhyme tune to be sung at Clan social gatherings;
   3. 4 mins: 1 & 4 interview 3;2 & 5 are asked to complete the anthem, if necessary, and
                then draw up proposals for a forthcoming Clan social gathering;
   4. 4 mins: 1 & 4 interview 5;2 & 3 are asked to decide what jobs they feel 1 & 4 would
                best be suited for in serving the clan and who of the 5 should be spokesman
                for the clan at inter-clan gatherings.
   5. 4 mins: All Clan meets together, 1 & 4 to inform others of the jobs they feel they
                are best fitted for, the others to teach the clan their new anthem and to
                suggest jobs for 1 & 4 as well as selecting the clan spokesman.
                Can they all agree about these matters?

B Read bottom half of front of card, not forgetting the top half information
   "All good friends and jolly good company"
   Now is the time of the year when you have to make plans together for the
   National Clan Holy-day when you celebrate the Feast of the Ancestors. Your
   task now is to plan the celebratory party after the observances.
   5. 10 mins: You must decide:
                a. what sort of party you want (disco?,games, cabaret, music, food);
                b. who is to be responsible for invitations, M.C., food, music, games;
                c. who will be seated next to whom for the traditional grand Feast.

C Read top half of back of card (which has picture) not forgetting previous facts
   "In the shadow of our ancestors: rules and meanings"
   6. 5 mins: Every clansman is allowed to bring one member of another clan to the Feast
                of the Ancestors. Such a member should be someone whom he could happily
                spend the rest of his life with, either in friendship, marriage or in
                work-business partnership. You have only 5 minutes.
   7. 10 mins: You are sitting together with your chosen partner, before the Feast day,
                when you read in the newspaper that the Holy Day is going to be used by the
                Clan Council for a "Cleanup the Clan" Campaign, when each clan is called
                upon to make an example of at least one of its members who is disobeying
                the Clan code of conduct.
                While clan members attempt to do that together, it could be that those clans-
                men (the controller announces) who feel threatened and misunderstood could
                meet together in groups of similar interests and try to make others more
                sympathetic to their point of view, perhaps even forming new organisations,
                with manifestos, to demonstrate at the Feast Day of the Ancestors.

D Read bottom half of back of card, not forgetting previous information
   "United we stand ... there is a tide in the affairs of man ..."
   8. 12 mins: Above the din, the controller calls for silence to make the following
                announcement in role.
                "Attention. Attention.
                This is an important B.B.C. News Flash. I repeat. This is an ....
                News has just been received that will be of grave concern to all our peoples.
                A disaster looms over our community.
                There is an imminent threat of total extinction. It comes from without.
                Society's only hope is to build a 4 foot high newspaper barrier in a box
                of four sides, with no gaps or crannies that would admit the power of
                extinction. In this the entire community can shelter together. Materials
                can be simple. Chairs may be used and other furniture for support, as well
                as string, sellotape, scissors, glue and paper clips. The Disaster is
                threatened to strike exactly 12 minutes from the termination of this news
                flash. I repeat. You have only 12 minutes before extinction from now."
                Controller to give 'countdown' at 10,5,4,3,2,1 zero minutes.

you are *Gronk* one

You loathe the national sport of tiddliwinks.

GRONKS enjoy company; they react strongly to fellow clansmen.
Gronk 2 is a trouble maker; you blame him if things go wrong.
Gronk 3 is a great bore who makes you yawn; he is often angry.
Gronk 4 is known as a wit and a comic and makes you laugh.
Gronk 5 is very popular and you want to be his best friend.

GRONKS are a law-abiding clan. They conform to its customs.
a. It is forbidden to wear any kind of head covering.
b. Clansmen must see the world clearly through both eyes.
c. It is traditional to be clever and quick on the uptake.
d. Clan members are expected to stay young; age is unwelcome.

---

you are *Gronk* two

You are very old move slowly and need support

GRONKS enjoy company; they react strongly to fellow clansmen.
Gronk 1 you look to as your leader to make decisions for you.
Gronk 3 is a great bore who makes you yawn; he is often angry.
Gronk 4 is known as a wit and a comic and makes you laugh.
Gronk 5 is very popular and you want to be his best friend.

GRONKS are a law-abiding clan. They conform to its customs.
a. It is forbidden to wear any kind of head covering.
b. Clansmen must see the world clearly through both eyes.
c. It is traditional to be clever and quick on the uptake.
d. A true clansman enjoys the national sport of tiddliwinks.

---

you are *Gronk* three

Sadly you're dim & need everything to be repeated

GRONKS enjoy company; they react strongly to fellow clansmen.
Gronk 1 you look to as your leader to make decisions for you.
Gronk 2 is a trouble maker; you blame him if things go wrong.
Gronk 4 is known as a wit and a comic and makes you laugh.
Gronk 5 is very popular and you want to be his best friend.

GRONKS are a law-abiding clan. They conform to its customs.
a. It is forbidden to wear any kind of head covering.
b. Clansmen must see the world clearly through both eyes.
c. A true clansman enjoys the national sport of tiddliwinks.
d. Clan members are expected to stay young; age is unwelcome.

---

you are *Gronk* four

You love hats; always wear one & always have

GRONKS enjoy company; they react strongly to fellow clansmen.
Gronk 1 you look to as your leader to make decisions for you.
Gronk 2 is a trouble maker; you blame him if things go wrong.
Gronk 3 is a great bore who makes you yawn; he is often angry.
Gronk 5 is very popular and you want to be his best friend.

GRONKS are a law-abiding clan. They conform to its customs.
a.   Clansmen must see the world clearly through both eyes.
b. A true clansman enjoys the national sport of tiddliwinks.
c. Clan members are expected to stay young; age is unwelcome.
d. It is traditional to be clever and quick on the uptake.

---

you are *Gronk* five

You have worn an eye patch ever since birth

GRONKS enjoy company; they react strongly to fellow clansmen.
Gronk 1 you look to as your leader to make decisions for you.
Gronk 2 is a trouble maker; you blame him if things go wrong.
Gronk 3 is a great bore who makes you yawn; he is often angry.
Gronk 4 is known as a wit and a comic and makes you laugh.

GRONKS are a law-abiding clan. They conform to its customs.
a. A true clansman enjoys the national sport of tiddliwinks.
b. Clan members are expected to stay young; age is unwelcome.
c. It is traditional to be clever and quick on the uptake.
d. It is forbidden to wear any kind of head covering.

GRONKS are exaggeratedly courteous when talking abroad;
They are very patriotic and loyal to their clan traditions.
All Gronks dislike the nearby KNYBES clan
but are very good friends with the TWERGS.
Other clans are tolerated.

Abroad you have a reputation for being artistic.
You are the only clan allowed to handle scissors, clips and glue;
you are not allowed to touch newspapers, string or sellotape,
or to move any chairs or furniture.
Be Gronks always.

GRONKS are exaggeratedly courteous when talking abroad;
They are very patriotic and loyal to their clan traditions.
All Gronks dislike the nearby KNYBES clan
but are very good friends with the TWERGS.
Other clans are tolerated.·

Abroad you have a reputation for being artistic.
You are the only clan allowed to handle scissors, clips and glue;
you are not allowed to touch newspapers, string or sellotape,
or to move any chairs or furniture.
Be Gronks always.

GRONKS are exaggeratedly courteous when talking abroad;
They are very patriotic and loyal to their clan traditions.
All Gronks dislike the nearby KNYBES clan
but are very good friends with the TWERGS.
Other clans are tolerated.

Abroad you have a reputation for being artistic.
You are the only clan allowed to handle scissors, clips and glue;
you are not allowed to touch newspapers, string or sellotape,
or to move any chairs or furniture.
Be Gronks always.

GRONKS are exaggeratedly courteous when talking abroad;
They are very patriotic and loyal to their clan traditions.
All Gronks dislike the nearby KNYBES clan
but are very good friends with the TWERGS.
Other clans are tolerated.

Abroad you have a reputation for being artistic.
You are the only clan allowed to handle scissors, clips and glue;
you are not allowed to touch newspapers, string or sellotape,
or to move any chairs or furniture.
Be Gronks always.

GRONKS are exaggeratedly courteous when talking abroad;
They are very patriotic and loyal to their clan traditions.
All Gronks dislike the nearby KNYBES clan
but are very good friends with the TWERGS.
Other clans are tolerated.

Abroad you have a reputation for being artistic.
You are the only clan allowed to handle scissors, clips and glue;
you are not allowed to touch newspapers, string or sellotape,
or to move any chairs or furniture.
Be Gronks always.

SCRUDS enjoy frequent body touching when talking abroad.
They are very patriotic and loyal to their clan traditions.
All Scruds dislike the nearby PLARMS clan
but are very good friends with the SFINX.
Other clans are tolerated.

Abroad you have a reputation for being superstitious.
You are the only clan allowed to handle the sellotape;
you are not allowed to touch newspapers, string, scissors,
clips and glue, or to move chairs or any furniture.
Be Scruds always.

SCRUDS enjoy frequent body touching when talking abroad.
They are very patriotic and loyal to their clan traditions.
All Scruds dislike the nearby PLARMS clan
but are very good friends with the SFINX.
Other clans are tolerated.

Abroad you have a reputation for being superstitious.
You are the only clan allowed to handle the sellotape;
you are not allowed to touch newspapers, string, scissors,
clips and glue, or to move chairs or any furniture.
Be Scruds always.

SCRUDS enjoy frequent body touching when talking abroad.
They are very patriotic and loyal to their clan traditions.
All Scruds dislike the nearby PLARMS clan
but are very good friends with the SFINX.
Other clans are tolerated.

Abroad you have a reputation for being superstitious.
You are the only clan allowed to handle the sellotape;
you are not allowed to touch newspapers, string, scissors,
clips and glue, or to move chairs or any furniture.
Be Scruds always.

SCRUDS enjoy frequent body touching when talking abroad.
They are very patriotic and loyal to their clan traditions.
All Scruds dislike the nearby PLARMS clan
but are very good friends with the SFINX.
Other clans are tolerated.

Abroad you have a reputation for being superstitious.
You are the only clan allowed to handle the sellotape;
you are not allowed to touch newspapers, string, scissors,
clips and glue, or to move chairs or any furniture.
Be Scruds always.

SCRUDS enjoy frequent body touching when talking abroad.
They are very patriotic and loyal to their clan traditions.
All Scruds dislike the nearby PLARMS clan
but are very good friends with the SFINX.
Other clans are tolerated.

Abroad you have a reputation for being superstitious.
You are the only clan allowed to handle the sellotape;
you are not allowed to touch newspapers, string, scissors,
clips and glue, or to move chairs or any furniture.
Be Scruds always.

you are **SCRUD** one	SCRUDS enjoy company; they react strongly to fellow clansmen.
	SCRUD 2 is a trouble maker; you blame him if things go wrong.
	SCRUD 3 is a great bore who makes you yawn; he is often angry.
	Scrud 4 is known as a wit and a comic and makes you laugh.
	Scrud 5 is very popular and you want to be his best friend.
You loathe the national sport of tiddliwinks	SCRUDs are a law-abiding clan. They conform to its customs.
	a. It is forbidden to wear any kind of head covering.
	b. Clansmen must see the world clearly through both eyes.
	c. It is traditional to be clever and quick on the uptake.
	d. Clan members are expected to stay young; age is unwelcome.

you are **SCRUD** two	SCRUDS enjoy company; they react strongly to fellow clansmen.
	Scrud 1 you look to as your leader to make decisions for you.
	Scrud 3 is a great bore who makes you yawn; he is often angry.
	Scrud 4 is known as a wit and a comic and makes you laugh.
	Scrud 5 is very popular and you want to be his best friend.
You are very old move slowly and need support	SCRUDs are a law-abiding clan. They conform to its customs.
	a. It is forbidden to wear any kind of head covering.
	b. Clansmen must see the world clearly through both eyes.
	c. It is traditional to be clever and quick on the uptake.
	d. A true clansman enjoys the national sport of tiddliwinks.

you are **SCRUD** three	SCRUDS enjoy company; they react strongly to fellow clansmen.
	Scrud 1 you look to as your leader to make decisions for you.
	Scrud 2 is a trouble-maker; you blame him if things go wrong.
	Scrud 4 is known as a wit and a comic and makes you laugh.
	Scrud 5 is very popular and you want to be his best friend.
Sadly you're dim & need everything to be repeated	SCRUDs are a law-abiding clan. They conform to its customs.
	a. It is forbidden to wear any kind of head covering.
	b. Clansmen must see the world clearly through both eyes.
	c. A true clansman enjoys the national sport of tiddliwinks.
	d. Clan members are expected to stay young; age is unwelcome.

you are **SCRUD** four	SCRUDS enjoy company; they react strongly to fellow clansmen.
	Scrud 1 you look to as your leader to make decisions for you.
	Scrud 2 is a trouble maker; you blame him if things go wrong.
	Scrud 3 is a great bore who makes you yawn; he is often angry.
	Scrud 5 is very popular and you want to be his best friend.
You love hats; always wear one and always have	SCRUDs are a law-abiding clan. They conform to its customs.
	a. Clansmen must see the world clearly through both eyes.
	b. A true clansman enjoys the national sport of tiddliwinks.
	c. Clan members are expected to stay young; age is unwelcome.
	d. It is traditional to be clever and quick on the uptake.

you are **SCRUD** five	SCRUDS enjoy company; they react strongly to fellow clansmen.
	Scrud 1 you look to as your leader to make decisions for you.
	Scrud 2 is a trouble maker; you blame him when things to wrong.
	Scrud 3 is a great bore who makes you yawn; he is often angry.
	Scrud 4 is known as a wit and a comic and makes you laugh.
You have worn an eye patch ever since birth	SCRUDs are a law-abiding clan. They conform to its customs.
	a. A true clansman enjoys the national sport of tiddliwinks.
	b. Clan members are expected to stay young; age is unwelcome.
	c. It is traditional to be clever and quick on the uptake.
	d. It is forbidden to wear any kind of head covering.

KNYBES are formal and stand some way off when talking abroad;
They are very patriotic and loyal to their clan traditions.
All Knybes dislike the nearby GRONK clan
but are very good friends with the PLARMS.
Other clans are tolerated.

Abroad you have a reputation for being fair.
You are the only clan allowed to handle any of the furniture,
except chairs; you are not allowed to touch newspapers, string,
scissors, sellotape, clips and glue.
Be Knybes always.

KNYBES are formal and stand some way off when talking abroad;
They are very patriotic and loyal to their clan traditions.
All Knybes dislike the nearby GRONK clan
but are very good friends with the PLARMS.
Other clans are tolerated.

Abroad you have a reputation for being fair.
You are the only clan allowed to handle any of the furniture,
except chairs; you are not allowed to touch newspapers, string,
scissors, sellotape, clips and glue.
Be Knybes always.

KNYBES are formal and stand some way off when talking abroad;
They are very patriotic and loyal to their clan traditions.
All Knybes dislike the nearby GRONK clan
but are very good friends with the PLARMS.
Other clans are tolerated.

Abroad you have a reputation for being fair.
You are the only clan allowed to handle any of the furniture,
except chairs; you are not allowed to touch newspapers, string,
scissors, sellotape, clips and glue.
Be Knybes always.

KNYBES are formal and stand some way off when talking abroad;
They are very patriotic and loyal to their clan traditions.
All Knybes dislike the nearby GRONK clan
but are very good friends with the PLARMS.
Other clans are tolerated.

Abroad you have a reputation for being fair.
You are the only clan allowed to handle any of the furniture,
except chairs; you are not allowed to touch newspapers, string,
scissors, sellotape, clips and glue.
Be Knybes always.

KNYBES are formal and stand some way off when talking abroad;
They are very patriotic and loyal to their clan traditions.
All Knybes dislike the nearby GRONK clan
but are very good friends with the PLARMS.
Other clans are tolerated.

Abroad you have a reputation for being fair.
You are the only clan allowed to handle any of the furniture,
except chairs; you are not allowed to touch newspapers, string,
scissors, sellotape, clips and glue.
Be Knybes always.

you are KNYBE one
You loathe the national sport of tiddliwinks

KNYBES enjoy company; they react strongly to fellow clansmen.
Knybe 2 is a trouble-maker; you blame him if things go wrong.
Knybe 3 is a great bore who makes you yawn; he is often angry.
Knybe 4 is known as a wit and a comic and makes you laugh.
Knybe 5 is very popular and you want to be his best friend.

KNYBES are a law-abiding clan. They conform to its customs.
a. It is forbidden to wear any kind of head covering.
b. Clansmen must see the world clearly through both eyes.
c. It is traditional to be clever and quick on the uptake.
d. Clan members are expected to stay young; age is unwelcome.

you are KNYBE two
You are very old move slowly and need support

KNYBES enjoy company; they react strongly to fellow clansmen.
Knybe 1 you look to as your leader to make decisions for you.
Knybe 3 is a great bore who makes you yawn; he is often angry.
Knybe 4 is known as a wit and a comic and makes you laugh.
Knybe 5 is very popular and you want to be his best friend.

KNYBES are a law-abiding clan. They conform to its customs.
a. It is forbidden to wear any kind of head covering.
b. Clansmen must see the world clearly through both eyes.
c. It is traditional to be clever and quick on the uptake.
d. A true clansman enjoys the national sport of tiddliwinks.

you are KNYBE three
Sadly you're dim & need everything to be repeated

KNYBES enjoy company; they react strongly to fellow clansmen.
Knybe 1 you look to as your leader to make decisions for you.
Knybe 2 is a trouble maker; you blame him if things go wrong.
Knybe 4 is known as a wit and a comic and makes you laugh.
Knybe 5 is very popular and you want to be his best friend.

KNYBES are a law-abiding clan. They conform to its customs.
a. It is forbidden to wear any kind of head covering.
b. Clansmen must see the world clearly through both eyes.
c. A true clansman enjoys the national sport of tiddliwinks.
d. Clan members are expected to stay young; age is unwelcome.

you are KNYBE four
You love hats; always wear one & always have

KNYBES enjoy company; they react strongly to fellow clansmen.
Knybe 1 you look to as your leader to make decisions for you.
Knybe 2 is a trouble maker; you blame him if things go wrong.
Knybe 3 is a great bore who makes you yawn; he is often angry.
Knybe 5 is very popular and you want to be his best friend.

KNYBES are a law-abiding clan. They conform to its customs.
a. Clansmen must see the world clearly through both eyes.
b. A true clansman enjoys the national sport of tiddliwinks.
c. Clan members are expected to stay young; age is unwelcome.
d. It is traditional to be clever and quick on the uptake.

you are KNYBE five
You have worn an eye patch ever since birth

KNYBES enjoy company; they react strongly to fellow clansmen.
Knybe 1 you look to as your leader to make decisions for you.
Knybe 2 is a trouble maker; you blame him if things go wrong.
Knybe 3 is a great bore who makes you yawn; he is often angry.
Knybe 4 is known as a wit and a comic and makes you laugh.

KNYBES are a law-abiding clan. They conform to its customs.
a. A true clansman enjoys the national sport of tiddliwinks.
b. Clan members are expected to stay young; age is unwelcome.
c. It is traditional to be clever and quick on the uptake.
d. It is forbidden to wear any kind of head covering.

TWERGS always stand very close & smile when talking abroad.
They are very loyal and patriotic to their clan traditions.
All Twergs dislike the nearby SFINX clan
but are very good friends with the GRONKS.
Other clans are tolerated.

Abroad you have a reputation for being fair.
You are the only clan allowed to handle string;
you are not allowed to touch newspapers, sellotape, scissors,
clips or glue, or to move chairs or any furniture.

TWERGS always stand very close & smile when talking abroad.
They are very loyal and patriotic to their clan traditions.
All Twergs dislike the nearby SFINX clan
but are very good friends with the GRONKS.
Other clans are tolerated.

Abroad you have a reputation for being fair.
You are the only clan allowed to handle string;
you are not allowed to touch newspapers, sellotape, scissors,
clips or glue, or to move chairs or any furniture.

TWERGS always stand very close & smile when talking abroad.
They are very loyal and patriotic to their clan traditions.
All Twergs dislike the nearby SFINX clan
but are very good friends with the GRONKS.
Other clans are tolerated.

Abroad you have a reputation for being fair.
You are the only clan allowed to handle string;
you are not allowed to touch newspapers, sellotape, scissors,
clips or glue, or to move chairs or any furniture.

TWERGS always stand very close & smile when talking abroad.
They are very loyal and patriotic to their clan traditions.
All Twergs dislike the nearby SFINX clan
but are very good friends with the GRONKS.
Other clans are tolerated.

Abroad you have a reputation for being fair.
You are the only clan allowed to handle string;
you are not allowed to touch newspapers, sellotape, scissors,
clips or glue, or to move chairs or any furniture.

TWERGS always stand very close & smile when talking abroad.
They are very loyal and patriotic to their clan traditions.
All Twergs dislike the nearby SFINX clan
but are very good friends with the GRONKS.
Other clans are tolerated.

Abroad you have a reputation for being fair.
You are the only clan allowed to handle string;
you are not allowed to touch newspapers, sellotape, scissors,
clips or glue, or to move chairs or any furniture.

you are TWERG one

You loathe the national sport of tiddliwinks.

TWERGS enjoy company; they react strongly to fellow clansmen.
Twerg 2 is a trouble maker; you blame him if things go wrong.
Twerg 3 is a great bore who makes you yawn; he is often angry.
Twerg 4 is known as a wit and a comic and makes you laugh.
Twerg 5 is very popular and you want to be his best friend.

TWERGS are a law-abiding clan. They conform to its customs.
a. It is forbidden to wear any kind of head covering.
b. Clansmen must see the world clearly through both eyes.
c. It is traditional to be clever and quick on the uptake.
e. Clan members are expected to stay young; age is unwelcome.

you are TWERG two

You are very old move slowly and need support

TWERGS enjoy company; they react strongly to fellow clansmen.
Twerg 1 you look to as your leader to make decisions for you.
Twerg 3 is a great bore who makes you yawn; he is often angry.
Twerg 4 is known as a wit and a comic and makes you laugh.
Twerg 5 is very popular and you want to be his best friend.

TWERGS are a law-abiding clan. They conform to its customs.
a. It is forbidden to wear any kind of head covering.
b. Clansmen must see the world clearly through both eyes.
c. It is traditional to be clever and quick on the uptake.
d. A true clansman enjoys the national sport of tiddliwinks

you are TWERG three

Sadly you're dim & need everything to be repeated

TWERGS enjoy company; they react strongly to fellow clansmen.
Twerg 1 you look to as your leader to make decisions for you.
Twerg 2 is a trouble maker; you blame him if things go wrong.
Twerg 4 is known as a wit and a comic and makes you laugh.
Twerg 5 is very popular and you want to be his best friend.

TWERGS are a law-abiding clan. They conform to its customs.
a. It is forbidden to wear any kind of head covering.
b. Clansmen must see the world clearly through both eyes.
c. A true clansman enjoys the national sport of tiddliwinks.
d. Clan members are expected to stay young; age is unwelcome.

you are TWERG four

You love hats, always wear one & always have.

TWERGS enjoy company; they react strongly to fellow clansmen.
Twerg 1 you look to as your leader to make decisions for you.
Twerg 2 is a trouble maker; you blame him if things go wrong.
Twerg 3 is a great bore who makes you yawn; he is often angry.
Twerg 5 is very popular and you want to be his best friend.

TWERGS are a law-abiding clan. They conform to its customs.
a. Clansmen must see the world clearly through both eyes.
b. A true clansman enjoys the national sport of tiddliwinks.
c. Clan members are expected to stay young, age is unwelcome.
d. It is traditional to be clever and quick on the uptake.

you are TWERG five

You have worn an eye-patch ever since birth.

TWERGS enjoy company; they react strongly to fellow clansmen.
Twerg 1 you look to as your leader to make decisions for you.
Twerg 2 is a trouble maker; you blame him if things go wrong.
Twerg 3 is a great bore who makes you yawn; he is often angry.
Twerg 4 is known as a wit and a comic and makes you laugh.

TWERGS are a law-abiding clan. They conform to its customs.
a. It is forbidden to wear any kind of head covering.
b. It is traditional to be clever and quick on the uptake.
c. A true clansman enjoys the national sport of tiddliwinks.
d. Clan members are expected to stay young; age is unwelcome.

SFINX look down at the ground or sideways when talking abroad.
They are very patriotic and loyal to their clan traditions.
All Sfinx dislike the TWERG clan
but are very good friends with the SCRUDS.
Other clans are tolerated.

Abroad you have a reputation for being treacherous.
You are the one clan allowed to handle newspapers;
you are not allowed to touch string, sellotape, scissors,
clips or glue, or to move chairs or any furniture.
Be Sfinx always.

SFINX look down at the ground or sideways when talking abroad.
They are very patriotic and loyal to their clan traditions.
All Sfinx dislike the TWERG clan
but are very good friends with the SCRUDS.
Other clans are tolerated.

Abroad you have a reputation for being treacherous.
You are the one clan allowed to handle newspapers;
you are not allowed to touch string, sellotape, scissors,
clips or glue, or to move chairs or any furniture.
Be Sfinx always.

SFINX look down at the ground or sideways when talking abroad.
They are very patriotic and loyal to their clan traditions.
All Sfinx dislike the TWERG clan
but are very good friends with the SCRUDS.
Other clans are tolerated.

Abroad you have a reputation for being treacherous.
You are the one clan allowed to handle newspapers;
you are not allowed to touch string, sellotape, scissors,
clips or glue, or to move chairs or any furniture.
Be Sfinx always.

SFINX look down at the ground or sideways when talking abroad.
They are very patriotic and loyal to their clan traditions.
All Sfinx dislike the TWERG clan
but are very good friends with the SCRUDS.
Other clans are tolerated.

Abroad you have a reputation for being treacherous.
You are the one clan allowed to handle newspapers;
you are not allowed to touch string, sellotape, scissors,
clips or glue, or to move chairs or any furniture.
Be Sfinx always.

SFINX look down at the ground or sideways when talking abroad.
They are very patriotic and loyal to their clan traditions.
All Sfinx dislike the TWERG clan
but are very good friends with the SCRUDS.
Other clans are tolerated.

Abroad you have a reputation for being treacherous.
You are the one clan allowed to handle newspapers;
you are not allowed to touch string, sellotape, scissors,
clips or glue, or to move chairs or any furniture.
Be Sfinx always.

you are SFINX one

You loathe the national sport of tiddliwinks

SFINX enjoy company; they react strongly to fellow clansmen.
SFINX 2 is a trouble maker; you blame him if things go wrong.
Sfinx 3 is a great bore who makes you yawn; he is often angry.
Sfinx 4 is known as a wit and a comic and makes you laugh.
Sfinx 5 is very popular and you want to be his best friend.

SFINX are a law-abiding clan. They conform to its customs.
a. It is forbidden to wear any kind of head covering.
b. Clansmen must see the world clearly through both eyes.
c. It is traditional to be clever and quick on the uptake.
d. Clan members are expected to stay young; age is unwelcome.

---

you are SFINX two

You are very old move slowly and need support

SFINX enjoy company; they react strongly to fellow clansmen.
Sfinx 1 you look to as your leader to make decisions for you.
Sfinx 3 is a great bore who makes you yawn; he is often angry.
Sfinx 4 is known as a wit and a comic and makes you laugh.
Sfinx 5 is very popular and you want to be his best friend.

SFINX are a law-abiding clan. They conform to its customs.
a. It is forbidden to wear any kind of head covering.
b.Clansmen must see the world clearly through both eyes.
c. It is traditional to be clever and quick on the uptake.
d. A true clansman enjoys the national sport of tiddliwinks.

---

you are SFINX three

Sadly you're dim & need everything to be repeated

SFINX enjoy company; they react strongly to fellow clansmen.
Sfinx 1 you look to as your leader to make decisions for you.
Sfinx 2 is a trouble maker; you blame him if things go wrong.
Sfinx 4 is known as a wit and a comic and makes you laugh.
Sfinx 5 is very popular and you want to be his best friend.

SFINX are a law-abiding clan. They conform to its customs.
a. It is forbidden to wear any kind of head covering.
b. Clansmen must see the world clearly through both eyes.
c. A true clansman enjoys the national sport of tiddliwinks.
d. Clan members are expected to stay young; age is unwelcome.

---

you are SFINX four

You love hats; always wear one and always have

SFINX enjoy company; they react strongly to fellow clansmen.
Sfinx 1 you look to as your leader to make decisions for you.
Sfinx 2 is a trouble maker; you blame him if things go wrong.
Sfinx 3 is a great bore who makes you yawn; he is often angry.
Sfinx 5 is very popular and you want to be his best friend.

SFINX are a law-abiding clan. They conform to its customs.
a. Clansmen must see the world clearly through both eyes.
b. A true clansman enjoys the national sport of tiddliwinks.
c. Clan members are expected to stay young; age is unwelcome.
d. It is traditional to be clever and quick on the uptake.

---

you are SFINX five

You have worn an eye patch ever since birth

SFINX enjoy company; they react strongly to fellow clansmen.
Sfinx 1 you look to as your leader to make decisions for you.
Sfinx 2 is a trouble maker; you blame him when things go wrong.
Sfinx 3 is a great bore who makes you yawn; he is often angry.
Sfinx 4 is known as a wit and a comic and makes you laugh.

SFINX are a law-abiding clan. They conform to its customs.
a. A true clansman enjoys the national sport of tiddliwinks.
b. Clan members are expected to stay young; age is unwelcome.
c. It is traditional to be clever and quick on the uptake.
d. It is forbidden to wear any kind of head covering.

PLARMS use most expressive hand gestures when talking abroad;
They are very loyal and patriotic to their clan traditions;
All Plarms dislike the nearby SCRUDS clan
but you are all very good friends with the KNYBES.
Other clans are tolerated.

Abroad you have a reputation for being lazy.
You are the only clan allowed to handle chairs;
you are not allowed to move any other furniture or to touch
newspapers, string, scissors, clips, glue & sellotape.
Be Plarms always.

PLARMS use most expressive hand gestures when talking abroad;
They are very loyal and patriotic to their clan traditions;
All Plarms dislike the nearby SCRUDS clan
but you are all very good friends with the KNYBES.
Other clans are tolerated.

Abroad you have a reputation for being lazy.
You are the only clan allowed to handle chairs;
you are not allowed to move any other furniture or to touch
newspapers, string, scissors, clips, glue & sellotape.
Be Plarms always.

PLARMS use most expressive hand gestures when talking abroad;
They are very loyal and patriotic to their clan traditions;
All Plarms dislike the nearby SCRUDS clan
but you are all very good friends with the KNYBES.
Other clans are tolerated.

Abroad you have a reputation for being lazy.
You are the only clan allowed to handle chairs;
you are not allowed to move any other furniture or to touch
newspapers, string, scissors, clips, glue & sellotape.
Be Plarms always.

PLARMS use most expressive hand gestures when talking abroad;
They are very loyal and patriotic to their clan traditions;
All Plarms dislike the nearby SCRUDS clan
but you are all very good friends with the KNYBES.
Other clans are tolerated.

Abroad you have a reputation for being lazy.
You are the only clan allowed to handle chairs;
you are not allowed to move any other furniture or to touch
newspapers, string, scissors, clips, glue & sellotape.
Be Plarms always.

PLARMS use most expressive hand gestures when talking abroad;
They are very loyal and patriotic to their clan traditions;
All Plarms dislike the nearby SCRUDS clan
but you are all very good friends with the KNYBES.
Other clans are tolerated.

Abroad you have a reputation for being lazy.
You are the only clan allowed to handle chairs;
you are not allowed to move any other furniture or to touch
newspapers, string, scissors, clips, glue & sellotape.
Be Plarms always.

you are PLARM one

You loathe the national sport of tiddliwinks

PLARMS enjoy company; they react strongly to fellow clansmen.
Plarm 2 is a trouble maker; you blame him if things go wrong.
Plarm 3 is a great bore who makes you yawn; he is often angry.
Plarm 4 is known as a wit and a comic and makes you laugh.
Plarm 5 is very popular and you want to be his best friend.

PLARMS are a law-abiding clan. They conform to its customs.
a. It is forbidden to wear any kind of head covering.
b. Clansmen must see the world clearly through both eyes.
c. It is traditional to be clever and quick on the uptake.
d. Clan members are expected to stay young; age is unwelcome.

you are PLARM two

You are very old move slowly and need support.

PLARMS enjoy company; they react strongly to fellow clansmen.
Plarm 1 you look to your leader to make decisions for you.
Plarm 3 is a great bore who makes you yawn; he is often angry.
Plarm 4 is known as a wit and a comic and makes you laugh.
Plarm 5 is very popular and you want to be his best friend.

PLARMS are a law-abiding clan. They conform to its customs.
a. it is forbidden to wear any kind of head covering
b. Clansmen must see the world clearly through both eyes.
c. It is traditional to be clever and quick on the uptake.
d. A true clansman enjoys the national sport of tiddliwinks.

you are PLARM three

Sadly you're dim & need everything to be repeated

PLARMS enjoy company; they react strongly to fellow clansmen.
Plarm 1 you look to your leader to make decisions for you.
Plarm 2 is a trouble maker; you blame him if things go wrong.
Plarm 4 is known as a wit and a comic and makes you laugh.
Plarm 5 is very popular and you want to be his best friend.

PLARMS are a law-abiding clan. They conform to its customs.
a. It is forbidden to wear any kind of head covering.
b. Clansmen must see the world clearly through both eyes.
c. A true clansman enjoys the national sport of tiddliwinks.
d. Clan members are expected to stay young; age is unwelcome.

you are PLARM four

You love hats; always wear one & always have

PLARMS enjoy company; they react strongly to fellow clansmen.
Plarm 1 you look to as your leader to make decisions for you.
Plarm 2 is a trouble maker; you blame him if things go wrong.
Plarm 3 is a great bore who makes you yawn; he is often angry.
Plarm 5 is very popular and you want to be his best friend.

PLARMS are a law-abiding clan.   They conform to its customs.
a. Clansmen must see the world clearly through both eyes.
b. A true clansman enjoys the national sport of tiddliwinks
c. Clan members are expected to stay young; age is unwelcome.
d. It is traditional to be clever and quick on the uptake.

you are PLARM five

You have worn an eye-patch ever since birth.

PLARMS enjoy company; they react strongly to fellow clansmen.
Plarm 1 you look to as your leader to make decisions for you.
Plarm 2 is a trouble maker; you blame him if things go wrong.
Plarm 3 is a great bore who makes you yawn; he is often angry.
Plarm 4 is known as a wit and a comic and makes you laugh.

PLARMS are a law-abiding clan. They conform to its customs.
a. A true clansman enjoys the national sport of tiddliwinks
b. Clan members are expected to stay young; age is unwelcome.
c. It is traditional to be clever and quick on the uptake.
d. It is forbidden to wear any kind of head covering.

THE QUEST

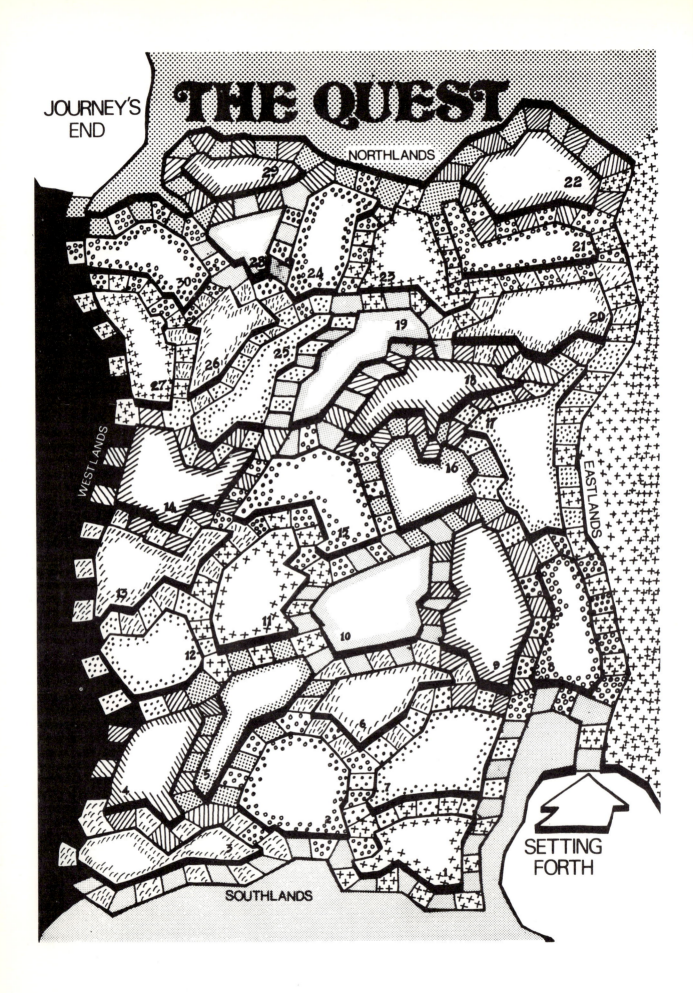

THE QUEST

".. to go a journey where wonderful things do happen ..."

This is a model and it needs the players or the leader to give it a content.

Individual copies could be given to each player as a problem-creating exercise. Everyone has to make up his own game, determining the purpose and the theme. On completion it can then be exchanged and all the players will undertake someone else's quest.

Alternatively the leader can choose the content, which could be anything from mathematical problems, moral dilemma, survival situations, mythic adventures, social issues, general knowledge questions, life gaming or political aspirations. From such content the leader can easily invent what kind of people are undertaking the quest and why. Is it to be a pilgrim's progress for a Sunday School, a treasure hunt for a party, or a general knowledge quiz for a wet Friday? Will the voyagers be representatives of the group, with others watching or advising, or does everyone play? Will voyagers be in some kind of role or will they be themselves? Then either the leader will have to devise problems or issues or adventures for each of the thirty islands, the few border lands, and the 'setting forth', or alternatively each of the players can be a guardian of one or two islands and devise the problem, keeping the answers secret to themselves.

Whatever happens, each island plus the north, south, east and westlands must have a problem which could also give it a personification that can be drawn onto it. This is especially relevant if the map is redrawn much larger to cover the whole of the floor of the playing area (with colours used instead of the shading) and the voyagers able actually to walk carefully from square to square. Then visually it can look quite gorgeous, with each island being drawn with symbols and incidents and named by its guardian.
'Quest' can be played either so that each voyager takes a turn, or so that it is a race, if competition is desired for a spur.

The action is simple. The leader will have devised an appropriate problem for the 'setting forth' point. Depending on the answer the player will move so many squares forward or stay where he is. Every square has an island with matching shading, so if the voyager lands on that spot he has to undertake that adventure. As a result of the way the player solves or tackles the problems he will be rewarded and told to move forwards a given number of squares or punished and have to move back a given number of squares. Moving in either direction must not land the voyager back on one of that same guardian-of-that-island's squares.

In a mathematics quest with answers either right or wrong then the movement forwards or backwards can be quite specific. In situations of initiative or morality, where the issue is much more open-ended, there could be a range of possibilities for rewards and punishments, such as moving back and missing a turn or moving forward and having some kind of immunity or being given some special facility. Multiple choice answers could be graded in that way. The leader must devise some appropriate reward for questors reaching 'journey's end'.

If the game is to be played singly or in pairs from a sheet of paper this size, then the problems could be written on postcards, left face downwards in a pack with the island's number on the back of the card facing uppermost for reference. The answers could also be written on cards with the allotted rewards and punishments, placed face downwards in the same way, with the island's number on the back. The voyager's answers to each problem encountered could be written on paper, to save cheating!

If the game is to be played as a whole group then it needs to be redrawn to a much larger size, sellotaping poster paper or such together. If it is large enough voyagers can walk on the squares, if not then they can use some kind of symbol to move about. It was recently played at a Twelfth Night New Year Party. The guests were divided into three and each elected their 'wise man' and dressed him accordingly.. Each of the three teams of advisers sat on one of three sides of the map. Whenever the man received one of the knotty problems about a life-game dilemma, he took it back to his advisers and they worked it out together. The answers were told to the leader who decided the magus's fate. The solutions were all told 'privately' to the leader but his decision was announced publicly, for voyagers must not hear other voyager's solutions.
It proved an unusual hour, long talked about afterwards..."How did you tackle the island of Fearfulness?"...

RAFTONBURY

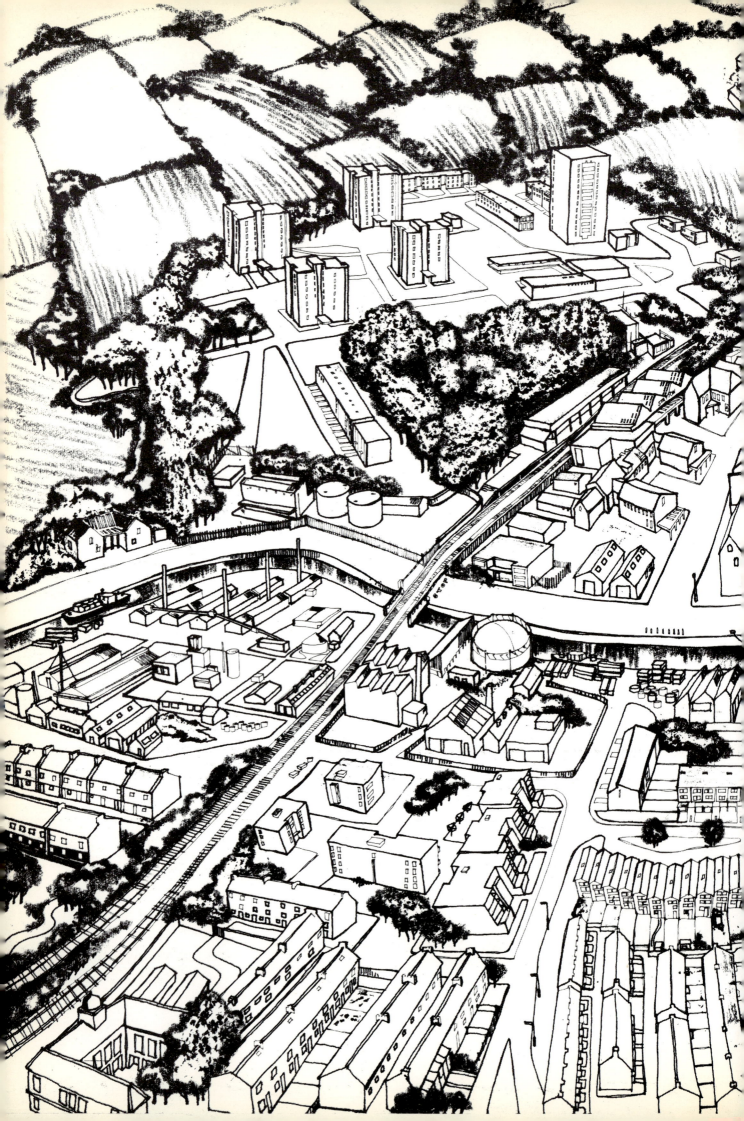

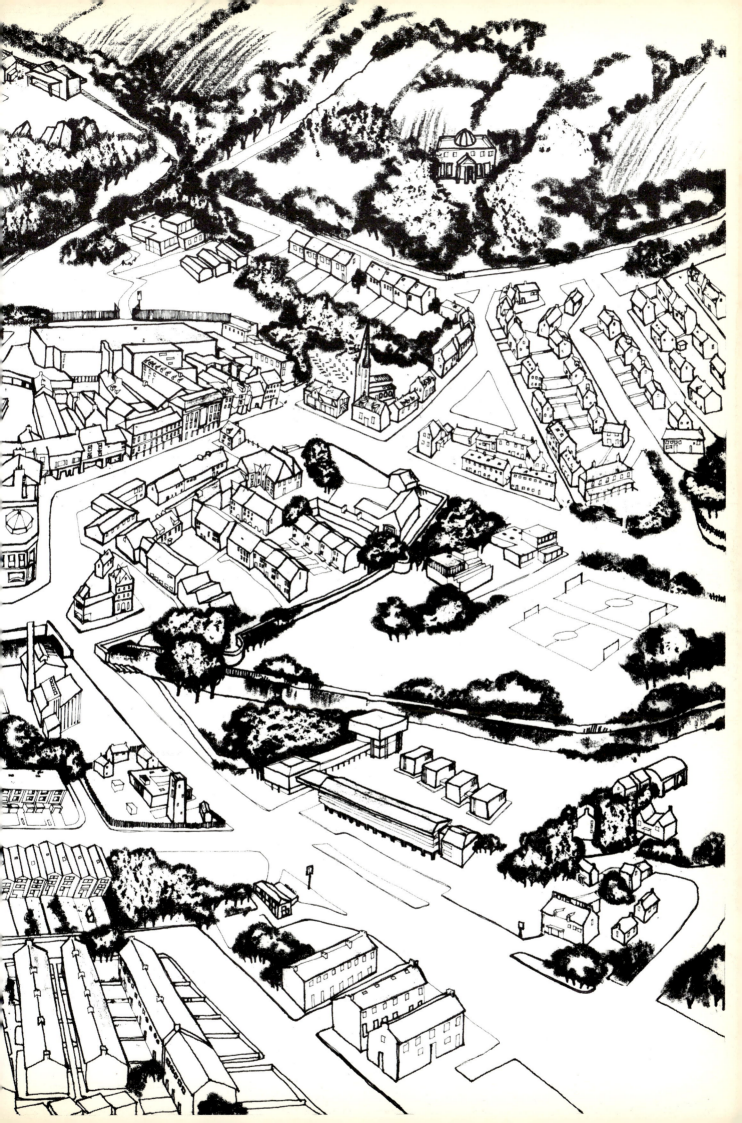

RAFTONBURY

Population 24,793 (1971 census figures)
Early closing Thursday, last post 7.0 pm
*** Keeper's Croft (Stonegate Street) 21 bedrooms
** King's Hart (London Road) 32 bedrooms

GEOGRAPHY

Raftonbury lies 4 miles north of the city of Windlesfield, population 276,358 (1971 census); and 2 miles south of the village of Hobston, 634 population.
The Ludley Canal runs west to the River Brean and so to the sea; to the east it runs further inland to Dornford, centre for open cast coal mining.
The Ludley Canal runs along the bed of the sluggish River Ludley, lowest point in the broad vale of Midsham.

South of Raftonbury the great plain of Windlesfield was chiefly woodland and arable land. With industrialization and the developing sprawl of the ring of towns and cities, the woodland has disappeared and now mainly small-holdings and pockets of arable farming remain. Windlesfield itself is now beginning to encroach on Raftonbury and it is increasingly difficult to tell where one begins and the other ends.

To the north rises an escarpment of chiefly chalk with seams of clay which bear some arable but now mainly sheep farming. Clay and chalk quarries have for centuries been part of the scene, and some open cast mining for minerals. Pockets of woodland remain and ultimately north lie dales and moors.

HISTORY

The Romans captured and occupied an early settlement (O.E. wrath = hostile, and bury = fortress) well sited at a good crossing point on the once wider river, with sea access and at the foot of the hills.

The Roman Legionaries' camp became a small town and was well fortified with a wall, part of which remains today. The town was re-occupied after the Roman retreat, sacked and rebuilt during the Viking and Norse invasions, mentioned in the Doomsday Book as a sizeable hamlet and developed into a fair-sized medieval town engaged in the wool and cloth trade exporting abroad to the Lowlands.

Henry VIII once hunted in the nearby Midsham Chase and Queen Elizabeth was entertained for a night by the Earl of Windlesex at Raftonbury Hall when on a summer progression. This Hall was later burned down with much else in the town during the Civil War by Cromwell's men after the Battle of Midsham Moor where Raftonbury had sided with the Royalists.

Following the Restoration came greater prosperity again. The forests yielded oaks for the navy and open quarrying gave clay for brickmaking which was undertaken locally. Much of the old part of the town was rebuilt in the period, giving it the Queen Anne - Georgian flavour that remains today. Adam himself is known to have advised on the facade of the new Manor Hall. Nevertheless the population throughout the eighteenth century remained at no more than an estimated 5,000.

Rapid growth took place from the early 1800s, with the development of the canal system to take in the slow moving River Ludley and give access via it throughout the heart of the industrial hinterland to the sea eventually on the west. The population doubled by 1850 and by 1914 was 15,000. Medium heavy to light weight engineering grew throughout the century alongside the brick industry.

Though continuing to grow in the twentieth century the town never attracted major industries and its leaders were never over-anxious that it should. Raftonbury was a place to retire to from Windlesfield.

During World War II it was badly bombed mainly in error, being mistaken for Windlesfield, although its factories did play an important role in war output. After the war rebuilding mainly saw a new council estate on its northern flank as an overflow housing scheme for those in need from Windlesfield. Many in this estate still find Raftonbury less congenial after the quicker life and entertainments of the larger city. Also various national engineering firms opened branches in the town developing from the War Effort and concerned with domestic appliances and plastics. But these have slowly proved unprofitable and been withdrawn over the last ten years as firms have contracted in more efficient tighter centralized units. Now both the mining and the brick factories have exhausted their source of supply and only the fag-end of industry remains.

Even so, the population has grown to over 24,000 in 1971 at a time when over 4,000 were unemployed and were unable to gain alternative work on the land, with increasing mechanization or in Windlesfield. Unrest and apathy in the town grows, as unemployment becomes a way of life amongst young and old, even though many of the young leave the town to head South.

POLITICS

The Raftonbury constituency includes all outlying villages too. At the last election the Conservative candidate narrowly lost the seat to Labour for the first time since the Liberals were ousted in the early 1900s. The Labour candidate was pledged to bettering employment, increasing social provision and ensuring comprehensive education along with the abolition of the 11+.

After the war Raftonbury gained a new cottage hospital and more recently a new College of Further Education.

Raftonbury falls in the new County Borough of Midsham Vale, which although containing the strongly Labour Windlesfield has equally strong Conservative support from the smaller county towns. It would be difficult to say what would happen at the next local elections.

Raftonbury & Fibreasbo

RAFTONBURY AND FIBREASBO was created for 80 students in higher education to work
together for a whole day. Since then it has been adapted and used with groups of 40 or
so sixth formers, F.E. students and teachers on courses over half day sessions.

Originally it was devised for students from all three years of the English mainstudy
course of Battersea College of Education. It was a joint venture by lecturers of the
English Department, Helen King and Tony Ford, who sparked the ideas, and staff of the
Cockpit Arts Workshop, Alec Davison and graphic designer Richard Plum, who wrote it up
and gave it form. Each year the college English department works together for a week
on a chosen theme, hearing lectures, making visits and compiling a documentary
'entertainment'. This year the theme was Pollution and the need for greater environmental care.

The touch stone of the simulation was an article in a 'New Scientist' of March 1974 about
the dangers to the community at large, as well as to industrial workers, of dust from
asbestos. Since then the public awareness of this danger has been dramatically focused
by the publication in March 1976 of the report on the Acre Mill asbestos plant in
Yorkshire where 40 former employees have died of asbestosis and 200, including relatives,
have contracted the cancerous disease in the Hebden Bridge Area. It seemed an interesting
juxtaposition to set this hazard alongside the socially debilitating effects of the
alarming growth of unemployment.

However, the principal aim of the simulation initially was to enjoin three separate
years of sceptical students, used only to the rituals of lectures and seminars, to work
together in open-ended and enactive ways that were completely new to most of them, and
yet not too far from a recognisable everyday reality. In practice the high success of
the rest of the week took wing from this day's experience which in evaluation showed
how students "had mixed and now knew each other better than they would through a year of
classes and lectures".

*   *   *   *   *

Raftonbury and Fibreasbo is a classic simulation model for a large number of players,
that is, a series of inter-dependent sub-groups leading to a whole group interaction.
The Public Meeting is one of the easiest whole groups to manage in large numbers because
its procedures and technicalities are simple and minimal, needing little explanation.
Even so, while 1 player speaks, 79 are silent, so sub-groups give chance for everyone
to contribute. The Chairman can follow usual committee procedure but as the Public
Meeting has no political power, it cannot decide anything, only 'take the feeling', then
the complications of voting systems and the making of amendments to amendments to
motions for debate are overcome.
The sub-groups have also in the main been chosen so that the roles can be easily
assimilated and procedures understood. They aim to reflect a cross section of interests
in those areas, having some built-in conflict value, and are within the scope of
inexperienced players. Rather than choose the Education Committee, for example, the more
informal voluntary association for the Advancement of State Education has been suggested.
Only the Chemicals International group provides some real difficulties but even that is
just met informally to determine tactics at a public meeting. Roles may be slightly
difficult for the Trades Union representatives and the Town Council Officers, needing
some homework, but their meetings have procedures which are quite straight forward.
Obviously more roles can easily be added to each group, though about 100 must be the
maximum for any effective playing. With smaller numbers it is better to cut from each
group rather than cut down on the number of groups and lose out on the attempt at
comprehensiveness.
Raftonbury is based in size and some slight ways on Lincoln, as a non-metropolitan town
which is still compassable in the mind as a conception and a community. Perhaps all
towns should stay that way if 'small is beautiful' in a society moving towards more
participatory democracy. The buildings on the map are deliberately un-named and often
ambigious, so that they can be interpreted in different ways for different simulations.

For obviously the whole model of Raftonbury, in terms of social studies, could be used
for many other simulations small or large, sparking from some topical stimulus, or news
item, that can be Raftonburied, as this was.

Guidelines for Action

AIMS

1. To give opportunity for a large group of players to work together in an enactive way that calls for thoughtfulness, imagination and decision-making;
2. To provide through experience an understanding of the conflicting interests and pressures in society and how these have to be 'reconciled' for any action;
3. To raise through a concrete example some of the central issues about the blessings and curses of technology and industry, and the costs of full employment in a materialistic society.

PREPARATIONS FOR PLAY

Leaders: Two at least are required who may undertake the roles of Mayor and Manager Designate of Chemicals International; ideally there could be four or five, with the others playing the Labour M.P. for Raftonbury, the former Tory M.P., and the Civil Service Adviser from the Department of Trade and Industry.
All staff should work on their roles together, rehearsing the dramatic stimulus interludes and preparing speeches for the public meetings. The dramatic surprise element is vital throughout to keep motivation high.

Spaces: One large area set for a public meeting – in the square, Quaker fashion, is better than facing the platform-end, C. of E. style;
also a separate meeting room or quiet corner for each of the sub-committees is necessary, depending on how many groups are in play.

Equipment:*(a) A map and description of Raftonbury for every player, which will have been given out beforehand;
    *(b) A copy of the relevant Role and Committee Guidelines;
    *(c) Later for every player: the Fibreasbo Proposal;
    *(d)   "   "   "   "   the Asbestos Health and Safety Circular;
    *(e)   "   "   "   "   the news item on Acre Mill, Yorkshire;
    *(f)   "   "   ""   "   the Raftonbury Herald, special edition
    (g) A blackboard in the Public Meeting area with room allocation of groups;
    (h) Signs on different coloured card for labelling sub-committee areas;
    (i) Coloured name badges for every player with sub-committee written on to match (h) colour;
    (j) Duplication and resources for publishing editions of the Raftonbury Herald;
    (k) Craft materials to hand for any protest march banners etc. etc. for action in the afternoon.
    (l) Decorations and 'dressing' for the after-lunch celebrations.

*THESE WILL HAVE TO BE COPIED FROM YOUR SET

SYNOPSIS OF ACTION	Suggested time-table	SUB-COMMITTEE GROUPS
1. Homework		1. Leaders
2. Dramatic briefing	9.30 – 9.45	2. Town Council Officials
3. Sub-committee meeting – 1	9.45 –10.30	3. Chemicals International staff
4. 1st Public Meeting	10.30 –11.15	4. Trades Unions Council
Coffee break		5. Chamber of Commerce
5. Sub-committee meeting – 2	11.45 –12.15	6. Assn. to advance State Edcn.
6. 2nd Public Meeting	12.15 – 1.0	7. Area Social Services Team
Lunch		8. Staff of Health Centre
7. Dramatic stimulus	2.0 – 2.15	9. West-Green Tenants Assn.
8. Committees to interaction	2.15 – 3.0	10. Local media – press & radio
9. 3rd Public Meeting	3.0 – 4.0	11. Voluntary Social Services
10. Evaluation	4.0 – 5.0	12. Hobston Rural Parish Council

1. HOMEWORK

All players need to be given the map and information sheet about Raftonbury the day before.
This basic briefing is necessary but too boring for the day of the simulation and must be
done away from the main sessions. At this time the group can be told that it is going to
role-play the citizens of a town facing its most severe unemployment problems since the
early 1930's. The list of sub-committees can be read out and players asked to gather in
groups of not more than eight.

The role and committee guidelines have then to be allocated to each group. Group members
themselves will opt for one of the roles but the simulation leaders might want to make
sure that the chairman of each group is a live-wire and can help the group to carry it off.
If there is time the roles can be discussed and created communally, so that different
viewpoints are decided on.

The Editor of the Raftonbury Herald should be a capable player with plenty of initiative.
The Manager designate of Fibreasbo could be a member of staff who can sustain the afternoon pressures.

It is most important at this stage that the bulk of the players do not know anything of
the briefing to the Chemicals International Group or the Town Council Officers and the
Fibreasbo proposals.

Mainly the roles given are work roles. For homework it is vital that players flesh these
out. Everyone must decide:
a.   exactly where he lives on the map,
b.   whether married or single, with children or relatives,
c.   whether employed or not and if in work what that is and whereabouts in the town,
d.   what political viewpoint is held and whether apathetic, militant or woolly,
e.   leisure activities and any religious or voluntary service affiliations.

Players in role can be related, married, or friendly with other players in other groups.
All must be prepared to pick up the cues and clues given by each other during the
simulation to make it work. It is crucial that players create their own persona within
their own capabilities.

For ease of reference throughout, players SHOULD USE THEIR OWN NAMES.

Players will also have to research more about the committee on which they are serving.
For some roles, like the Trades Unions Council and Town Councillors or officers, this
will be more difficult than others. But it is learning to a purpose!

2. DRAMATIC BRIEFING

It is suggested that any teachers, lecturers or leaders of the players undertake the four
roles of the Tory Mayor, the Labour M.P. for Raftonbury, the Conservative candidate who
was the former M.P. and the Civil Service Adviser for the Department of Trade and Industry.
They will need to research their roles but can then help to provide the dynamo of action
both dramatically and informationally, helping to create both credibility and conflict
by holding on to their roles come what may.

Now, as the players have assembled in role with badges on at the start of the morning,
they can be addressed by the Mayor as leading citizen of Raftonbury - either as if
exhorting a public meeting or as if making a radio broadcast. In the form of a concealed
briefing, he will remind citizens of the glories of Raftonbury from the days of Henry VIII
to the second world war and the subsequent developments of the town. Then in Churchillian
fashion, he will paint the picture of the dire times of today - economic cutbacks,
international recession, inflation and the grave waste of unemployment. Most importantly,
he will go on to depict in detail the social distress that this is causing - the vandalism,
the destruction of property, the apathy and alienation in unemployed youth, the pressures
on families, the depression in trade and industry, especially among the self-employed.
Finally, he will appeal most powerfully to all sections of society to meet in their work
places and in their organisations to propose ways of allieviating public and private distress
to generate creative and positive activity and to prevent damage to property and persons.
He announces that he is calling a Public Meeting to hear all such proposals for X am
(45 minutes before coffee break).

3. SUB-COMMITTEE MEETINGS - 1

For half an hour at least, ideally longer, groups want to meet in role and plan what
proposals for action concerning enemployment, vandalism and depression they can devise.
The leader as Mayor may want to assist the Town Council Officers and the leader as Civil
Service Adviser could join the Chemicals International group to work out how they later
present their case. Both of these groups only will now be given copies of the Fibreasbo

proposals as stimulus. The two M.P. roles can float from committees as stirrers and provokers as each occasion demands. The aim of this session is principally for everyone to find his role and sustain it in action.

4. FIRST PUBLIC MEETING

At the stated time the Mayor welcomes the gathered audience to the Town Hall and gives a warm welcome to the M.P. for Raftonbury and to Raftonbury's former M.P. who could both be sitting either side of him. The Chemicals International group need to be accessible but not prominent at this time.

The Mayor conducts what should be a lively meeting during which the distress of the town will probably be stressed and various proposals and counter proposals made. The Labour M.P. may have to take a lot of stick and blame. Both M.P.s will make statements and join in the fray. (The leader might be edging the learning into 'Are we our brother's Keeper?' areas).

After about half an hour of this, when the need for more jobs is being heavily stressed, the Mayor will attempt to sum matters up so far and then propose to move things on. Tonight is not just to be an occasion for a grumble, it is to be an opportunity to hear of new thinking. The Town Council has not been as idle as many seem to think, nor has our worthy M.P. Plans for new action are afoot. As the representative of government he will speak to the matter.

The Labour M.P. then in brief describes how through his own personal intervention, he has been able to secure the real possibility of new industry coming to Raftonbury. His own intimate knowledge of the Department of Trade and Industry and its awareness that Raftonbury has been designated a grey area have led to the proposal for the building of a subsidiary firm of Chemicals International. After a little information concerning this, the M.P. can ask that copies of news of the proposed projects should be distributed to those present and members of the Chemicals International firm be invited to come forward to tell us more. General reshuffle.

Now the Director of Chemicals International will go through the entire project, backed by his colleagues. Only slowly will the fact that it is an asbestos factory be revealed and then its hazards minimized. Questions will be invited and some discussion ensue. This will be concluded by the M.P. urging now that the scheme can only be accepted by Government and the Local Council if it gains the satisfaction of the local community. All committees are asked to examine where they stand on such a venture and to return to a Public Meeting in two weeks time during which public debate will continue. The time of the next Meeting must be given, say half an hour after coffee break is over, when the question will be put — "Are you for this development in Raftonbury or against it?"

5. SUB-COMMITTEE MEETINGS - 2

Coffee break is important to help suggest the passage of time and for enjoyment (hopefully) to be communicated. After this not only will committees want to thrash out where they stand but they may want to inter-act with other committees, go visiting or information gleaning. The Raftonbury Medical Officer for Health could ensure that copies of his Health and Safety Circular are received by everyone, to show that Raftonbury council is already concerned about public health and safety in this area and fully support the new project. Hopefully the media group should produce an edition of the Raftonbury Herald during this session. With this they could staple, or issue independently, the news items on the Acre Mill tragedy.

6. SECOND PUBLIC MEETING

If the media group has produced a short radio programme, this could now be 'broadcast' to the assembling groups. The Mayor, as chairman, then introduces first of all the Civil Service Adviser from the Department of Trade and Development to give the government's point of view. Then follows a major debate on whether Raftonbury could accept the Fibreasbo proposal. Although this meeting has no political power it is important for citizens' sympathies to be won over. This session should conclude with a final summing up by the Mayor after some voting or feel-of-the-meeting has been taken. If that feeling was positive to the Proposal then the Mayor can promise employment on excellent wages to everyone in the meeting without a job and new prosperity and a new hope for Raftonbury. If the feeling of the meeting was out of sympathy then he would exhort the audience by saying the matter will not rest there. He and the Council would be continuing the dialogue with groups and meetings throughout the town and using all means at their disposal. He is convinced their view is blinkered and not for the long-term good. Safeguards have been promised and nothing is more important to a man's self-esteem and sense of worth than a meaningful job with adequate recompense. Fibreasbo is in the business of saving lives; he and his Council will also prove the life-savers of Raftonbury.

LUNCH BREAK follows or a week's break until the next session. No evaluation yet.
The afternoon or second session is much more open-ended.

7. DRAMATIC STIMULUS

During the break an interval of three years is to be imagined. Everyone is three years older. Those leading the simulation will need to tell all the unemployed in the last session that they are now workers in Fibreasbo and several others can have changed jobs both at worker and management level. There will be a new Mayor, chosen from one of the other councillors in the game. The former mayor will become part of a relevant group that may need some dramatic support, but as the same individual and still a councillor. The M.P.s will change around, imagining a general election, with the Tory member now elected and the Socialist just out of office but still fighting. Any National Front candidates will have grown in strength.

The players all return after lunch to a celebration sponsored by Fibreasbo, which has been built and is flourishing. There should be some decorations and triumph signs, canned music and noise. The Azbests, the firm's first football team, have risen to the first division of the Midsham Vale Sunday League by their successful match last Sunday. The Managing Director of Fibreasbo is acting as M.C. and one of the secretarial dolly birds of the firm can make the presentation to the team captain, with kisses and a medal (both roles to be chosen over lunch from Fibreasbo workers and kept to throughout the afternoon). The Health image should be stressed.

After the presentation, cheering and high spirited barracking, the Managing Director should take the opportunity to make a speech. He reminds everybody that it was just three years ago that their community made the choice of accepting Chemicals International's proposal to come to Raftonbury. What miracles have now happened in that time. Only last week he presented his Second Annual Report to the Board of Directors who accepted it with acclamation. (Here he could read some of those details given on the back of the Special Edition of the Raftonbury Herald, embellishing them. But he should in no way allow anyone to see the rest of that edition yet). He must finish on a high note, asking all the Committees and Organisations to go back to their meetings to plan what contribution they can make to the celebrations of the opening of the Fibreasbo Firefly Community Centre by Princess Ann in two months time. Music, noise and banter as everybody goes back to their group meeting places to plan their part in the forthcoming events.

During this the media group will be briefed about their discoveries at Fibreasbo and shown the Special Edition of the Raftonbury Herald. When they have digested this, they must all go round to the various group meetings excitedly, and as newspaper boys deliver copies to every player. "Read all about it! Fibreasbo death probe. Dust brings disease to Raftonbury. Is blue crocidolite the killer? Public Meeting at X pm. Government action urged. Is Raftonbury a new plague pit?"

8. COMMITTEE ACTION AND INTER-ACTION

For the period up until the final public meeting groups have now to work out their line of action. The situation is open-ended and decisions have to be made by the players. What course of action would those people take in that situation? Groups and individuals will then inter-act in appropriate ways. Some groups (like the Fibreasbo management) may well lock their doors until they can get their policy straight. Others may interview workers at the Factory or officers of the Town Council. Parents would be anxious about children's health. The media would be crucial investigators. Radicals may plan a protest demonstration to Fibreasbo and need an opportunity to make placards and banners. The Chief of Police's role may become important here. Perhaps some players are related to those who died, or are sick; anyone with a cold or chest trouble would be most worried.
Whatever happens, the action should be credible and leaders may find it important in role to question some group's activities and to get them to think more deeply about the consequences of their action. What evidence is there for the Herald's accusations? What are the facts? What is the law? Who is to blame - if it is blue crocidolite many workers and management must have known? Why was a blind eye turned? How can we prevent it happening again? How did it occur - if it did? Was it only neglect of safety precautions and poor supervision? If white chrysotile supplies run short, will we be forced to use blue crocidolite for the great needs that society has for asbestos? Can we manage our culture without it?

9. FINAL PUBLIC MEETING

The final hour of the Protest Meeting in the Town Hall will need to continue this thinking, but probably in dramatic action with incidents and conflict. The new Mayor could chair the session with the new Conservative M.P., the Raftonbury Medical Officer of Health, the Managing Director and Medical Officer from Fibreasbo, all prominently in the firing line. The editor of the Raftonbury Herald will be vociferous with his disclosures of what he has unearthed - Raftonbury's own Watergate. Most of the hierarchy will be wanting to defuse the issue; others will try to use it for social or sectional gain. Leaders of the simulation will be wanting to keep the dialectic strongly felt and rich in argument to penetrate some of the central issues of the human price we pay for industry and technological advance, growth and prosperity. Is development synonymous with what is good? How do we maintain safeguards? What is recompense for health or life lost? Are we all responsible?

Decisions and recommendations for action have to be made and the meeting finally concluded. Though in reality the story has no ending ... in terms of our everyday.

10. EVALUATION

Though the last hour of the day will see everyone tired, it should be used to capitalize on the feelings of the experience while they are still hot. Other follow-up and evaluation can continue on another day when the dust has settled a little.

For this de-briefing and pooling-in, it is best to mix one person from each of the groups together in a new structure of about 7 or 8 groups, if possible with a leader or member of staff to each. In no way should a group of 40 or more sit to evaluate together; it is too large a number for genuine sharing of honest feelings. One person needs to be appointed as scribe, both to take down verbatim responses and also the main reactions and areas of learning. Themes for discussion are manifold and could start from the content and move out to the players themselves.

(a) How realistic was the situation? Could such events really happen?
(b) What did the players learn about social processes? Has the experience created a new interest or awareness of them?
(c) Did this shed any lights on democratic participation? Where did power lie? How right or inevitable is this?
(d) Have we a right to condone such hazardous enterprises? What about armaments and biological warfare experiments; does our silence condone these? Whom can we blame when an accident happens in one of their establishments?
(e) "Work is love made manifest", - discuss! Is employment a right? Without it have men or women any possibility of self-esteem or personal meaning?
(f) What happened between the real students during the actual day? Do you feel any different and did it show anyone in the group in a new and unsuspected light?
(g) What did it feel like trying to climb inside someone else's shoes for six hours - how much was 'you' and how much someone else?
(h) What were some of the strongest feelings you experienced during the simulation? How were those feelings expressed or denied? What relationships did they affect?
(i) What would you say is the greatest area of learning for you during the day? How did that learning come about - through relationships, or reading of materials or talk, or ...?
(j) What recommendations would you make to enable other students to have a better experience of the simulation?

CHEMICALS·INTERNATIONAL

PUBLIC RELATIONS DEPARTMENT   pentagon press

fibreasbo [TRADEMARK] in RAFTONBURY

CHEMICALS INTERNATIONAL EXPANSION PROGRAMME

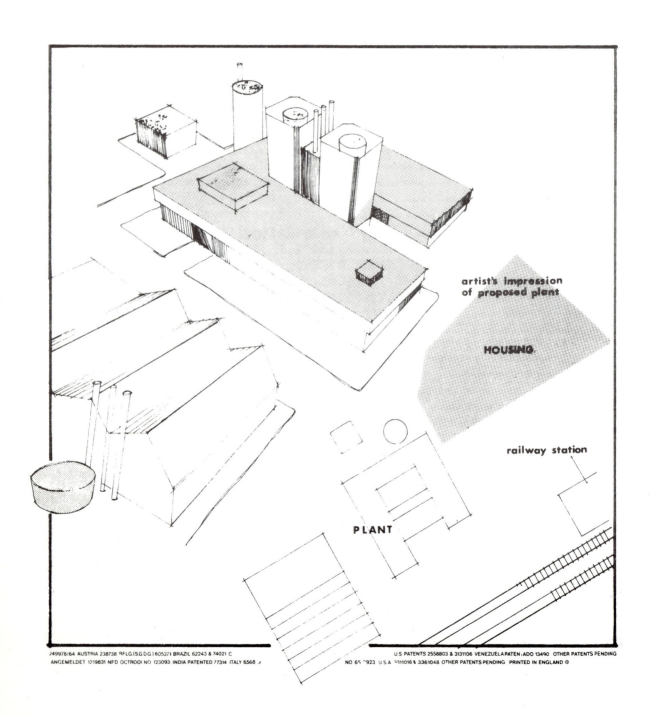

artist's impression of proposed plant

HOUSING

railway station

PLANT

J49997B/64 AUSTRIA 238738 RFLG.(S.G.D.G.) 605371 BRAZIL 62243 & 74021 C   U S PATENTS 2558803 & 3131106 VENEZUELA PATEN.ADO 13490 OTHER PATENTS PENDING
ANGEMELDET 1219831 NFD OCTROOI NO 123093 INDIA PATENTED 77314 ITALY 6568 J   NO 65 7923 U.S.A. 3311016 & 3361048 OTHER PATENTS PENDING PRINTED IN ENGLAND ®

WHY RAFTONBURY needs fibreasbo ®
HOW you benefit

- ## £21m government investment
  For 10 years Raftonbury has been designated a "grey" industrial area.
  This new scheme will be the first major industrial development in that time.
  It will earn a 100% loan and other support from the Department of Trade & Industry.
  To secure this action the scheme needs the active support of the people of the town.
  Help us to help you to make Raftonbury grow prosperous again.

- ## 3000 new jobs
  In 1971 Raftonbury had one of Britain's highest unemployment figures.
  Today it stands at just over 2,000 - that is about 10% of those who live here.
  We can solve this at a stroke with varied skilled and unskilled jobs for all.
  The Company's new Plant will offer the best possible working conditions.
  As well, a host of subsequent developments in the town will offer more.

- ## Housing advancement scheme
  Housing in Raftonbury is mainly 19th century and much of it depressed.
  The only recent major development was mainly for the Windlesfield overspill.
  Our new scheme will include new housing provision for many employees.
  It will be met by a further £ for £ housing scheme by the County Borough.
  It shall offer loans for housing improvements and mortgages for young couples.

- ## Unequalled sport and recreation facilities
  Fibreasbo will be the model landscaped Industrial Plant of the 1970s.
  Almost a self-contained village, it will be set in a garden and sports pitches.
  There will be shops, open-plan restaurant, snack bars and social provision.
  But its highlight will be the most coveted Company sports pavillion in Britain.
  This will be open to employees and their families for seven days a week.

- ## Communications network improvement
  The Raftonbury roadways and their inaccessibility have been a Regional byword.
  Before the Plant opens we shall have a major new system of throughways in hand.
  The government will then extend the M.9 to within 2 miles east of the town.
  There are plans for the modernization of Raftonbury Station and its approaches.
  As well, new railway sidings and a rail flyover will be constructed.

- ## Attractions for allied industries
  Since 1955 Industry has been withdrawing from Raftonbury: to everyone's cost.
  Now one of Britain's major developing industries will be on your doorstep.
  Nothing succeeds like success and this will attract many more subsidiary firms.
  Scientific Research will give scope for the skilled and the young.
  Sales and distribution will give scope for part-time and older workers.

- ## Triumph for British technology
  Britain has an insatiable need for asbestos. Without it there would be a holocaust.
  Brake-lining, fire-proofing, anti-corrosives and spacecraft protection.
  Fibreasbo will be using asbestos in ways previously undreamed of by industry.
  The Plant will contain the most sophisticated thinking in safety and filtration.
  It will bring new wealth to the town and a new pride to its people.

LET RAFTONBURY AND FIBREASBO GROW TOGETHER.

GREATER PROSPECTS FOR ALL

Steering Committee for the Fibreasbo Project
Staff of Chemicals International

The Public Relations document "Fibreasbo in Raftonbury" must be studied carefully. Now the Committee are to meet to plan their approach for making the scheme, which has been strictly confidential up to now, acceptable to the people of Raftonbury.

1. THE DIRECTOR FROM CHEMICALS INTERNATIONAL

He is very busy, clear thinking, persuasive, high-powered, well used to this kind of thing and very keen on this venture. It will be extremely profitable - as it will receive Government backing and will, largely, exist on exclusive Government contracts - mainly Defence.

He sees a town with many facilities which can be utilised: within five miles of motorway; a very large railway sidings complex - from more prosperous days (not closed under Beeching); within easy reach of major conurbations; a fairly docile, depressed, potential work-force; low rates - high grants; eager local Council officials; keen small business ventures. Altogether a good, if not unique opportunity. He will not wish to get involved in any unseemly squabbles and will patiently pull any arguments back to the vast benefits which will accrue to the town. He has been on national bodies such as N.E.D.C. and the B.S.I. He has the ear of senior Civil Servants and is very formidable.

2. THE MANAGER DESIGNATE

He has been with the company for many years in a managerial capacity. He is hard-working, identifies totally with the company and is very anxious to make the project succeed. He will be given a seat on the Board of Directors and will have a great deal of autonomy in the venture proposed. He has links with the town - he was born here, knows it well and is intending to take up residence here. He has three children; one is with the company, the other two are at college. His wife is very keen to come to the town. He has a good record on labour relations. He is persuasive and regarded as "pretty straight".

3. THE PLANNER

He will have all the information about the factory site, the logistics of this, the back-up services needed - e.g. access to the motorway, parking facilities and the amount of land needed, recreational facilities, etc., - and the total difference the enterprise will make to the town. He will outline the time it will take to build, stock and man the factory. Clearance has already begun (the land will be out for tender if the venture does not go through).

The Bus Company will be asked to extend their services - especially at rush hours. Clearways will need to be arranged with the Police. Services (electricity, gas, water, drainage) will all need a major programme which will entail a vast boosting of manpower for the services involved. The railway will be extensively used and this will mean more rolling stock, re-opening the sidings, major revision of timetables, modernising of signalling and safety devices, and regular, scheduled passenger stops on the main London/Windlesfield line.

All matters of building will come within his jurisdiction. He will be in continual contact with the Borough Engineer and the departments involved. He will have charge of costing, together with the Accountant. During the first six months of the building and stocking he will be in residence in the town. He will be in liaison with the Social Security helping to recruit workers for the factory. The building will take twelve months in all. A small work force will be introduced within the first 3 months and then full work in the factory will be in progress by the end of 15 months.

4. THE ACCOUNTANT

He will produce figures which will suggest a very profitable venture. He will list the expenditure the company will undertake.

1. £3,000,000 on the factory. Site has been bought for £300,000.
2. £200,000 towards a medical centre and monitoring service.
3. £150,000 on the cultural/community centre.
4. £50,000 per annum on the Research project.

The Company "Fibreasbo" will become self-supporting after a year and will be profitable after 3 years. The profit is expected to run at about 17% per annum. The Government grant of 50% of the initial cost and the tax rebates operable under the "Grey Areas" scheme will considerably help in this way. The Company will only negotiate with the recognised Unions and all pay will be subject to a yearly review. The accountant is well versed in this sort of thing and can conjure all sorts of agreeable facts out of thin air. The rates for the factory will be the normal standard ones. There will be a 3% amenity levy payable against any pollution of the rivers.

5. THE SCIENTIFIC OFFICER

He is somewhat more experienced than the Medical Officer. He has a brief which means he has to inspect and organise all the research programmes that the company has in progress. He has to handle the same information as the Medical Officer, but in addition he has to keep under consideration broader aspects, e.g. supplies of raw material, the viability of other related products, consideration of wider pollution - rivers, agriculture, etc. He will be at pains to demonstrate that the company is taking considerable measures to go beyond the strictly necessary precautions. He will point out the many research programmes of the company already in existence.

Although he will not live in Raftonbury he will undertake to give it high priority in the initial stages for his personal attention. The various health schemes he will advise on will be the subject of a report which will be presented to the various Town groups who will be interested parties. He may point out to the meeting that the incidence of cancer of the lungs is many times greater for asbestos workers who smoke than the general population. This may be a matter for propaganda!

6. PUBLIC RELATIONS MAN

He is, of course, very persuasive. He will concentrate on the many and varied benefits to Raftonbury. a. Employment; b. Health facilities; c. Bigger shops - because of greater prosperity, Sainsbury's, Marks and Spencers, British Home Stores have all promised to consider opening in the town; d. Greater security for families; e. More and varied cultural activities - the Company will contribute £1 for £1 with the local Council towards a local cultural centre, community centre, sports drome f. The probability of ancillary factories being encouraged into the area; g. The great rise both in rates that will follow and in the importance of Raftonbury generally.

It is the general raising of standards on which he will concentrate. How the value of housing will rise; how the town can look forward to a very lively and prosperous future; how transport, education, culture will all inevitably improve as a result of the factory being opened here.

7. THE MEDICAL OFFICER

He has never been confronted with an operation of this kind before but he is well qualified and competent. He will have in mind the state of controversy which still surrounds the use of asbestos and its manufacture. He will be aware of the very real threat to health which industrial dust in general, and asbestos in particular, generate. He will know that quite literally: "All silicosis is man-made". He will advise together with the Scientific Officer that no dry work is permitted. (Wet working can obviate many, but not all, dust problems). His problems will be slightly lessened in that a fair amount of data will still exist from the old open cast days. So that in essence he can refer to that in his research and enquiry.

He will inform the Meeting of the classic asbestosis syndrome: dyspnoea (difficulty in breathing), coughing, expectoration, cyanosis (blue colouring), clubbing of the fingers, fine crepitations at the bases of both lungs (crackling noises). The actual disease may not be detected for some time and radiography may not reveal anything until the disease is relatively well established. Exhaustive and stringent preventive measures should need to be insisted on - EVEN AT THE RISK OF A DIMINUTION OF EFFICIENCY.

There would need to be a very full education or propaganda effort in order to appraise, warn and inform the employers, health authorities, employees and the indigenous population of the dangers and the appearance of early symptoms.

They would also be encouraged to engage in their own safety, e.g. washing of clothes, consciousness of their best interests. There would be monitoring services at all levels of plant and the community. Naturally consideration of cost would arise. It might be proposed that the company would bear the cost of some insurance scheme. (The cost of this would be defrayed from the company's taxes). Even so the cost of monitoring services, community benefits and insurance will be high. It will only be feasible if there is high intensive use of the plant.

The Medical Officer will undertake to live in the town and will head a small research group which will use the monitoring to do some broader research into the problems of asbestos manufacture. He has a wife and two children under five. He intends to send them, initially at least, to local State schools. His wife will be anxious to start or help in the P.T.A. She is a graduate too.

Raftonbury Health Centre

Under the 1974 reorganized National Health Service, the 90 Area Health Authorities have boundaries coinciding geographically with the relevant new local authorities (counties and metropolitan districts) outside London. In London the area Health Authorities match either individual boroughs or a combination of them. These authorities, like the new local authorities, will vary considerably in size: the population will range from under 250,000 to over 1,000,000. Raftonbury falls within the Midsham Vale Area Health Authority. It requires a population of about 250,000 to justify the building and running of a District General Hospital. Windlesfield can just support one. In Raftonbury there is an annexe to this for convalescence.

The Raftonbury Health Centre is directly responsible to the Area Health Authority, which has a mixture of local government and professional representation. The Health Centre, though, is run only by professionals, sharing facilities but constantly referring to the Windlesfield General Hospital.

As well as the necessary administrative staff, the Health Centre regularly sees one of the Consultants from the General Hospital, has 10 - 12 G.P.s based there, plus health visitors, midwives, a baby/women's clinic, care for elderly, dental services, chiropody, a psychiatric outpatients and some pharmaceutical facilities.

The staff occasionally come together for meetings about practice and policy but major decisions are referred to the Area Health Authority. One of the Community Physicians who is represented on the new Community Healty Council, which is a kind of public watchdog on health affairs could take the chair at such meetings but he would not be based at the Centre himself.

HEALTH CENTRE COMMITTEE MEETING

1. Chairman: COMMUNITY PHYSICIAN, Dr and hospital consultant from Windlesfield, specialist in respiratory diseases.

2. G.P. DOCTOR, practice is on new West-Green Council Estate, comprising the five large tower blocks in the main. Young.

3. G.P. DOCTOR, practice is in the old centre of the town. Elderly.

4. HEALTH VISITOR throughout Raftonbury

5. MIDWIFE, liable to be called anywhere in Raftonbury

6. FAMILY PLANNING DOCTOR/WOMEN'S CLINIC, based at Health Centre, sex educator

7. FAMILY NURSE, able to be called into families and live-in occasionally, otherwise based at the Centre.

8. PHARMACIST, based at Health Centre, radical activist in medical politics.

The Politicians

The town council of Raftonbury has a conservative majority which has been the case for much of this century. But the growing problems that the town has not been able to solve have changed a great many attitudes and the socialists have high hopes for the next local elections. The County Borough of Midsham Vale overall has a Labour majority. This was reflected in the last General Election when for the first time the M.P. who includes Raftonbury in his constituency became a Socialist Member and not a Tory.

1. MAYOR OF RAFTONBURY - former alderman; mayor for one year only, conservative councillor for last twleve years; an Executive of Henslow Scientific Instruments Ltd., in East Raftonbury.

2. SOCIALIST M.P. FOR MIDSHAM VALE NORTH (including Raftonbury) You have lived in Raftonbury for the last 15 years, worked your way through the Stanley Plastics Factory becoming a trades union official then Area Organiser for the Transport and General Workers Union. Married with children. Succeeded at third attempt to Parliament.

3. PROSPECTIVE PARLIAMENTARY CONSERVATIVE CANDIDATE FOR MIDSHAM VALE NORTH. Recently moved to Raftonbury from the South, where had been local councillor for eight years; banker, working in Windlesfield Trust Company.

4. CIVIL SERVICE ADVISER FROM THE DEPARTMENT OF TRADE AND INDUSTRY, invited from Whitehall for a series of meetings in Raftonbury, including the Public Meeting.

Victims of the deadly dust

Greater London Council planners and architects will today begin to search their files for details of buildings in which cancer-causing blue asbestos was used.

Valley where they die by millimetres

by LAURENCE MARKS

A GOVERNMENT inquiry into the tragedy of the Yorkshire valley hit by an epidemic of the deadly industrial disease of asbestosis has been demanded by Mr Max Madden, Labour MP for Sowerby, in a letter to Mr Michael Foot, the Employment Secretary.

A High Court judge was told by a chest physician last week that people living in the valley were watching their friends and families 'die by millimetres.'

Asbestosis is one of the pneumoconiosis group of lung diseases caused by inhaling dust. It can lead to a slow and painful death. Although it was recognised as a killer more than 50 years ago, the number of people who are known to die from it and the number of new cases diagnosed every year are increasing.

The Department of Health and Social Security says that 688 workers in the asbestos industry were diagnosed as suffering from pneumoconiosis in 1972. In one company alone, a survey of 100 asbestos workers found 65 with X-ray abnormalities.

About 10,000 workers in the asbestos industry are in daily contact with the material, but altogether around 100,000 people could be at risk in various occupations.

According to Patrick Kinnersly's 'The Hazards of Work,' published last year,* there is a danger of contracting the disease in any job in which asbestos is handled extensively. These include:

Dock and transport workers who handle sacks and bales.
Steelworkers, shipbuilders and power station workers engaged in lagging and de-lagging.
Engineers, boilermakers and carriage builders who install various forms of insulation.
Paper-makers producing filter papers and grinding rollers.
Factory workers handling and producing linoleum, floor tiles, rubber paints, plastics, adhesives and roofing compounds.
Motor industry workers grinding brake and clutch parts, and making battery cases and undersealing for cars.
And, of course, anyone in the building industry regularly handling asbestos products.

There are two main forms of asbestos. Blue asbestos (Crocidolite) is so lethal that its import into Britain was belatedly banned about 18 months ago. Some experts have claimed that five minutes' inhalation of blue asbestos dust can produce cancers up to 20 years afterwards.

But neither the import ban nor current research and development of a safe alternative industrial material disposes of the danger. Thousands of tons of blue asbestos have been built into old structures, ships and gasworks, lying in wait for demolition workers. It may be unrecognised. Its rich lavender blue fades when exposed to extreme heat and may not show up when mixed with other types of material.

White asbestos (Chrysotile) has somewhat less penetrative properties, but is still dangerous. Individuals vary in their susceptibility. Six weeks may be enough for a man working in a heavy concentration. Although such conditions have been illegal in factories since 1931, some asbestos firms continued to expose their workers to dense dust until comparatively recently.

New regulations were introduced in 1969. There have been more than 30 prosecutions for breaches in the past three years. But, as with other kinds of environmental pollution, the penalties do not seem to be heavy enough to discourage negligence. Last February a firm of contractors was fined £200 for leaving blue asbestos waste lying around a mill in which 10 men were working.

In another case in 1972 a factory inspector said he would have preferred an unleashed tiger to have been in the plant to the blue asbestos that was lying on the walkway and on the floor.

Not only the workers themselves, but their families may be at risk. A Dagenham woman, whose husband was killed by asbestosis in 1957, died of the same disease in April. The inquest was told that she used to wash all her husband's work clothes by hand, and in doing so had inhaled asbestos fibres.

There is a strong link between asbestosis and cancer. About half of those who contract asbestosis sooner or later get lung cancer. According to Dr Stephen Jones of Nottingham City Hospital, cigarette smokers who work with asbestos are 90 times more likely to suffer from lung cancer than workers in other industries.

Sufferers can claim compensation from the firm that employed them, but it is often difficult for a man to find witnesses to testify that he worked on a particular construction contract many years before.

The factory inspectorate is engaged in a long-term study of the disease. The health of present and former asbestos workers is nowadays carefully monitored.

Like coal miners' pneumoconiosis, it tends to afflict smallish communities around a particular work place. At Cape Asbestos Ltd's Wadsworth Mill near Hebden Bridge, the subject of last week's court case, 25 people have died after working there and 150 more cases have been diagnosed. It was closed in 1971.

Pluto Press, 90p.

RAFTONBURY HERALD

late special edition

THE HERALD HAS ALWAYS STOOD FOR THE GOOD OF THE PEOPLE. IT OPPOSED THE BUILDING OF THE NEW FIBREASBO PLANT EVEN THOUGH THIS WAS UNPOPULAR. WILL THIS NEW TRAGEDY MAKE RAFTONBURY THINK AGAIN?

THIRD VICTIM DEATH PROBE

FIBREASBO UNDER FIRE

A deathbed exclusive interview by Herald Reporter uncovers a threat to the people of Raftonbury that could mean murder

CAN WE ALLOW IT?

When you read this, Harry Benson, a Fibreasbo Mechanical Engineer, will have died. His cousin, reporter Tom Benson, reports.

I must have been one of the last of the visitors to see Harry Benson alive. We said little and he coughed blood. "This is more than fags," he gasped. "I took that risk and deserve what I got. This is more than that. It's up to you now, Tom. Tell them what's going on at the Plant. Find out about Frank Davies and Steve Jenkins. We should have listened to you blokes. It's a death factory."

Staff at Windlesfield General Hospital were not over forthcoming. The Consultant in charge, Doctor Trevor Henslow, 35 years, admitted that Harry Benson was dying of cancer. "This has never been a secret." Tests do not yet indicate its cause, though clearly there has been a sudden collapse over a very short period of time.

When questioned he would not admit that there was any connection between the two other recent cancer deaths of Fibreasbo workers, except that all three were heavy smokers. "But we are making a thorough investigation. "Mrs. Benson knew there would not be long to go. She has spent most of the last month by his bedside and she looked all in. "Why should it be our Harry?" she sobbed. "It's all been so quick. I thought cancer gave you warning. Still he won't have to bear the pain too long; that's good. "

Is blue croc — the killer?
our scientific adviser investigates

Blue crocidolite comes from S. Africa. It is one of the fibrous silicotic minerals out of which Asbestos is woven. It is the most resistent to corrosion but its exceedingly fine dust is the most lethal. Evidence shows it causes pulmonary scarring and lung cancer. For over a year now there has been a world-wide shortage of the alternative white chrysotile.

The Herald is opening a Harry Benson Fund to help his two sons through their schooling and to mark Harry's years of service to the Toc H.

EDITORIAL

INDUSTRIAL ACCIDENT ?

The deaths of Frank Davies and Steve Jenkins had not attracted public attention. Both bereavements were seen as occasions for family mourning and passed without society's intrusion. Cancer is not unique to Raftonbury and this region has traditionally had more than its fair share. But Harry Benson's dying fears have signalled grave doubts and cause for serious anxiety. Benson was a senior engineer with Fibreasbo and clearly had his suspicions.

PANIC IN SURGERY

Nor are the Herald's fears alleviated. Reactions from the medical profession seem to indicate that the idea of associating these deaths is not new. "We must beware of social panic", I was warned. Certainly, on checking all local doctors we were told of a "substantial increase" in chest and respiratory complaints throughout last winter put down to fog.

TOWN HALL'S 'NO COMMENT'

The Town Hall was no more informative. Some officials scorned the idea and said we should all have heard if there was something to be told. Some councillors reacted angrily at the allegations and said they would ask questions in Council without delay. The anger seemed not without guilt. Nowhere did the Herald find co-operation easy; a conspiracy becomes clear.

WHAT PRICE PROSPERITY ?

Tight security has always surrounded Fibreasbo. Now it is like a clam. Our staff cross-questioned over fifty workers in their homes this week. Many could recollect the change in style of mineral deliveries about 18 months ago. There is more than a growing conviction that this was a change to the use of the killer blue crocidolite. If this is true, and no one yet denies it , then the people of Raftonbury are living on the brink of a hellish pit from whose dread fumes no social wealth or Fibreasbo sheeting can protect us.

FIBREASBO PROFITS SOAR
SECOND ANNUAL REPORT

CHAIRMAN Norman Broughton's second annual report presented on behalf of the Fibreasbo Company, a subsidiary of the giant Chemicals International Group, last Thursday must have brought joy to the hearts of investors and shareholders. From out of the usual tangle of statistics and high finance emerges an impressive picture of growth, increased dividends and success. Sales have soared as Fibreasbo's products have increasingly eaten into an expanding market of demand but a diminishing international supply. Not only have the shareholders reaped benefit. The whole social amenities programme of the Plant is now complete and the Asbests, the firm's famed football team has risen to the first division in the Midsham Sunday League. The Firefly Community Centre, provided by the Company for the immediate neighbourhood, is now complete and will be opened, along with the new extension to the M.9 and the Raftonbury Civic Swimming Pool by Princess Anne on her visit this summer. Raftonbury basks in its new-found affluence.

ANGRY WIDOW TO SUE

Mrs. Frank Davies was shocked and amazed when it was suggested to her that her husband's death was anything other than smoker's lung cancer as she had been told. "He was always chesty and I said for years he should stop smoking. I've never doubted they were to blame. But if what Mr. Benson says is true then I'll get a solicitor right away and start to take action. "Mrs. Davies was obviously stunned by the news. "It's like opening up an old sore again. I thought I was just coming to terms with it. "

PUBLIC PROTEST MEETING
in Town Hall 6.0. pm tonight
CALL FOR GOVERNMENT INVESTIGATION URGED

Raftonbury
Department of Medical Health

HEALTH AND SAFETY BULLETIN No. 7 - GENERAL INFORMATION FOR ALL STAFF

From: Dr P.G. Wagner, Chairman Raftonbury Health and Safety Services Committee

Asbestos

There has recently been a great deal of attention given to the subject of asbestos in the working environment. Widespread media and press coverage has also shown its use and dangers in the home, in schools and all public buildings and in transport. The concern now of the Health Department is to present the facts, rather than the exaggerations of the situation, as a service to our many employees.

Type of asbestos

Asbestos is a mineral fibre which occurs naturally in many parts of the world but particularly in Canada, Russia, Southern Africa and America - in order of output. There are several different types of asbestos of which chrysotile (white asbestos), amosite (grey/brown) and crocidolite (blue) are the most common. Of the current world production about 93% is chrysotile. Although there are physical and chemical differences they have two features in common. They can be woven and are resistant to flames.

The most dangerous type, blue crocidolite is found in South Africa. No crocidolite (blue asbestos) fibres have been imported into the United Kingdom since 1970 although materials imported before that date may have been used in the 1970's.

History and Uses

Asbestos comes from the Greek for unquenchable. It was used by stone-age men for cooking utensils. The Egyptians used woven asbestos in order to retrieve the ashes of the corpse after ceremonial burning. The Industrial Revolution of course laid great stress on the need for such a material, and mining and usage is now running at about four million tons per annum. Countless human lives have been saved through its application.

Over 1000 uses for asbestos have been described. It is included in a wide range of insulation products for pipe lagging, cement sheets for building work, pipes and pressure pipes, floor tiling and ceiling tiling, and fireproof paints. Wool asbestos fibre is even used in the filter pads of certain types of respirator. (When finely woven it is a very efficient filter for beer, wines, medicines and for removing bacteria from drinking water). In brake linings and clutch facings the asbestos is usually reinforced with wire threads. Asbestos is widely used for fireproofing on bulkheads in ships, on girders in buildings and for improving the fire resistance of cellulose and other materials. It is also used in acid resisting filtering cloth, textiles, and in firefighting suits, firemen's helmets, theatre safety curtains. Domestic uses include linoleum, ironing boards, oven cloths , table and cooking mats.

Latterly the material has been used for covering the nose cones of space craft because of the intense heat on re-entry into the earth's atmosphere. Blue crocidolite was found to be useful fire-proofing for war ships in 1900 for the German Navy. It was resistant to corrosion and sea-water.

As far as Raftonbury Council is concerned the main uses of asbestos products are as insulating or fireproofing materials in the building and construction field. The Council's own Health and Safety Committee has set up an Asbestos Advisory Panel to investigate the extent of the use of asbestos and will make recommendations about the protection of employees and occupants as well as its treatment, replacement and disposal. The use of asbestos in new building operations has already been considered and lists of both permitted and prohibited asbestos-based building materials drawn up.

HEALTH HAZARDS

The specific diseases associated with exposure to asbestos are:-
1. Asbestosis (a form of fibrosis of the lungs).
2. Bronchial cancer (especially in association with cigarette smoking).
3. Mesothelioma (tumours of the linings of the chest or abdomen).
Although currently there is much uncertainty over the risks associated with other forms of asbestos, crocidolite (blue asbestos) is believed to be the most dangerous perhaps because of its very fine fibres. Usually diseases have resulted following periods of contact in factory or work conditions. However the differing medical opinions as to the actual health hazards resulting from the use of asbestos has led to the establishment by the Government of an Advisory Committee on Asbestos headed by the Chairman of the Health and Safety Commission. In the meantime the International Agency for Cancer Research recently published a major report on asbestos hazards. It concluded:-

"1. That all types of asbestos produce pulmonary scarring if there has been excessive exposure to the dust.
"2. Cancer of the lung occurs among workers who have had excessive exposure to all types of asbestos dust.
"3. Cancer of the lung is far more common among workers who are cigarette smokers. (The two carcinogens, asbestos and cigarette smoke, appear to combine multiplicatively in the production of lung cancer).
"4. Mesotheliomas of the pleura and the peritoneum (the lining of the abdominal cavity) are more common among those exposed to asbestos than the general population. More than 1000 cases have been reported in people exposed to asbestos.
"5. There is no evidence of an increased rate of mesotheliomas among miners, and those living in the vicinity of the mines, in any mining area except the crocidolite mines in the Cape Province in South Africa.
"6. In industry, crocidolite asbestos has been definitely implicated in the development of the mesotheliomas, and crocidolite asbestos has been identified in the lungs of asbestos workers with mesotheliomas from Germany, Italy, Britain, France, Holland, Sweden, South Africa, Australia, Canada and the United States.
"7. Mesotheliomas have occurred in people who have had neighbourhood exposure to asbestos dust either from living in close vicinity to mills and factories before the dust was controlled, or from the cleaning of protective clothing of relations who brought their overalls home before this practice was forbidden.
"8. It was shown that asbestos fibres could be recovered from the lungs of the majority of individuals living in urban communities. However, there was no evidence to suggest that anyone had developed disease from exposure to the ambient air.
"9. There was no evidence that exposure of the general population to the small amounts of asbestos fibre in beverages, drinking water, food or pharmaceutical preparations increased the risk of cancer."

Asbestos at work

The dangers associated with asbestos vary considerably, Some operations are quite safe whereas with others extensive precautions must be taken. Many regulations, codes of practice, recommended procedures, etc., exist to safeguard workers. It is the dust which is the danger and in Britain a significant safety improvement has been the introduction of "wet processing" of fibres for textile production.
Supervisors and managers engaged in work involving asbestos should be aware of all the new safety regulations or be prepared to seek advice. If all employees note the following advice any risk involved in working with or near asbestos will be minimised.
1. Notify your immediate supervisor of any suspected asbestos hazard including damaged or decayed materials.
2. Do not touch, disturb or damage asbestos materials.
3. Supervisory staff should notify Senior Management of the discovery of asbestos.
4. Before commencing work check with supervisory staff that the necessary precautions appropriate to the particular activity have been taken.
5. Always follow the instructions given.
At all times Raftonbury Council will endeavour to take full safety precautions including, where appropriate, notification to the Factory Inspectorate.
It is intended that employees should be kept informed of all new developments. With this in mind an Asbestos Joint Liaison Committee has been established. It is composed of representatives of the trade union and staff side bodies together with senior officers from various departments concerned with asbestos.

(Based on G.L.C. Service Circular No. 103 and 'New Scientist' article: 7.3.74).

The proposal for the new Fibreasbo Factory to be built in Raftonbury to help alleviate its acute unemployment problems is still highly confidential. There has been six months of backroom work to get matters to the stage when they can become public with any real chance of their outcome being successful. The site is on either side of the canal to the west side of Raftonbury and has been acquired by Chemical International successfully. The Department of Trade and Industry has already designated Raftonbury a grey area and fit for development. An Industrial Development Certificate and some Government financial backing will both be forthcoming if the local community is prepared to back the venture with its support. The project is first to be made public at a major meeting in the immediate future until then strict confidence is to be observed.

Although the Fibreasbo Factory will be built and paid for by Chemicals International, services must be provided by the Town Council and safety standards must be acceptable to the local authority. All government officers are aware of two factors:-
  a) The town badly needs investment; it is running down. Unemployment has become a way of life to too many people. Vandalism is reaching epidemic proportions.
  b) A thriving new industry will increase the size and importance of the town and this will increase the importance (and possibly the salaries) of its officers' positions.

The officers must go into the questions of what amenities and services would have to be provided for the new works, and decide, having weighed the pros and cons, what attitude to take up at the public meeting. Though they need not attend this, as it will not be a decision-making meeting, their presence may be very useful in case the official position from the council needs to be spelt out.

INFORMAL CONSULTATIVE MEETING OF OFFICERS

1. Chairman: BOROUGH ENGINEER
    In conjunction with the Borough Surveyor and the Chief Planning Officer, you are responsible for certain requirements and regulations, concerning the scheme. Provision must be made for water, electricity and gas services to be laid on, fire regulations must be observed, fire escapes, fire-doors, fire extinguishers. Access roads must be provided; crane-swings during building must not encompass any public thoroughfare; there must be adequate provision for waste-disposal; local interests must not be violated by the building, nor historical monuments and wild life destroyed. The factory must not be near enough to houses to constitute a health hazard and it must conform to practical and aesthetic standards with regard to height and size. The Medical Officer of Health's judgement on the health hazards is especially important. All the officers have become discouraged over the last five years in which their jobs have dwindled with less and less resources for public spending. A big new factory would mean a large increase in the rates coming into the Borough Treasurer. This would make possible a long over-due improvement to the sewage system, among other things.

2. THE CHIEF PLANNING OFFICER - see notes on Borough Engineer.
    Your department is nearly bereft of activity in the current recession. You are a visionary and feel with new prosperity the town could be made into an almost ideal environment for living with the addition of sport and leisure facilities, pedestrian ways for shopping and a small concert hall-cum-theatre.

3. THE BOROUGH SURVEYOR - see notes for the Borough Engineer and Planning Officer.

4. MEDICAL OFFICER OF HEALTH Last year you issued a Safety Report on Asbestos. In the event of an industry producing health hazards you would be obliged to investigate them and demand that adequate precautions were taken. You are torn between your awareness of the danger-potential of the asbestos factory and the possibilities of new prosperity coming to Raftonbury.

5. CHIEF INSPECTOR OF POLICE You have been invited to the meeting to advise on the problems of the increased traffic the factory will bring. You are concerned that the factory will have adequate parking facilities to keep cars off the road and adequate security guards so that your own men do not have to do extra patrol duty. The vandalism is already proving a headache in this respect.

6. MANAGER OF THE WATER BOARD Invited to the meeting because a major new factory will put pressure on industrial and domestic water supplies which come from a reservoir fed by the River Bream. Possible pollution from waste will be a problem.

7. MANAGER OF THE BUS COMPANY An improved service will be necessary.

8. MANAGER OF THE REGIONAL ELECTRICITY BOARD.

Raftonbury Area Social Services Team

Under the new Seebohm Committee recommendations, the areas that the Social Service teams relate to echo that of the new County and City Boroughs. There is a Director of Social Services responsible to and appointed by the Social Services Sub-Committee of the County Borough. Such a Director might be based in the Town Hall or main administrative centre. In this case it would be the Windlesfield Civic Centre. Then a series of sub-area teams serving a population of 20-50,000 would be based more locally, responsible to the Director.

The Raftonbury Area Social Services Team serves Raftonbury and all the outlying social areas. In the new service every kind of social need is dealt with by the team that is not health, education or housing. The team supervises any Family Advice Centres, Old People's Day Centres, Day Centres for the Physically Handicapped or former Mentally Ill patients. Some day nurseries, all foster homes and all daily child minders are their concern, and they would relate to but not supervise Children's Homes and Adolescent Hostels.

An area team would have 10 - 15 social workers who together would cover all social needs from cradle to the grave, although some social workers might specialise. The team would meet regularly for Case Conferences when difficult cases are described and the group gives advice on dealing with them, or for matters of policy and practical concern. In-service training may be given and conferences held.

Some social workers of the older school were trained on the job; nowadays some have very little training at all. Others,called case-workers, have a training in greater depth in understanding feelings and in psychological insight. Social workers give what practical aids they can, knowing of state provision and the constant change in law, such as helping with pensions, holidays away, domestic help, various appliances, meals on wheels, social security, legal aid, housing grants etc. etc., often just being a 'good neighbour'. They can also give emotional support to clients, not always be offering advice but by enabling the client to greater self-awareness and to see his problems in a new way.

Some radical social workers identify with clients and may well squat with them, if necessary, to fight the State; some traditional social workers were appointed in a period when the Lady Bountiful approach seemed strong; others will want to remain strictly professional, feeling that this helps the client to gain strength himself.

An area team comprises:

1. Area team leader; he/she would chair meetings and be directly responsible to the Regional Director;
2. Two Senior Social Workers of good standing and experience, perhaps with different complementary backgrounds;
3. Seven or more social workers, holding various responsibilities;
4. Administrative and support staff, sometimes community service volunteers.

All probation is part of the legal and court system but today the Raftonbury Team have invited in a local Probation Officer to join them for their special meeting.

WORKING PARTY MEETING OF AREA TEAM

1. <u>Chairman</u>: AREA TEAM LEADER, Wide experience, case-worker trained, worked with Children and Families as well as Mental Welfare. Read sociology at Oxford, working class background.
2. SENIOR SOCIAL WORKER, was in prison service in earlier days, now has responsibility for blind, deaf and specialist needs.
3. SENIOR SOCIAL WORKER, did early work in preventative case-work, now specialises in the area of Mental Welfare after working in an Adolescent Hostel for those dependent on drugs or alcohol.
4. SOCIAL WORKER, special concern for Children's welfare, adoptions, fostering.
5. SOCIAL WORKER, beginner in first year, radical attitudes.
6. PSYCHIATRIC SOCIAL WORKER is a counsellor in a clinic surgery set up as part of the Family Advice Centre.
7. PROBATION OFFICER, visiting the area team, responsible for young delinquents.
8. ADMINISTRATION OFFICER, takes minutes at meetings, runs office, deals with complaints from the public and helps social workers through administrations.

TRIAD *TEACHER TRAINING EXERCISE*

Authority Role	**Subordinate Role**	**Observer Role**

A 1   TEACHER OF SOCIAL STUDIES

You have asked one of your fifth form group to come to see you at 4.0 pm. You are not happy at all with his/her work and feel that he/she can do much better. You have always expressed an interest in the pupil and have often said that he/she has good potential that is not being fulfilled.

The presentation of work is quite neat but you feel that a lot of it is copied from his/her great friend Jack/ie Simmons, a very spontaneous pupil, or that too much comes straight from the text book without thought.

Recently the pupil has grown more sullen and you now want to say that if he/she doesn't pull her/his socks up then you cannot really recommend that he/she is entered for the G.C.E. O.L. examination.

B 1   FIFTH FORM PUPIL

You have been summoned to see your Social Studies teacher at 4.0 pm. You have never got on all that well with him/her because you have always felt that he/she has been unnecessarily critical of you. This is a pity because you enjoy a great deal of the work in Social Studies; you expect to do well in it in the forthcoming G.C.E. O.L. in the summer and might even go on to study it further in the sixth form.

You feel you are a diligent and hard-working pupil. You have not the flair of your best friend Jack/ie Simmons, who can get away with murder and who frequently borrows your homework to embellish his/her own when in urgent need. You feel that the Social Studies teacher wants you to stick very closely to the text books because you have been criticised in the past for putting down stupid ideas, though you felt these were quite original. You work hard and long at the subject, especially recently but have not received any just praise you feel. You hope now that at this meeting your teacher will say how well you've been doing and has noticed the improvement that you feel is there.

**C 1
OBSERVER**

B 2   HEAD OF SOCIAL STUDIES DEPARTMENT

You see yourself as a reasonably progressive head of department and have brought in some major changes and new thinking to the department over the last few years. However, you are not happy with one of the younger members of your staff still in his/her first year of probation.

You are especially concerned that the record book is rarely filled in, that the pupils' exercise books seem to be rather messy and ill cared for and that there is frequently too much noise from the classes. Recently you have received several complaints from members of staff in other departments whose judgement you respect.

You are especially concerned to keep up standards of rigour in the department to justify this new subject from antagonism from other members of staff. So far you have not been able to see your colleague teaching in the classroom but you have felt that the time has come to call him/her to task.

C 2   YOUNG TEACHER OF SOCIAL STUDIES

You are in your first year as a Social Studies teacher in a reasonably difficult inner city school. There are a host of social problems within most of the forms that you teach and you feel that you have been given some of the most difficult of the school's classes. In general you have worked hard and feel that you have coped well. Your Head of Department has now called you in to see him/her.

So far the Head of Department has not seen you teach, nor been very supportive; if anything, rather remote. You feel this is a pity because your prime concern in your subject is for the human relationships within the group and an awareness of those human relationships. You have generated a good workable relationship in most of your classes. They are not quiet but they are happy and many of the pupils seem concerned about many of the human issues. You admit to some behaviour problems in some of the classes but are aware that even experienced members of staff have similar difficulties. You have encouraged a great deal of outside visits with senior forms. You now anticipate some commendation from your Head of Department, aware that he has to recommend your probationary period.

**A 2
OBSERVER**

C 3 HEAD TEACHER OF NEW AMALGAMATED COMPREHENSIVE SCHOOL

You were the Headteacher of a former grammar school which has now been amalgamated with two smaller secondary modern schools to form a three site comprehensive school. You are in your late thirties, go-ahead in many ways and concerned that the best standards of the grammar tradition can be brought into the more human framework of the comprehensive. You are certainly still under pressure from parent and governor expectations to keep up the good record of examination successes and university entrance that your former grammar was noted for.

Recently you have had a problem with the Head of your Social Studies Dept. For he/she believes in senior pupils in fourth and fifth forms having rich first-hand experience in actual social service. Some fifth formers were working in the local hospital, helping the porters and nursing auxiliaries. However, they recently went on strike and the Head of Dept. felt this was a good opportunity for the pupils to stay in that situation and observe all the social pressures of what happens in a strike situation – interviewing all the parties involved, including the patients and seeing how it was resolved. However, you felt the situation was too politically 'hot' and withdrew the group two days ago.

The Head of Dept. has now made an appointment to see you and you know that he/she feels strongly about the issue. You feel it is now not the right time to get the school involved in such local politics so young in its new comprehensive life and when it is already facing antagonism from influential parents jealous of its academic reputation.

A 3 HEAD OF SOCIAL STUDIES DEPARTMENT

You have requested to see the Headteacher and it has been two days before you could get an appointment. Your Social Studies department is only three years old and in that time it has set about some excellent work and is slowly earning the respect from other more traditional colleagues on the staff.

You are especially concerned to have fourth and fifth formers for some of their subject time placed in valid real social situations, to help in practical terms and to become aware of human behaviour and social processes. You and your department have spent a long time setting many of these up. One group of fifth formers was placed working with the porters and auxiliary nurses at the local hospital. However, they recently went on strike. This you felt would be a real learning situation for the pupils to see what happened throughout this process, to interview all parties concerned and to make this a major project. But two days ago the Headteacher instructed that the pupils were to be withdrawn from the situation fearing their political involvement and the kind of criticism that the school might face. It is only three years since the two former secondary modern schools and a grammar school combined to form the comprehensive and the Headteacher was Head of the former grammar. He/she is a reasonably go-ahead leader and has previously backed you strongly and the work of your department. However, you now feel that you have been ridden over rough-shod and that this might be the thin end of the wedge with other 'interference' imminent.

B 3 OBSERVER

PROCEDURE

This is a training exercise for teachers to examine some of the dimensions of their everyday interactions. Every enactor has an opportunity to take part as the 'authority' role, 'subordinate' role and observer role in turn and the progression of the situations through a hierarchy structure adds other layers of role concern and ambiguity. Some situations are deliberately structured with discrepancies of expectation.

Clearly the 'social studies' content could easily be changed to any other subject area, as the 'teacher training' dimension could be changed for any other profession.

The exercise needs at least a period of 45 minutes or 1 hour. Every encounter needs to be at least 10 minutes and its evaluation 5 minutes immediately afterwards. There could also be a pooling back time when the whole group meets together at the end.

The group of enactors is divided into threes and each player decides whether he is to be role A, B or C, which he retains throughout.

The leader can call all the As to him and brief them with their roles only, either privately and orally reading from the sheet or can give them the information in a duplicated form for them to digest and then put away. The leader repeats this with the Bs and Cs. All triads start and stop together.

The Observers can either be told to consider a particular aspect of communication between the enactors, like eye contact, non-verbal communication, empathetic understanding, facilitation towards decision and action, listening etc. or asked to look at all aspects of the encounter. They should sit as anonymously as possible with paper and biro, writing actual verbatim responses which they will then share with the enactors in the evaluation afterwards in a positive and not a destructive way.

This Howse To Let

The gentry and leisured elite of Drury Lane

The poor, sick and beggars living in nearby alleys

The players in the Cockpit Plaie Howse

This Howse to Let

"THIS HOWSE TO LET" is an attempt to look in an unusual way at some of the social, political, religious and cultural divisions and conflicts of the mid-seventeenth century. The Cockpit Plaie Howse off Drury Lane becomes the symbolic cockpit of state, a microcosm for what was happening at large.

The players were arrested in costume in mid-performance in January 1649 and taken to prison by the soldiers who 'often times took the crown from his head who acted the King and in sport would oftentime put it on again.' Within a month Charles was beheaded and weeks later London's play houses were razed - the stage is empty and 'to let'. The shedding of the 'Divine' blood unleashed a political ferment of new ideas which is only paralleled in English history by our own situation today. Every central issue of our own times - the government of the state, power and equality, freedom and belief, sexual roles and family life, master and servant - was feverishly explored and attempted in action in those early years of the 1650's - levellers, ranters, shakers, quakers, diggers, masterless men, baptists, independents together turned their world upside down. On January 1649 all was poised on the brink of this ferment and this is the situation that the simulation explores.

The full materials make use of seventeenth century documentary material and the simulation could only be undertaken by groups who are immersed in the history of the period and want to bring their studies to life in a lively way.

The model is very similar to "Raftonbury and Fibreasbo". Every player is given a copy of Wenzel Hollar's map of N.W. London in the 1650's with the focus in the Drury Lane area where everyone is to determine where he lives and works. As well the map sheet has reminder information about the broad events in the Cockpit of State during the 1640's and also about the Drury Lane environment and surrounding courts and alleys. The players work in eight different groups of at least two members each and no more than six; so any number from 16 to about 50 can take part. Each group has a double sided role-and-information briefing sheet with an illustration at its top and a whole series of quotations from pamphlets and documents of the 1640's to help sustain attitudes and arguments.

This takes time for digestion.

The role sheet areas are:-

1. <u>Gentry and leisured elite</u> living in Drury Lane, recently returned; supporting King.
2. <u>Clergy and churchmen</u> from St. Giles in the Field and St. Clements; supporting King.
3. <u>Players</u> from the Cockpit Plaie Howse returned from the wars fighting for King.
4. <u>The poor, sick and crippled</u> living in the alleys off Drury Lane, raw survivors.
5. <u>Middle class merchants</u> living in smaller Drury Lane houses, working nearby; Parliament men.
6. <u>Citizens</u>, working in humble trades all around, radical attitudes, supporting army.
7. <u>Apprentices, masterless men</u>, young people; range of attitudes, trying new life style.
8. <u>Soldiers from New Model Army</u>, officers and other ranks, based in Whitehall, on duty.

<u>OUTLINE OF ACTION</u> (at least a double period to attempt part of it, preferably a whole morning)

1.	Getting into role:	possibility of making appropriate head gear, series of simple warm-ups, role-play exercise.
2.	Out in Drury Lane:	cold morning, January 1st; players surreptitiously distributing playbills about performance at 3.0 pm of Shirley's play 'The Traitor'.
3.	Back at home:	Each group planning how they can see the play, or in some way prevent it from happening by suppression of disturbance.
4.	3.0 pm at the play: (freedom and censorship)	All converge on the start of the performance. Chance for debate, argument about censorship of plays, 'sin' of theatre. At suitable time, the militia enter, arrest everyone, including audience, pros and antis, taken to Marshalsea Prison.
5.	Marshalsea Prison: (politics)	Questioning by soldiers of everyone in turn, while an altercation is structured based on the power of the army and the future of the state. During this it is announced that parliament have decided to try the King for treason. Implications teased out in role. All prisoners released with a fine each.
6.	St. Giles Church: (religion)	Sunday following. After the formal service, it was possible for a religious disputation to be engaged with visitors and intruders.
7.	Evaluation:	Plenty to talk through.

The Cockpit of State

THE WAR BEGINS

1639 'Bishops' War' in Scotland; Archbishop Laud and Charles attempt to impose the prayer book and Anglican worship on Presbyterian Kirk, army beaten by Scots.
> Cockpit Plaie Howse raided and players imprisoned for presenting a play which satirised Charles' political folly in the Scottish campaign.

1640 On Stafford's advice, Charles summons first parliament for 12 years to raise subsidies. This Short Parliament dissolved when the Commons demanded redress of grievances. In December the Long Parliament summoned, but this was more revolutionary.

1641 The Commons impeach Stafford, Charles' strongest support, but London mob forces Charles to betray him and Stafford is beheaded. Crown made subservient to Law.

1642 In January, King attempts to impeach five members of the Commons; they escape. King leaves protestant London; raises his standard at Nottingham.

WAR DECLARED - FIRST CAMPAIGN

Battle of Worcester, Edgehill, King victorious, makes Oxford his capital.
> In September all the London plaie howses are closed with the Beeston's Boys performance of Broome's "A Jovial Crew" at the Cockpit being the last. Most of the players enlist for the king and leave London.

1643 Battles of Gloucester, Bristol and Newbury and further victories for the King. Parliament still mainly anxious to curb and not kill the King, but divided aim.

1644 Archbishop Laud tried. King's chief adviser now his Catholic queen, Henrietta.

THE WAR WIDENS

Cromwell forms the New Model Army, the Ironsides; Fairfax made its commander-in-chief. At the Battle of Marston Moor, Prince Rupert and King's army defeated.

1645 Archbishop Laud beheaded. King now alone. New Model Army resoundingly defeated the King again at the Battle of Naseby.

1646 Fairfax marches on Oxford, the King flees, delivers himself to the Scots. Parliament supreme but dependent on the power of the Army which it pays poorly.
> The Cockpit Plaie Howse resident dramatist, James Shirley, uses the theatre as a school, himself as teacher.

1647 Scots surrendered and King held captive by Parliament. All fighting ceases and King presented with nineteen proposals as terms of peace; he secretly negotiates with France and Scotland to overthrow parliament. He escapes.
> The players return from the war and give illicit performances. Parliament issues an ordinance stating that actors caught flagrante should be imprisoned.

THE SECOND CIVIL WAR

1648 Charles recaught. Cromwell now victorious. King distrusted and found to be conspiring with England's enemies. Now is forced to accept Parliament's conditions. Army increasingly militant in attitude towards Parliament which vacillates about its future and about adequate pay. There is an attempt to send it to Ireland to suppress disturbances. Leveller faction grows in army.
Ordinance of 1647 expires, immediately plays performed again.
> Parliament then declares players as Rogues and Vagabonds with appropriate punishments. Many actors now move to France and join George Jolly's company performing to the Court-in-exile and touring.

The 30 years war in Europe finishes; more soldiers come to London. The army captures the King and marches on Parliament, forcing its terms. Increasingly it is seen that the King can no longer be negotiated with, that trust is impossible.
> In July firmer measures are taken to suppress the plaie howses.
> All stages, boxes, scaffolds, seats and forms are dismantled.
> Yet Performances continue and are well supported by audiences.
> In mid-December the Cockpit actors, Lowen, Taylor, Pollard, Burt and Hart are caught performing "The Bloody Brother" and briefly put in prison.

In December the army is responsible for Cromwell setting up the Rump Parliament, from which the most dangerous members of the House have been excluded.
Meanwhile the special problems following the Civil War are legion with London full of wounded former soldiers, beggars and the increasing poor. The year's harvest is very bad, prices are extremely high, wages have lagged behind.
There is widespread hunger and unemployment. The army is growingly restless.

1649 1st January The Cockpit players prepare to welcome the new year with a play. Parliament is meeting to decide its next move in its battle royal with the King.

7

Games in Mathematics and Science

Most of the examples of games so far presented have been drawn from the areas of personal relationships and decision-making on environmental problems. As we have already noted, the same techniques are now being used in most subjects of the curriculum. This chapter looks at mathematics and science to demonstrate how this work might be carried out, first with children of primary age, starting with familiar games, such as snakes and ladders and dice, and leading on to a more advanced approach for older pupils.

Change of perspective and change of rules
'Daddy, I've bought a pack of cards about British Birds at the jumble sale. Isn't this black and white magpie beautiful, with its purple and green feathers?' The pack contains thirty-six lovely coloured pictures of different birds, and perhaps these pictures were the first attraction for him. But the cards are not only attractive, they are also useful to identify birds when on holiday. The family has already played 'Snap' with them, which was easy because the cards are marked in families; for example the cards for all birds of the Finch family are marked with the letter A. This is because the game is designed as a version of 'Happy Families', so a naturalist would probably consider it to be a game about the classification of birds. Finally, in school the game might even be used to teach about classification, and it would then itself be classified as a 'task orientated' science game.

In the last paragraph, the same game has been described in several ways, ranging from an attractive set of artistic pictures to a resource for teaching about classification of birds. The encouraging fact is that these various descriptions of one game are *all* possible. The various descriptions are possible for different people who use the game in different ways, and they are also possible for one person if he or she can take a wide-ranging view of the many alternatives. Listing the various alternatives is not as easy as listing the alternative uses of a brick (eg. building a wall, resting on the dustbin lid on a windy day, a robber smashing a jeweller's window etc.) but it can be interesting to find these alternative uses or rules for a game.

Watch those children in the junior school playground and listen to them talking (expletives are censored). 'I can beat you in a race.' 'Go on, you're not as good—Pete and Don are the fastest in school.' Five of them race across the playground to the wall, and back again. 'You cheat, you didn't touch the wall,' 'I did, with my foot.' 'OK, all to kick the wall, it's faster.' One stands by the wall as umpire, one judges start and finish, and the other three race. Then they change places in some acceptable manner and another three race. An observer will realise that children of this junior age are inventive and not constrained by the correct and written rules.

When the group in action has decided on the rules of this game, they play to those rules for the next few minutes or few days. 'Kick the wall' is the rule, until they decide to change to a new rule! They are also satisfied by an empirical approach to deciding who can run fastest. Not for them the league table using groups of three runners out of five; they may run two more races than is theoretically necessary, but then running races is the game.

During the years before they leave school, most of these children will lose their inventiveness and imagination for games. They will learn to play to the rules designated by the rule-book, the teacher, the parent or the club-leader. In doing so they may learn to win a game, but they will lose some of the satisfaction of dynamic group decision making. They will be constrained to accept an offered game instead of being tempted to extend to new dimensions. Next time you go to a jumble sale and pay 5p for a game which has lost its set of rules, you've perhaps got better value than if the rules had been included. Next time you don't know what to do, take one of your games and change it. Noughts and crosses has already been changed into three-dimensional noughts and crosses, which is a more demanding game; could you change it into yet another game?

Of course, it is not desirable always to change everything. Our argument is that every player of games should realise that there is the possibility of change, and that it is interesting to follow up this possibility. Change can follow many directions and we are not supplied with a route map of gaming which will tell the place reached if we take any one route. We could not even use such a route map of gaming to find the best route to any one place of change, because when we start out the destination is unknown. In truth, change can begin a voyage of discovery rather than an experimental investigation of some already identified route or destination.

Dice
The change to a new dimension may be achieved by a change of the equipment used for a game. Many board games are played using a cube-shaped die numbered (or spotted) from one to six. What will be the effect if the game is played with either a differently numbered cube-shaped die, or with a die which has a different number of faces? You can find out if you use some of these multi-faced dice. There is not complete freedom of choice as the faces must all be the same size and

163 shape to give equal chances of scoring each number. Plato has shown that there can be only five such dice, and they are shown on this page. The instructions to make them are:

(1) Find, or cut out from firm card or plastic, an equal-sided triangle, square, or pentagon. These are the templates around which you draw.
(2) Using an old cereal packet, or similar card, mark one of the networks shown. This is fairly easy if you use a ruler and one of the templates.
(3) Cut along the outer lines of the network.
(4) Score along the inner lines of the network.
(5) Fold the network, joining with sticky tape to make the solid.
(6) Paint the solid, and write the chosen numbers on the faces.

The last instruction for making each die tells you to 'write the chosen numbers on the faces.' This is where you may wish to be rather conservative, and write the numbers from one to eight if the die has eight faces. Imagine that you have done this, and then use this die to play snakes and ladders. These are some of the differences you may find in the game. 'We've always started by throwing a six, shouldn't we now start by throwing an eight?' 'There's only one chance in eight of throwing an eight, so it'll take longer to get started. Let's start straight away because the extra numbers anyway will tend to separate the counters more.' 'I'm moving faster across the board.' 'I slid down a snake, threw a seven, and immediately slid down another. This board's not fair if you can throw a seven.' 'It's more difficult to throw the two I need to win.'

Five dice which may be used with board games.

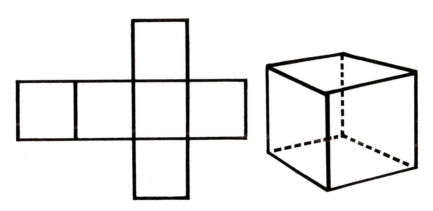

The network for................a Cube

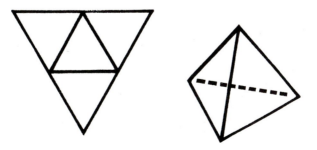

The network for..........a Tetrahedron

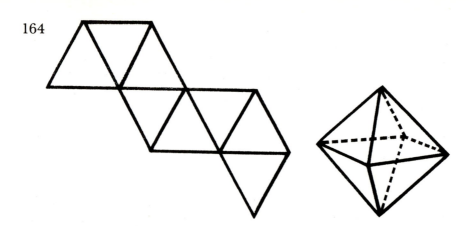

The network for.........an Octahedron

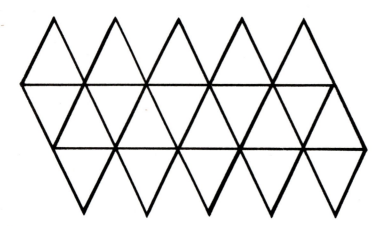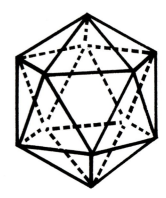

The network for...................an Icosahedron

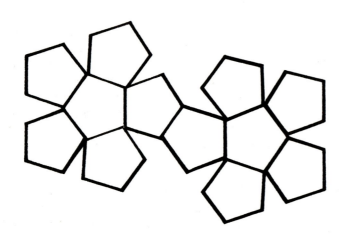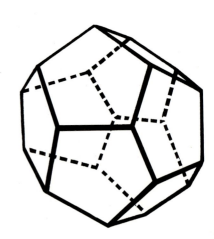

The network for...................a Dodecahedron

165   Instead of being conservative and writing the numbers one to eight, you may choose to include a zero, or even to write the numbers from minus two to plus five. Using these directed numbers really brings in a new dimension of change for a player moves backwards when he throws a negative number. New problems occur during play. 'My first throw is a negative number, how do I move?' 'I've moved backwards to the tail of a snake so I should be allowed to go up to its head.'

In the former game when a one-to-eight die was used one child's perspective was that 'this board's not fair if you can throw a seven.' What are other people's perspectives? There would probably not have been the same plea of 'not fair' from another child who had gone up two ladders instead of down two snakes. The person interested in games design considers the inter-relationship between the players, the equipment and the rules; why and how has the game developed to its present state? (This person, or another, might then make another change.) The teacher sees several possibilities for mathematical questions arising from the use of different dice. With a die from one to twelve is a game won in half as many throws as with a normal die? Should you place the snakes and ladders in different positions if the board is to be used with an abnormal die? What are these positions? Is there a standard position used on most boards for normal dice? What are the probabilities of various events? Does moving backwards and forwards on the board help the children to understand directed numbers?

Snakes and ladders has been used as a familiar example of a board game, but many others can also be used by the player who has made, or bought, some of these multi-faced dice. Take a voyage of discovery and you'll probably get new enjoyment from your board games. It does not matter whether they are games about mathematics, science or any other subject.

Arithmetic skills
$7 + 3 = 10;$ $8 + 2 = 10;$ $10 - 2 = 8;$ $5 \times 3 = 15;$ $6 \times 3 = 18;$
21, 24, 27, 30.
Parents and teachers are often concerned about children's ability in the basic skills illustrated here. After a child has experienced numbers and number patterns, regular practice will help to fix these basic skills so that they can be recalled when they are needed. This regular practice can include the use of several task-orientated games, such as those mentioned here and in the resource list. For each task (eg. multiplication tables) variety may be introduced in two ways: (i) because there are several suitable games, and (ii) because each game can be played several ways. Most of these games use a pack of cards (or plastic tiles) each of which is marked with a number. Some of the cards may be spread or stacked on the table, and each player may be dealt a hand of cards. The aim of most games is for each player to collect, or play, sets of cards which correctly represent the arithmetic skill being practised.

Tens rummy
'7 and 4 do make 10 don't they Sir?' 'They don't Sir, he's a cheat.' Tens rummy is one way to provide practice in the pairs of numbers whose sum is ten (eg. $7 + 3$). From a pack of playing cards select those numbered one to nine, and shuffle them. For two players, perhaps parent and child, deal ten cards to each player. The rest of the cards (the stock) is placed face downwards in the centre of the table, and the top card of it is turned face upwards and laid beside the stock to start the discard pile. Each

player in turn must pick up either the unseen top card of the stock, or the known top card of the discard pile, and then put down a card from his hand on to the discard pile. The aim of the game is to make pairs of cards whose numbers sum to ten, exposing them on the table as each pair is collected. The winner is the first player to expose correctly all the cards from his hand.

Tens fish

Tens fish is another way to provide practice in the pairs of numbers whose sum is ten. From a pack of playing cards again select those numbered one to nine, and shuffle them. For up to four players, spread out the cards face downwards on the table, so that no card is on top of another. Each player in turn must select two cards and turn them face upwards. If the two numbers sum to ten, the player keeps that pair of cards. Otherwise he turns them face downwards again, leaving them in the same place on the table. The winner is the player with most cards when all the cards have been correctly paired.

The game of Tens Fish

167   Contrasting these two card games, *Tens fish* also provides practice in memorizing the position of cards on the table. This is a skill which primary school children have enjoyed demonstrating, and it tends to concentrate their attention on the game even when it is another player's turn. The rules for *Tens fish* are very simple, whereas the rules given for *Tens rummy* are more complex and have purposely been left incomplete. What happens if a player exposes an incorrect pair of cards (eg. 6 + 5); should he just replace them in his hand or should there be an extra penalty? These extra rules can be decided as the game is played.

Once a complete set of rules is thought to have been made, it is an interesting exercise to try to write them down in a simple and logical way. They can then be given to some people who have never played the game. If these people now succeed in playing the game, the rules can be considered to be satisfactory. This task of writing rules is not as easy as it is often imagined, and both the child and the adult may benefit from it. Even with the logical game of *Mastermind,* the rules provided with the original sets were apparently ambiguous. This will come as no surprise to the many students who have since attempted to write computer programs to play *Mastermind.* One difficulty is with the logical reasoning needed to interpret the placing of black and white pegs. The claim 'I can write a program to solve *Mastermind* within six rows' has rarely been followed by 'Here is a successful program which I have written'.

A computer can be a useful tool, or playmate, for the person interested in games and simulations. Using the rules of a game, the computer can be programmed to simulate the actions of one or more players. It thereby provides opponents who behave in a consistent and pre-specified way, and can be used to help to evaluate the game or just as something against which to play.

Adventurous Equations

'I could never choose new rules for a game.' 'Then why not choose just one new rule?' This choice is the start of *Adventurous Equations* which is a development of Layman Allen's game of *Equations.* Each player begins by choosing a new rule which is either a rule which he has invented or a rule taken from a list of potential new rules. These additional rules are used together with the original rules to produce a new variation of the game.

Equations uses sets of six-sided coloured dice each of which is marked with a selection of numbers and operations. For example, the red dice are all marked with 0, 1, 2, 3, +, −. Playing with twelve of these red dice gives the easiest game, but more difficult variations can be played by using other groups of dice. For each game the group of dice is thrown on the table and players use the symbols on the uppermost sides to build up a correct equation. There are certain rules and restrictions about the use of the symbols but the aim of the games is to give experience in elementary mathematical operations.

If young people have enjoyed simple games like *Tens Fish,* the parent or teacher could buy a commercial game like *Equations* which can provide several variations of a basic game. However, some care should be taken to select one at the right level of complexity for the child or children.

Bingo

'Please, can we play *Bingo* again?' was an enthusiastic cry from several of the class. The teacher was pleased at this willingness to practise addition, subtraction and multiplication, for this was why he let them play *Bingo*. It was home-made equipment, illustrated on this page. A description of the *Subtraction Bingo* cards will show readers how to set about making one of the three games.

  There are three kinds of cards. Firstly, there is a Checker's card which is marked with the numbers 0 to 99. Secondly, there is a set of one hundred different Caller's cards. If all the cards are used they cover every square on the Checker's card. For children getting practice with two-figure numbers most of these Caller's cards give the subtraction of

The three kinds of cards used for Subtraction Bingo

The Checker's Card

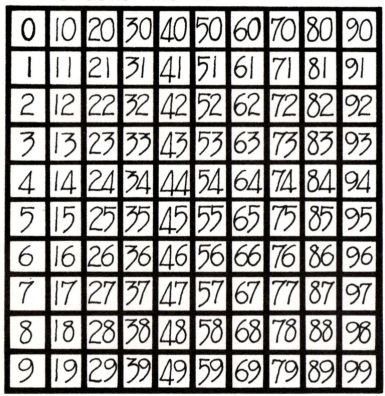

Two Caller's Cards

$$97 \\ -3$$

$$44 \\ -16$$

The cards should be the correct size to fit the squares on the Checker's Card.
Each card may have the answer written on the back.

A Player's Card

Each row contains five numbers.
Each card has a different combination of numbers.

one two-figure number from another. The numbers are chosen to give questions ranging from the easy (eg. 97 − 3) to the difficult (eg. 44 − 16). Thirdly, there is a set of thirty different Player's cards, which are not on card but on duplicated paper. The top row contains answers to the easy questions, the bottom row contains answers to the difficult questions, and the middle-range questions give answers in the middle row.

The game is played like ordinary *Bingo*, and children may take it in turn to be Caller, Checker, and Players. The winner is the player who first completes either one, two or three rows of a Player's card.

The other two games of *Bingo* mentioned before are made in a similar way. For *Addition Bingo* the same Checker's card and Player's cards may be used. New Caller's cards must be made; this should again give easy, moderate, and difficult questions, and should also reinforce the commutative property of addition (eg. sometimes calling 36 + 5 and sometimes calling 5 + 36). For *Multiplication Bingo* new cards of all three kinds (Checker's, Caller's and Player's cards) have to be made; this is because there are only forty-two different answers from multiplying the numbers from one to ten.

Skill in thinking

Most of the games described in this chapter can be used for fun, and for learning or practising facts in mathematics or science. However, there is one group of non-factual games which encompasses both the logic in mathematics and the scientific method. These games aim to develop a skill in thinking by introducing a problem or a series of problems. There is fun in solving each problem, and this satisfies the immediate needs of each player. But some designers or users hope that, by solving the given problems, the players will be better prepared to think about and solve other problems. The most popular game in this group is probably *Mastermind* which is one of the most successful games to be marketed in this decade. Two factors have contributed to its success. Firstly there is its simple, robust and attractive design, and secondly its versatility. It is enjoyed by both young and old and is played in clubs, homes and schools. A player's way of breaking the code can range from trial and error to a logical scientific approach. This range of methods of solution is the attraction for many parents and teachers. Each person can play it at his present level, yet may progress towards a higher level which demands more logical thought. Each new game is a new challenge as there is no easy rule which a player can apply to reach a solution; it has already been mentioned that few people manage to write a computer solution. Over a sequence of games, most players appear to develop a skill which leads to more success at future games of *Mastermind*. If the skill also leads to more success at solving other challenges and problems, then *Mastermind* has provided a much more valuable benefit for those players.

A personal benefit is claimed for players of three games developed by Edward de Bono. These games are designed to give practice in 'thinking as a skill.' *The L-game* is for two opponents whereas *The Option-game* and *Sequence Blocks* are for individual players.

The equipment for *Sequence Blocks* is a number of sets of blocks and a handbook of instructions. The blocks are often made of coloured plastic but wooden ones may be used. They nearly all have a triangular or quadrilateral shape. The pieces in each set have to be put together in a specified sequence to make various unspecified patterns. Each new piece represents a new piece of information, which the player has to combine with the pieces (information) which have already been placed in a pattern. The new pattern may be achieved by putting the new piece alongside the old pattern, but at other times a rearrangement of the existing pieces (information) may be required before a new pattern is evident. The idea behind the game is that the sequence of pieces used by the player is a simulation of items of information used in thinking. When building a new pattern, the player is simulating the re-ordering of information to produce a new idea or understanding.

Sequence Blocks is an example of a geometry game, which uses a combination of shapes which is now a familiar part of school mathematics. The children tend to concentrate on fitting the pieces together, with only the occasional comment like 'Is this pattern right?' The other two games each have a non-numerical version, so that all three could appeal to players who think that they are 'numbskulls at numbers.' So do not despair, you non-mathematicians and non-scientists who are still reading this chapter. If you start by using games for 'thinking as a skill' it could be the easy pathway into mathematical and scientific games. It could also be the first step to inventing a 'thinking as a skill' game for another subject or category.

The Games in Action board
The *Games in Action* board is shown on page 171 and is quite easy to make. It is designed to be used in any situation where items of factual knowledge are to be tested. The items are written on two packs of plain-faced cards with different coloured backs. These may be purchased (from Waddingtons) or cut from pastel coloured card. On one pack are written easy questions, and on the other are written harder questions. Examples of questions are 'Which city staged the 1976 Olympic Games?' (for a test of general knowledge); 'What is the aorta?' (for a test on the blood system); or 'Water boils at 100° on what temperature scale?' (for a test on temperature). For any group of players, questions are chosen so that some are classified as easy and some are classified as harder. Each question card should also be numbered to correspond with a list of answers.

To start the game the two packs of cards are placed face downwards in the centre of the board. The game is between two players or two teams of players, one with red counters and the other with blue counters. Up to four counters of each colour may be used, depending on the time available for the game. These counters are placed on separate squares in the 'red start' and 'blue start' regions. Each player or team, in turn, throws a die to decide how many adjacent squares any one of the counters may move. If that counter lands on a shaded square, the player must choose to turn over the topmost easy card or harder card. The player then answers the question on that chosen card. The rules for rewarding a correct answer may be decided by the organiser or players. When an early version was tested the rules were: two extra throws of the die for a correct answer to a harder question, one extra throw of the die for a correct answer to an easy question, and the counter remaining on that shaded square for an incorrect answer. However, some better players would have liked to see an incorrect answer punished by the counter being moved back to the previous shaded square, so that the player then had to choose another question! This last rule might benefit the weak player by making him answer more questions.

The game is won when all the counters of one colour have moved once round the board to the finish squares for that colour. Various other rules for the game will probably be needed. We will suggest some possible ones,

The 'Games in Action' Board

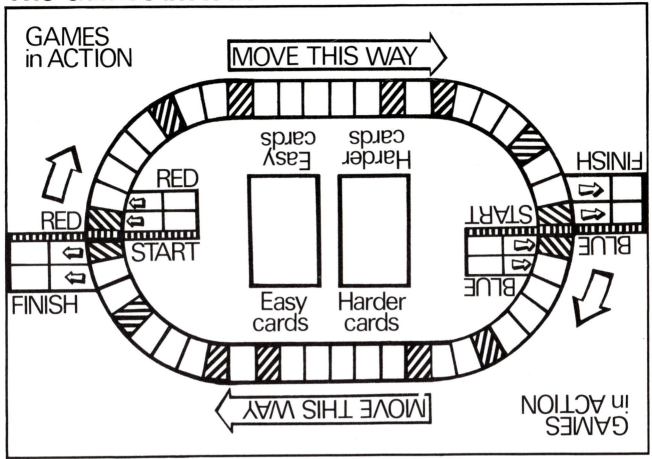

171   and the players should then try developing and amending these rules to provide the best game in their own circumstances. The possible rules include:

(1) *The no-overtaking rule.*
    One counter may not overtake another counter (of either colour) as a result of one throw of the die.

(2) *The piggy-back rule.*
    If a throw of the die allows one counter to finish moving at an already occupied square, the new counter may rest on top of any counter(s) already there. Subsequently, no counter can move if another counter is resting on top of it.

(3) *The complete-move or no-move rule.*
    If no counter can move the complete number of squares shown on the die, then all the counters must remain where they are.

The 'Games in Action' board, counters and die can be used time and time again. For each different game all that have to be prepared are two packs of question cards (one easy and one harder) and a corresponding list of answers. In many clubs, this preparation can be done by a teenager who would thereby get enjoyment and interest, by, for example, his suggesting, 'I'll do some question cards on football.'

This is a card game in which each player tries to collect in his hand a complete set of attribute cards. For example, if the player were collecting attribute cards of a Robin Redbreast, he would keep cards printed 'Has a red breast,' 'Eats worms,' and 'The female lays eggs,' but would get rid of a card printed 'Has webbed feet.'

As shown by the example of a Robin, this game is very suitable for attributes of the animal and plant kingdoms, but it can as easily be used for other branches of science and for other subjects. In economics, for instance, we have seen it applied to the attributes of financial institutions; 'Sir, does a Building Society provide day-to-day cash withdrawal?' was one question that the teacher had to answer. The reader will probably see how the game described in the next paragraphs can be applied to some of his or her own interests. For each interest or topic, the game can also be played at many levels of knowledge. The first example above is of quite elementary questions about the Robin, suitable for the average child. If the game were being played by more knowledgeable bird-watchers, two attribute cards could be printed 'Has white eggs, speckled with red-brown' and 'Eggs have a 13–14 day incubation period.'

For an *Attribute Game* about birds, the equipment needed is a set of pictures of birds, a set of attribute cards and a list of the birds and their attributes. There must be three more pictures in the set than there are players. These pictures could be from a set of cards (e.g. the British Birds cards mentioned earlier), or they could be cut from magazines and posters, or they could be photographs. One game which was played had photographs taken at the London zoo. For each picture, an equal number of attributes should be listed. From this list the attribute cards are then made. Some of these attribute cards will be unique to one picture (e.g. 'Has a red breast'). Other attribute cards will apply to several pictures and the game designer should include fewer of these cards than the players could use. For example, if the game designer has listed seven attributes for each of eight pictures, he may only make forty-five attribute cards. The game could then be played by up to five players each collecting six attribute cards.

To begin this game, shuffle the pictures and deal one face downwards to each player. The rest of the pictures are placed face downwards in the centre of the table. Shuffle the attribute cards and deal six face downwards to each player. The remaining attribute cards (the stock) are placed face downwards in the centre of the table, and the top card of it is turned face upwards and laid beside the stock to start the discard pile. Each player now looks at his picture, and replaces it face downwards by his place. Each player then holds in his hand the six attribute cards, and sorts them into cards to keep (i.e. cards with an attribute corresponding with the picture) and the other cards which will be discarded.

The game continues as each player in turn may do one of three things:
 (1) place his picture under the picture pile, and pick up the unseen topmost picture
 (2) pick up the unseen top card of the stock, and put down a card from his hand on to the discard pile
 (3) pick up the known top card of the discard pile, and put down a card from his hand on to the discard pile.

When the stock is finished, the discard pile is shuffled to make a new stock. The aim of the game is to collect a picture and six corresponding attribute cards. The first player to declare these is the winner.

173   From this description an *Attribute Game* can be prepared and played. The players may wish to make a more detailed list of the rules of play which suit their particular circumstances. For instance, what happens if a player declares a win but the attribute cards do not all correspond to the picture?

Conclusion

This chapter has used mathematics and science to illustrate ideas about games and their rules. The reader can make or collect the equipment for these games, and decide their rules, just as we have done. The ideas, and much of the equipment, can also be applied to other subjects. Details of other games and simulations will be found in the Resources list at the end of the book.

8
Evaluation

Why evaluate?

Many claims are made for the effectiveness of games and simulations. Some of these are based on apparent enjoyment by students participating in the activity. The fact that the students' dependency on the teacher in learning situations is lessened by gaming demonstrates well the advantage of this method. Similarly, the nature of the educational experience itself, which involves problem-solving and decision making, can be said to add a new dimension to the classroom climate.

There has, however, been increasing concern over the apparent lack of rigour in testing some of these and other assumptions. Perhaps the most significant research has been that of Cherryholmes (1966) who examined the findings of six simulation studies carried out in the United States. Five major hypotheses were formulated with the intention of testing them against the findings: that students taking part in a simulation will take a greater interest in the exercise than in ordinary class lessons: they will learn more facts and principles of information and these will be retained longer than by more conventional teaching means: students will become more flexible in their thinking and decision-making: and their attitudes will be significantly altered.

While recognising that there are some dangers in generalising from six separate studies, Cherryholmes nevertheless concluded that a number of these claims cannot easily be substantiated. On the first point, it was true that students' interest was greater but this was counterbalanced by the finding that students did not learn significantly more facts or principles. Nor is the retention of information superior to other methods. No evidence of a gain in critical thinking or problem-solving skills, the fourth hypothesis, was found. Likewise, attitude alteration was not more effective through the medium of games than other conventional classroom exercises.

Such a study although of great interest must be cautiously considered. The sample was small, not all the studies were concerned with testing these five particular hypotheses and the length of time devoted to the studies varied from one day to twelve weeks. What emerges from it however is that there is some confusion on the effectiveness of games; this in turn stems from a failure to spell out the criteria by which games should be judged.

There are a number of stages which a teacher should be aware of in evaluating any educational process and these are particularly appropriate in assessing games.

All evaluation involves some form of *measurement*. The most obvious kinds are examinations and assessment, though, as will be discussed later, they may not be the most appropriate form in this context. What is required is the spelling out of the *aims and objectives* in using a simulation for a group. This should ideally be done in a context of the desired outcomes or behaviours of the students. Of course, it will not be possible nor is it always educationally desirable, to foresee all the likely outcomes, intended or unintended, of teaching. One of the difficulties in evaluating games is precisely this: as most of them are deliberately constructed in an open-ended manner, behavioural objectives are more difficult to forecast.

This does not invalidate the need for objectives as without this stage, the selection of appropriate content and method becomes more difficult. Objectives should be concerned with what is practicable within a school or classroom context and relate to the skills, interests, age groups and background knowledge of the students. Attempts have been made to break down educational objectives in an ordered way. Notable among these is the classification by the psychologist Benjamin Bloom in his book *Taxonomy of Educational Objectives* (1956 and 1964). Bloom framed objectives under two broad headings or domains—the cognitive domain, that is, relating to knowledge, comprehension, analysis and synthesis—and the affective domain, which is concerned with values, beliefs and attitudes. Although the suggested framework is too complex for practical purposes in evaluating games, the stating of objectives in terms of the two aspects of knowledge and values gives a broad indication of the factors involved.

It is obvious that it will be more difficult to write down easily the affective type objectives which the teacher would hope to accomplish in a game. For one thing, the intended outcomes depend on the students being aware of which objectives are to be achieved. Another consideration is the climate of the school which is exemplified in the rules, organisation and teacher-student relationships. Two further considerations mentioned by Nicholls and Nicholls (1972) are important. Much depends on whether the teacher has in mind short-term or long-term objectives. In the case of games, this might be regarded in the former case as a novel teaching technique or one useful to illustrate a particular theme in the curriculum. Long-term objectives might be more concerned with them, for example, as an intrinsic part of the teaching method.

The stress here laid on the need for objectives is deliberate. As Ralph Tyler (1949), one of the earliest writers to develop a rationale for evaluating educational experiences, wrote 'It is only after the objectives have been identified, clearly defined, and situations listed which give opportunity for the expression of the behaviour desired that it is possible to examine available evaluation instruments to see how far they may serve the evaluation purposes desired.'

As the objectives stated will affect both the content of the game chosen and the method which is to be used, certain general rules should be followed in choosing them. Wiseman and Pidgeon (1972) put forward four principles. Objectives must be directly and appropriately related to the learning experience provided on the course; they must be capable of being achieved; they should be stated in terms of observable behaviour; and objectives must be appropriate to the level of instruction aimed at in the course.

Further, clear learning objectives as Elder (1973) has pointed out 'provide valuable guidance for the designer and prospective users of an instructional game. They also aid students as they prepare for and participate in the exercise. They facilitate the administration of the game and provide guide lines for the post-game review. Moreover, goal learning objectives also serve as criteria for evaluating both student performance and the overall adequacy of the exercise, pointing to fairly specific ways in which both can be improved.'

Nevertheless, the problems of evaluation in gaming are not always concerned solely with learning objectives. The literature of gaming is, within the last few years, increasingly aware of other less measurable factors. For instance, Kasperson (1968) has challenged the possibility of successfully evaluating games in the following terms:

'In games it is difficult to establish evaluation criteria as to what the game is in fact teaching and to create tests capable of discriminating among the various types of learning. Since games are not closed systems players may introduce unanticipated and often unrecognizable values, behaviours and rules, thus thwarting evaluation efforts.'

In order to examine the statements made by Kasperson and others it will be useful next to look at some of the principles on which games are constructed. This will help towards a later consideration of types of evaluation which have been put forward.

The structure of games—what is involved?
Many writers on games have spelled out the recipe for constructing a successful game. By the same token, the teacher can use the criteria stated for assessing the potential usefulness of games which may be available in the school. Similarly for teachers who will wish to make their own games, the 'rules' governing their construction should be considered.

Obviously, there will be differences of emphasis according to the type of game. 'Academic' games will be less open-ended in their objectives than say, a social studies type which may be more concerned with making the student aware of social interaction and relationships. But there are general principles underlying the construction of games which are widely applicable.

It is a remarkable fact that many of the commercially available games fail to spell out the designers' aims and objectives, thus leaving the teacher to speculate about the purpose of the game and without evidence of its effectiveness during its experimental stages.

At a general level, it is important to consider the following questions:
(a) Are the rules simple and easy to follow? Some games have manuals for both players and the teacher which require much pre-game time and preparation. Over-sophisticated explanations and complex instructions may be a barrier to student participation.

177 (b) Is the time span allowed for the game realistic? There is a real problem in schools and colleges in fitting playing sessions into a tightly-scheduled timetable. Some games such as the Esso Business Game allow for continuity over a period of time without any noticeable loss of interest. Where there is a more open-ended interaction game it is not easy nor is it considered desirable, to re-start or repeat the situation at a later time. Of course the time allocated should allow not only for playing the game but for the debriefing session which follows it.

(c) Does the game allow for progressive development?—that is, can the rules be developed and new factors built into the game if desirable? Rigidity and narrowness can make for an uninteresting experience.

(d) Is the material itself simple? The needs can vary from the use of a computer down the scale to mere verbal instructions. Considerations of the resources available will rule out certain games. The majority of games are of the board variety or consist of printed instructions. One should also consider under this heading the space required for a game, either large open areas, the need for groups of tables and chairs or a set of adjacent rooms.

(e) Does the game generate interest? This is a difficult factor to judge in advance of playing. In the course of the game itself, the key question will be how far is the interest sustained? The novelty of the situation in the form the game is presented and the nature of the materials if interestingly devised carry with them initial motivational advantages. A good game will allow scope for the instructor to vary his approach where the situation warrants it.

(f) This leads on to the question—how flexible is the game? Will the main objectives be distorted if, for example, chance factors are introduced? Does the game allow for the insertion if necessary of additional information or for participants to change some of the rules where required? This point is of special interest in role playing situations, where more information can be fed into the activity or withheld according to the judgment of the controller.

(g) Does the game reflect a tolerably realistic situation acceptable to the participants? The more remote the exercise is from their experience, knowledge and their credibility, the greater the chance of failure. This applies less in the case of games which deliberately put the players into a strange or ambiguous position in order to illustrate a process. This does not exclude contrived situations so long as the students can accept them as bearing a relation to reality.

(h) How far do all the participants undergo the same experiences, regardless of their diverse backgrounds, abilities and interests? Ideally, there should not be a range of experiences shared out amongst the players; this makes for difficulties in defining objectives and for generalizing experiences in discussion later.

(i) What is the nature of the experience of players during the course of the game? If one of the advantages of this technique can be justified, the game should allow for autonomy in decision-making, for possible modification of decisions by fellow students; and for the interpersonal relationships to become easier as a result of the experience. Some constraints are placed on participants by the style of presentation—for example, if the game involves interaction between only a limited number of students, if desks are required and by the size of the group.

178 (j) How is the teacher able to judge the purposefulness of the activity during the game's progress? This is one aspect of evaluation which will be dealt with later. Much depends on the role allocated to the organizer by the nature of the game. Some require the constant involvement with the group, such as explaining the next stage, answering procedural points as they arise and introducing from time to time new information. It is fairly clear that the involvement of the instructor has both advantages and disadvantages. On the one hand, the greater the closeness to the game, the greater the possibility to observe the progression of the activity; on the other hand, this does not allow for the necessary detachment in assessing the dynamics of the game or the subtleties of interaction between the players which might lead later to an improvement in the structure of the game.

(k) What opportunities does the game afford for feedback by the students? The previous points have been mainly oriented to the teacher's needs in assessing a game. It is essential that time is allowed for a debriefing session where students can express their reactions and report back their experiences and opinions. According to the structure of the game, the value of this session varies. If the students are more concerned with who won or lost rather than with some of the central issues which the game was designed to explore, then this detracts from the value of the activity. The organisation and procedural rules of the game are less important for discussion than the principles embodied in the game. For this reason, they should play a lesser part in the debriefing session.

This final point ties up a number of strands concerning the construction of games. If any judgment on the efficacy of a particular game is to be aimed at, the teacher should, first, be in a position to consider the criteria which make for a generally successful game and second, be able to assess as a result of playing and the following debriefing, how far the game fulfilled the initial objectives. One of the difficulties in operating this procedure is that the teacher's own criteria of success may not necessarily be acceptable in more than impressionistic terms. Rightly or wrongly, writers on gaming and simulation are increasingly questioning the validity of such unscientific and unstructured evidence. Because of this, the last section of this chapter will consider the forms of evaluation which are available and some of the problems which they entail.

Evaluation Techniques

No evaluatory instrument or instruments can readily encompass the many different dimensions of behaviour and experience mentioned earlier which gaming involves. In a school setting, for instance, where simulation techniques are used in a variety of different departments, this will make for a more natural setting than a once-for-all session conducted by an enthusiastic individual. (The increasing use of games in a range of Schools Council material is an encouraging sign here.) To what extent this activity is integrated into the wider learning context will also affect the evaluation of the experience. Staff support for innovatory work is another obvious factor.

Less is known of the effects of differences between the sexes in gaming. The few studies which have been made are inconclusive on this point. In a group setting, individual players' personalities, their attitudes towards playing the game and characteristics of the groups themselves seem to be of more consequence to a successful outcome. Again, the level of performance of the teacher in translating a game into actuality is subject to wide variations. Of course these variables in both teachers and students are not peculiar to gaming and are equally relevant in all learning situations.

Two other factors ought to be mentioned here. There are difficulties in identifying the precise range of skills in a game which are being evaluated and in assessing other skills which may be an unexpected spin-off from the activity. In addition, account must be taken of the size of the group being tested, the duration of the evaluation and the instruments to be employed. In sum, it seems unlikely that any one assessment method is capable of encompassing and recording the range of activities which are subsumed under gaming; because of the nature of the activity at the best only a partial picture emerges.

At this stage of development in gaming and simulations, only home-made instruments are available for testing. These range from simple pencil and paper test items to computerized analysis and may be concerned with the outcome either of a single simulation exercise or of a series. Alternatively, comparisons are made between conventional class instruction and the use of simulation.

An example of the latter is described by Baker (1968) in the teaching of pre-Civil War American history. The evidence of this study suggests that the traditional method of teaching American history may be a less efficient way of communicating to children historical facts, concepts and attitudes. However the experiment was a limited one involving only four classes over 15 days and is no more than an interesting finding.

Most evaluation studies are concerned with the effectiveness of games. One of the commonest procedures is the pre- and post-testing of students. This is particularly so with learning games, which teach the skills of thinking; attitude change in students is another much tested area.

The majority of the instruments are devised by the originator of the game. These items may be based on facts to be recalled from the session, often in the form of a multiple choice test. A more flexible approach was used by Arthur (1973) in a geography project. The first stage of the evaluation was to identify the factual and conceptual content of the game; this was followed in a number of schools by a common introductory lesson, a common post-game and a post-sample consolidation lesson. The multiple choice assessment test consisted of five factual items and five essentially reasoning questions. One test was administered immediately after the consolidation lesson and the other a month later. Comparison was made between the two groups in terms of the items tested and between the first and second testing. In this experiment, for reasons discussed later, the non-game groups achieved better scores than the game groups.

In the field of cognitive learning, testing can measure factual gains or losses in a number of ways. A study by Thompson in the United States (1968) of economics teaching used a multiple regression analysis technique. By this it was possible to hold constant factors such as age and ability of the students while measuring the relationship of the experimental variable (games participation versus non-participation) to the cognitive performance of the students.

At Johns Hopkins University, Boocock (1968) carried out an interesting study of the learning effects of two games with simulated environments, a Life Game and a Legislature Game; a multi-variate analysis displayed some of the effects of the game, taking into account sex, age, father's education and the student's college year group.

So far, the studies mentioned have provided information for the teacher or games designer based on students' reactions. A strategy put forward by Cherryholmes (1966) places the pupil in an evaluative role. He suggests that one of the major benefits of taking part in a simulation may be the opportunity for the participants to design it. Alternatively, they could redesign a simulation based upon their evaluative findings.

There are obvious practical difficulties in making this possible, not least among them the students' inexperience of gaming technique, the principles of construction, and the lack of time available for this activity. Some help towards achieving this aim can be offered by presenting students with incomplete games; the task would be to devise further rules and to encourage critical reaction to the original design. On a more elaborate scale, Cherryholmes quotes a study of Garvey at North-Western University, where students were presented with a completed model of the United States Congress in the 1960s. A contemporary Congress was simulated at the beginning of the university year. Later, students were given historical materials relating to an early twentieth century Congress to be redesigned and subsequently evaluated.

Increasing use is being made of computers in gaming, especially in the business management and economics field (Jones 1972). Two games by Wing (1968), one to teach secondary pupils the basic principles of economics in Neolithic Mesopotamia, and the other for the experimental group, the Sierra Leone Development Game, concerning an emergent nation, contained computerized material. No differences in the amount of learning were noticeable between the experimental and control groups, the latter of which followed conventional classroom methods. On the other hand, the computer group achieved the same amount of learning in half the time taken by the other group.

We have so far been considering the evaluation of cognitive learning by the use of games. Perhaps more attention has been paid by games designers to what is often considered the major benefit of gaming: improvement in students' attitudes and motivation.

It is not easy to show that attitude change can be induced by gaming except by asking participants to state their subjective views after the game. For example, Zaltman (1968) in playing an economics game, *Consumer,* claimed that 'experience-induced learning is associated with the degree of participation in basic games process.' Attitudes towards borrowing were tested on a pre- and post-game questionnaire for both teenage and adult players. Involvement in the game itself, which was concerned with teaching players how to borrow, made participants more conservative in attitude than before. Other studies have reported favourably on the impact of games on affective learning. Here, the instruments of measurement are even less reliable, i.e. even more subjective than in the cognitive domain. Better evidence would be the long term effects of games on attitudes. It must also be remembered that students are playing in a game context and may be more concerned to appear democratic or liberal minded than they would be in a non-group context.

A cautionary tale is reported by Wentworth and Lewis (1973) which demonstrates the difficulty of forecasting intended outcomes in gaming. Students' attitudes were more favourable towards the poor after they played a game called *Ghetto,* but at the same time there was a significant decline in their interest on the subject of poverty. It is also known from

181 psychological researches that direct attempts to bring about attitude change can be counter-productive. Another difficulty in reporting the results of affective aspects of gaming is the unique nature of each group experience; this makes replication very difficult. Once more, it becomes apparent that the measuring instruments are fairly crude and that such testing is only on a small scale.

Evaluatory instruments have the disadvantage of testing in a post hoc way the attitudes of the group. Neil Rackham (1970) has devised a means of in-game evaluation which provides information to the controller of the game. Participants are supplied with assessment blanks, consisting of four rating scales, on which students are asked to score their perceived enjoyment, information, relevance and duration on a seven point scale. These scales are used at different stages in the game, and take only a few seconds to fill in: the analysis of the results is made while the game is in progress. This enables immediate feedback to take place. Individual profiles can also be 'mapped' by this process throughout the course of a game and ratings correlated with intelligence quotient. This could be useful in ascertaining whether the game is suitable at a given ability level. Rackham puts forward three findings based on group session assessment: first, a trough occurs in enjoyment during the course of a game: this will vary according to the complexity of the game. Second, coincident with the enjoyment trough there is a levelling out or depression in the student's understanding of data; this rises again as the game continues. Third, these techniques help in deciding at what point to end a game; that is when there is a noticeable falling off of interest. Such ongoing evaluation, as Rackham admits, would not show the effectiveness of the game, unless it were supplemented by pre-test information on the background performance of students and also a post-test follow-up; both aspects are prohibitive in terms of cost and complexity.

Problems of evaluation
This last example illustrates some of the difficulties encountered in assessing the effectiveness of games. One of the most obvious ones is that we can measure only the apparently testable aspects of the game; many of the subtleties of the experience are not easily susceptible to measurement.

There is a danger, as Garvey (1971) has mentioned, that by attempting to quantify the facts and information which the student acquires in simulation, we are in danger of evaluating the student and not the technique. The evaluation of technique should be directed therefore to seeing how teachers achieve their teaching objectives. This too raises further difficulties. Gillespie (1973) shows that the experience may fail, for example, through the inability of the teacher to organize the environment of the game adequately. The teacher remains the judge of whether the game fails so desperately on one criterion that it should not be used again. It should be mentioned that the quality of the teacher-student relationship is not easy to evaluate in considering the success or failure of a simulation exercise.

Variations in teacher performance can affect attempts to standardize validation procedures. Arthur in the study mentioned earlier attributes the indeterminate nature of his findings on the learning gains by the control and experimental groups to differences in teachers' performances.

The very nature of gaming raises problems in looking at objectives. How far are we really comparing like with like when considering the control group learning by conventional classroom methods and the experimental group which works in a very different way? For example, the motivation engendered by simulations cannot be measured in any objective form. Other problems are raised by Taylor and Carter (1971). The students assigned to two groups for evaluative purposes may be randomly chosen, but it is possible that they are self-selecting in some way. There is also the danger of artificiality, in the comparative situation, of the teacher of the control group unconsciously competing with the experimental group, thus obtaining a better result than would normally ensue.

Research Design

One of the weaknesses of evaluation procedures is the lack of consensus by researchers. We have already mentioned the difficulty of measuring a process which is often open-ended, demanding a high degree of interaction between students and involving non-verbal cues, by pencil and paper methods. Both objective and subjective tests are appropriate, provided they are sufficiently rigorous. Walford (1974) believes it to be possible to evaluate specifically identifiable parts of the aim of a simulation by certain existing objective tests without yielding more than partial knowledge about the activity. He sees some merit in exploring subjective evaluation by experienced observers.

Taylor (1974) takes this idea one stage further. Given the wide range of evaluation from a single small scale experience evaluated by the designer with his own standards to the large scale statistical studies which use a battery of tests, he sees the need to accept much more than hitherto the systematized subjective judgments of experienced observers. Subject area panels consisting of experienced designers and users would classify and publish their findings in simulation directories, indicating 'best buys' (and otherwise) for consumers. This would give rise to discussion and useful feedback to all who are interested in gaming.

This approach accords closely with the recently expressed view that the predominant conventional evaluation model is inappropriate as an aid to practical decision-making. Parlett (1974) has described what an alternative paradigm given the name 'illuminative evaluation' should look like. It would examine the actual school situation in which an innovatory programme is being operated; what those concerned see as its strengths and weaknesses; document what it is like for both teacher and pupil to participate in the scheme; and discuss the most significant features of the innovation. In another paper the advantages of this approach are listed as follows:

It aims to be both adaptable and eclectic. The choice of research tactics follows not from research doctrine, but from decisions in each case as to the best available techniques: the problem defines the methods used, not vice versa.

Because of its comparatively recent introduction as an activity, information on simulation is fragmentary. The reader can find reviews of some games in the United Kingdom in a few journals and weeklies, notably *The Times Educational Supplement, Programmed Learning* and *Educational Technology, Games and Puzzles* and the publications of the Society for Academic Gaming and Simulation in Education and Training. But with the mushrooming of new games, not enough information is available for judging their efficacy. A model which might well be emulated is the Schools Council Evaluation Project (1973), in which the teams involved in curriculum development material described evaluation

183 procedures in terms of the objectives and philosphy of the projects.

Jacquetta Bloomer (1973) has drawn attention to educational games that 'are already proliferating (and) which have vaguely stated aims, cryptically worded rules and structures which permit mechanical success without any mastery of the principles involved.' There are however optimistic signs: the recent appearance of a series of teaching games in a number of subject areas is evidence of collaborative work amongst designers in this field. Dissemination of information on the nature of gaming and simulation at all levels is being carried out through courses in educational institutions, training centres and subject association conferences, and feedback is becoming increasingly available.

Boocock (1966) concludes her study with the remark, 'Games design is not only not a science, it is hardly a craft, but rather an "art" in the sense that we have no explicit rules to transmit'. It is in order to make gaming more readily accessible and appropriate to teachers' needs that evaluation techniques as well as the objectives to be achieved by gaming and simulation need to be assessed.

This does not mean, however, that the teacher should be deterred from using games because of an imperfect awareness of these techniques. Teaching styles, students' personalities and the particular background to the game about to be played differ from classroom to classroom. The judgment of appropriateness to the situation and the intended outcomes of the activity must in the end be left to the individual teacher's judgment.

References

Arthur, R., 'An Objectives Evaluation of Gaming in Geography Teaching' in *Cambridge Journal of Education* Vol. 3 No. 1 1973.

Baker, E. M., 'A Pre-Civil War Simulation for Teaching American History' in Boocock, S. S. and Schild, O. *Simulation Games in Learning*, Sage, Beverly Hills, California, 1968, pp. 135–142.

Bloom, B. et al., *Taxonomy of Educational Objectives*. Vol. 1 Cognitive Domain, Longmans 1956; Vol. 2 Affective Domain N.Y., 1964.

Bloomer, J., 'What have Simulation and Gaming got to do with Programmed Learning and Educational Technology?' in *Programmed Learning and Educational Technology*, Vol. 10, No. 4 July 1973.

Boocock, S. S., 'An Experimental Study of the Learning Effects of Two Games with Simulated Environments' in Boocock, S. S. and Schild, O., op. cit. pp. 107–133.

Cherryholmes, C. H., 'Some current research on effectiveness of educational simulations: implications for alternative strategies.' *The American Behavioural Scientist*. Vol. 10 No. 3 Oct. 1966.

Elder, C. D., 'Problems in Structure and Use of Educational Situations', *Sociology of Education* Vol. 46, Summer 1973.

Garvey, D. M., 'Simulation: a catalogue of judgments, findings and hunches' in Tansey, P. J. *Educational Aspects of Simulation*, McGraw Hill, 1971.

Gillespie, J. A., 'Analyzing and Evaluating Classroom Games', *Social Education*, January 1972.

Jones, G. T., *Simulation and Business Decisions*, Penguin 1972.

Kasperson, R. E., 'Games as Educational Media', *Journal of Geography*, Vol. 67, No. 7 October 1968.

Nicholls, A. and Nicholls, H., *Developing a Curriculum, A Practical Guide*, Allen and Unwin, 1972.

184 Parlett, M., 'The New Evaluation', *Trends,* July 1974.

Parlett, M. and Hamilton, D., 'Evaluation as Illumination: a new approach to the Study of innovatory programs.' Occasional Papers No. 9, Centre for Research in the Educational Sciences, University of Edinburgh, n.d.

Rackham, N., 'The Effectiveness of Gaming and Simulation Techniques' in Armstrong, R. H. R. and Taylor, J. L. *Instructional Simulation Systems in Higher Education,* Cambridge Monographs on Teaching Methods No. 2, Cambridge Institute of Education, 1970.

Schools Council, *Evaluation in Curriculum Development: Twelve Case Studies,* Macmillan, 1973.

Taylor, J. L. and Carter, K. R., 'Some Urban Gaming-Simulation Assessments' in Armstrong, R. H. R. and Taylor, J. L. *Feedback on Instructional Simulation Systems,* Cambridge Institute of Education, 1971.

Taylor, J. L., 'Preliminary Observations on Improving the Performance of Environmental Simulation Systems in Higher Education' in *Programmed Learning and Educational Technology,* Vol. 11, No. 4, July 1974.

Thompson, F. A., 'Gaming via Computer Simulation Techniques for Junior College Economics Education'. Final Report, Riverside, California 1968.

Tyler, R., *Basic Principles of Curriculum and Instruction.* University of Chicago Press, 1971 edn.

Walford, R., 'Evaluation', in SAGSET Journal Vol. 5 No. 1, 1975, pp. 20–22.

Wentworth, D. R., and Lewis, D. R., 'A Review of Research on Instructional Games and Simulations in Social Studies Education.' *Social Education,* May 1973.

Wing, R. L., 'Two Computer-Based Economics Games for Sixth Grades' in Boocock, S. S. and Schild, O., *op. cit.* pp. 155–165.

Wiseman, S. and Pidgeon, D., *Curriculum Evaluation,* NFER, 1972.

9
Resources

This list is in two parts. The resources are grouped: first by the headings of the categories explained in Chapter 6 and second, by the headings of subjects.

A Board Games

(i) *Confrontation*
An international crisis with the threatened use of nuclear weapons. Secondary pupils, up to three hours. Possibly for whole class if working in two to four groups. Devised by Philmar.

(ii) *Conservation*
Published by the Royal Society for the Protection of Birds, this board game, lasting one hour, is designed to show the difficulties facing bird life in Britain. The aim is to make conservations i.e. a set of male, female and young of the same species in an appropriate environment. Ingenious. From 7 years of age upwards. By Gosford Games.

(iii) *Diplomacy*
Large board game, for seven players, representing a European country in 1901. The aim is to gain control over the majority of Europe both diplomatically and militarily. Simple rules but cheating, rumours and breaking alliances are encouraged. Takes about four hours. All ages. By Philmar.

(iv) *Security*
Based on Monopoly, using dice, chance cards etc. Deals with problems of unemployment and opportunities in further education. For older

secondary pupils. Obtainable from Community Service Volunteers, 237 Pentonville Rd., London N1.

(v) *Snakes and Ladders*
Based on the ups and downs of the rich and the poor. For two to four players. From Christian Aid Publications, PO Box 1, 2 Sloane Gardens, London SW1.

(vi) *Speculate*
A stock market game, age range 14 to adult, two to five players. Participants are small investors dealing in shares. The aim is to amass wealth. Realistic simulation. Playing time two hours. By Waddington.

B   Task Oriented

(i) *Caribou Hunting: Seal Hunting*
Two board games for primary age pupils which simulate some of the difficulties encountered by Eskimos in securing an adequate supply of food. They form part of Bruner's 'Man: A Course of Study.' From Educational Development Centre, 55 Chapel St., Newton, Massachusetts, U.S.A.

(ii) *Decisions*
A package of guides, maps, charts and data for simulating basic business decision processes for twenty students. One term's material for sixth formers and beyond. Three problems presented are: 1. Siting an Air Terminal, 2. Coastal Tankers, 3. Marketing. From B.P. Educational Services, PO Box 21, Redhill, Surrey.

(iii) *Election*
Gives some notion of the issues involved in a General Election. It is played on a map of Great Britain and consists of six players representing different parties who operate in ten regions. The game culminates in an election following campaigns for vote-catching. From fourteen upwards, taking about three hours. By Intellect Games, 49/50 Great Marlborough St., London W1.

(iv) *The Game of Nations*
No winners but a struggle to survive. The continent of Kark is rich in oil and the problem is how each nation will try to exploit it. For fourteen years upwards, taking two to three hours. By Waddington.

(v) *Railway Pioneers*
A simulation devised by Rex Walford dealing with the building of the North American railway in the 1860s and the attendant problems which arose. Clear printed rules, maps and background information supplied. For secondary students, up to 30 players. From Longman.

(vi) *North Sea Exploration*
Also by Rex Walford. Considers both gas and oil exploration in the North Sea. Enough material for whole class. Longman, produced by SGS (Education) Ltd, 1973.

(vii) *Street*
A kit based on a housing project for nine- to thirteen-year-olds. There are four units: Our Street, Change for the Better, Who Decides? and the last one looks at the families who have been rehoused. Much good visual and tape material as resources. From Shelter Youth Education Programme, 86 Strand, London, W.C.2.

(i) *Generation Gap*
To give some understanding of the strategies of negotiation and the conflict between the different points of view between parents and children. Simulations of these two roles are undertaken. For adolescent groups of four to ten players and lasting an hour. By E. O. Schild and S. S. Boocock, Johns Hopkins University, Baltimore, Maryland, 2128 USA.

(ii) *Grasslands*
An ecology simulation based on card-deck logic by Michael Chester for the Santa Cruz County Education Office USA. It demonstrates what happens when the national balance of life on the prairie is disturbed by the introduction of cattle. Secondary pupils, working in pairs. Full details in *Gaming/Simulation/News* November 1972.

(iii) *Help!*
An exercise in crisis decision-making and communication. Players take turns in role-playing responses to common household emergencies in a non-threatening situation. For primary schools. By Abt Associates, 55 Wheeler St., Cambridge, Mass. 02138 USA.

(iv) *Life-Line—Schools Council's Moral Education Project*
The project was designed to produce materials 'to help children in secondary school to adopt a considerate style of life, that is to adopt patterns of behaviour which take other people's needs, interests and feelings into account as well as their own.' The first of the three groups of material *In Other People's Shoes* include 'Sensitivity', 'Points of View', and 'Consequences', three sets of cards which encourage people to take other people's point of view. Played in groups of two to four. Age range 13–16 + . By Longman, Burnt Mill, Harlow, Essex.

(v) *Propaganda*
A sociological game with a serious underlying message. Players are presented with statements which exemplify different propaganda techniques, becoming more subtle as the game proceeds. From thirteen years to adult. Lasting over one hour and for up to four players. A good introduction to this area. By Wff'n Proof Inc., Box 71, New Haven, Connecticut, USA.

(vi) *Sierra Leone*
To make lower secondary pupils aware of aspects of national economic development in underdeveloped countries in Africa. Decisions proceed from elementary to more complex tasks as the country develops. For a single player. From Westchester Board of Co-operative Educational Services and Research, 845 Fox Meadow Road, Yorktown Heights, New York 10598 USA.

D   In-tray Exercises

(i) *And Gladly Teach*
An in-tray exercise by W. Taylor and S. Moore involving role play for teachers: provides insights into the sociology of the classroom. From EVR Partnership, 1 Hanover Square, London WC1.

(ii) *European Environment 1975–2000*
Explores issues such as pollution, the expected duration of natural

resources: decisions to be taken by a governing body. Available from the Conservation Society, 21 Hanyards Lane, Cuffley, Potters Bar, Herts.

(iii) *Heading for Change*
Concerned with the management of innovation in secondary schools. This takes the form of a Headmaster's in-tray at 'Severnside Secondary School' with letters and memoranda which require action. There are useful discussion notes included. By William Taylor, and published by Routledge & Kegan Paul, 1973.

(iv) *Malthusania*
Problems facing a new industrialising state through four stages of population growth. Groups of eight make decisions from options. Upper secondary. From Longman Group, 35 Tanner Row, York.

(v) *Nonsuch Youth Club*
Devised by the Wiltshire Training Agency, it was used in training part-time youth workers in a rural area. Centres around decisions to be made by a management committee of a youth club. Available on loan from Youth Service Information Centre, 37 Belvoir St., Leicester, Leics.

E Committee Structures and Case Studies

(i) *Aid Committee Game*
The players study one developing country and its developmental needs using background papers. Decisions have to be made on which projects should be financed. For lower secondary age. Takes four periods. Obtainable from Oxfam, 274 Banbury Road, Oxford.

(ii) *Control in A School*
Uses simulated documents to build up a picture of an English high school, its staff and students. Units 1 and 2 cover nine different case studies. From General Studies Association, c/o Longman Subscription Enquiries, Journals Division, 43/45 Annandale St., Edinburgh, Scotland.

(iii) *Crisis in Lagia*
This is a simulation of a fictional war consisting of four case studies—the outbreak of war, morale and attitudes, the concept of a just war and protest. There are four follow-up discussion sessions with details of suggested procedure given. For upper secondary age. Devised by John Elliott of CARE, University of East Anglia, Norwich, Norfolk.

(iv) *The Development Game*
For up to 60 players. Groups play the roles of governments of several developing countries and draw up development plans. Plenary session for presentation of requests to a committee. For 16–18-year-olds. One day required. From Oxfam, 274 Banbury Rd., Oxford.

(v) *Greenham District Council Game*
Basically a simulation of a Council meeting. Looks at the balance between community need and personal interests. Needs some insight into how councils function to be successful. From Community Service Volunteers, 237 Pentonville Rd., London N1.

(vi) *The Poverty Game*
Players in groups represent farmers from villages in West Africa. Crops are planned and dice determine weather and other circumstances. Can

189 the village survive? Obtainable from Oxfam, 274 Banbury Rd., Oxford.

(vii) *Volunteers Clash with Council*
Role-playing in small groups at secondary level. Based on protest to local councillors about neglect of their housing when volunteers called in to redecorate old people's bedrooms. From Community Service Volunteers, 237 Pentonville Road, London N1.

F   Trading Game Structure

(i) *Breed or Breathe?*
A simulation with a strong emotional stimulus. Deals with the progression of population growth and exploitation of world resources from the 1970s to 2000. Requires an evolving series of decisions on a world-scale. Devised by Cockpit Arts Workshop and available from the ILEA Media Resources Centre, Highbury Station Road, Islington, London N1.

(ii) *Culture Contact*
A trading expedition lands on an isolated island inhabited by a non-industrial tribe. Deals with problems arising from the potential for conflict when two different cultures meet. For 20–30 players of secondary age. From Abt Associates Inc., 55 Wheeler St., Cambridge, Mass 02138, USA.

(iii) *Pi*
A simulation for 11- to 15-year-olds. The aim is to enable participants to experience some aspects of greed, selfishness, power etc. Fairly complicated procedure with two trading sessions. Fully described in *SAGSET Journal* July 1975.

(iv) *Ratrace*
A three-circuit game, representing three social classes. Each circuit has its own appropriate status symbols. These can be traded with other players and some social mobility is possible. Amusing and with clear instructions. Eight years of age upwards. Two to six players and taking an hour and a half. By Waddington.

(v) *Streets Ahead*
Deals with city problems and designed for secondary pupils. Six players. It can be played at two levels. One, Short Cut, lasts an hour: Long Way Round, either a term or a year. From Priority, Harrison Jones School, West Derby St., Liverpool 7.

(vi) *Starpower*
The classical interaction game by Garry Shirts for 18–25 players. Simulates the relationship between wealth and power in human societies. From Simile II, 218 Twelfth St., PO Box 910, Del Mar, Ca 92014, USA.

(vii) *Outsider*
An adaptation of another Shirts game. It explores the way in which we perceive a culture or nation different from our own within an anthropological framework. For large numbers. In G. I. Gibbs & A. Howe, eds. *Academic Gaming and Simulation in Education and Training*, Kogan Page 1975.

(viii) *Tenement*
A simulation concerning seven families and their negotiations with the landlord with assistance from welfare agencies. From 13 years onwards.

G Whole Class Meetings and Enquiries

(i) *International Relations Game*
Concerned with diplomacy and tension between imaginary countries.
Can be obtained from T.E.A.M. 7 Cathedral Close, Exeter.

(ii) *Man in his Environment*
Basically a board game but which leads out to explore the effects on the
environment of a marina, a shopping precinct and a hydro-electric dam.
Attractively presented, allows for understanding of political power. From
The Coca-Cola Export Corporation, Stapleton House, 28/33 Scrutton St.,
London EC2.

(iii) *Mental Health Dispute*
Concerns the problem of building a mental health hostel in a community:
will the plan be rejected or accepted? From Community Service
Volunteers, 237 Pentonville Rd., London N1.

(iv) *New Steel Site—but where?*
On a national scale this simulation deals with some of the constraints and
limitations of possibilities on where steel industry can be sited. From
Community Service Volunteers, 237 Pentonville Rd., London N1.

(v) *Raftonbury*
A large scale simulation for up to 100 players which can last all day. A
community is faced with the choice of unemployment or the siting of an
asbestos factory within it and its subsequent health hazards. From
Cockpit Arts Workshop, Gateforth St., Marylebone, London NW1.

(vi) *Spring Green Motorway*
Designed as a role-playing game to bring out the various reactions of the
inhabitants of Spring Green to a proposed motorway route through the
village. Leads up, from roles established in pairs, to a full public meeting.
For upper secondary pupils. From Community Service Volunteers, 237
Pentonville Rd., London N1.

(vii) *Unesco Project in Education for International Understanding*, Paris
1974.
Handbook developing an innovative approach to social science and
integrated studies curricula to promote international understanding.
Contains 24 different units which make use of role play. Some useful
ideas.

(viii) *Who's to Blame?*
Places youth club member or senior secondary age pupils in a situation
where they have to be concerned about explaining acts of vandalism and
devising responsible ways of preventing their reccurrence. From Cockpit
Arts Workshop, Gateforth St., Marylebone, London NW1.

H More Complex Simulations

(i) *Cassandra: You are the survivors!*
The game is intended to create an environment where the participants
were the last known survivors of a nuclear accident. A number of groups
in different rooms have to make critical decisions. Suitable for sixth

formers and above. Full instructions in *Simulation/Gaming/News.* September 1972.

(ii) *The Coffee Game*
For sixth formers and students 'to illustrate the complexity of the dynamics of international trade and aid, as they are operative around the commodity of coffee, and show how they bind us to the lives of people in other lands.' Obtainable from VCOAD. Education Unit, Parnell House, 25 Wilton Rd., London SW1.

(iii) *Inter-Nation Simulation*
A long-playing simulation (up to 30 hours) for older secondary pupils which deals with foreign relations and world politics. Available from Science Research Associates, Maidenhead, Berks.

(iv) *Macroeconomic Game*
Developed by J. N. Robinson of Reading University. Players take the part of governments trying to achieve a number of targets such as full employment and balance of payments by a variety of policy instruments. Can be played at different levels. Local schools compete over a period of two terms. Budget decisions are sent to the University: in return they receive a computer print-out of decisions of other countries. Schools can enter free of charge. Details from the author, c/o Faculty of Letters and Social Science, University of Reading, Whiteknights, Reading. Details in *SAGSET* Journal April 1975.

(v) *Smog*
An ecological game. Two to four players are given roles and decide on policies which will satisfy the environmentalist, the voter and so on. New elements can be introduced and its complexity reflects the problems of an industralized society. Upper Secondary, 2 hours or more. By Urban Systems Inc. 1033 Massachusetts Ave, Cambridge Massachusetts 02138 USA.

(vi) *Ulster in Your Hands*
Aims to show young people (older secondary age) how political decisions are made and what were the chief aims of all the groups involved in the Ulster situation. Players are divided into three groups and subdivisions— the cabinet, political parties, the press—with background information. From the General Studies Association. Longman, Subscription Enquiries, Journals Division, 43/45 Annandale St., Edinburgh, Scotland.

(vi) *Social Services Resource Allocation Game*
Focuses on the interplay between decision-making and political bargaining which occurs when allocating scarce resources within a local authority social services department. Eight key decision makers negotiate over a number of rounds and are 'observed' by others. Takes about three hours with young adults. Published by the National Institute of Social Work by the National Council for Social Service, 26 Bedford Square, London WC1.

SOME EXAMPLES OF GAMES AND SIMULATIONS
UNDER SUBJECT HEADINGS

Careers

(i) *Framework*
A newspaper format adopted by the Schools Council Careers Education and Guidance Project for its Foundation Course trial materials. Each issue contains two lesson units for thirteen to fourteen-year-olds. Decision making units include Lost Underground (Framework 3) and Thiston By-Pass and Community Election Time in Framework 5. From the Project, c/o The Village College, Impington, Cambridge.

(ii) *Speedcop*
(iii) *Deciding*
Speedcop is a careers simulation aimed at teaching eight important aspects of any job. *Deciding* looks at decision-making skills within the curriculum, including those relating to education, careers and leisure, on an individual and group basis. For older secondary pupils. Obtainable from Careers Research and Advisory Centre, Hobsons Press (Cambridge), Bateman St., Cambridge.

Economics

(i) *Bank Loan*
Sponsored by Lloyds Bank, this simulation puts pupils in the position of a bank manager making decisions on loans for five clients. Good background information included. For fourteen-year-olds upwards and lasting about two hours. From Longman Group Resources Unit, 35 Tanner Row, York.

(ii) C. T. Sandford and M. S. Bradbury et al. *Case Studies in Economics: Projects and Role Playing in Teaching Economics* Macmillan, 1971.
A useful book for teachers, containing fourteen projects and role-playing case studies. Can be adapted to suit different school contexts.

(iii) *Economic Decision Games*
A series of booklets for upper secondary pupils dealing with a number of topics in economics. Easy to use as only pencil and paper is required and booklets can be re-used. From Science Research Associates, Maidenhead, Berks.

(iv) *Esso Service Station Game*
Large-scale game dealing with the siting and operating of service stations in a new town. A whole class can participate but requires a good length of time to play. From Hobsons Press (Cambridge).

(v) *Profit and Loss*
An economics board game for older secondary pupils with business studies connections. Lasts about four hours and for up to ten players. Available from Economics Association, Hamilton House, Mabledon Place, London WC1.

English

(i) *Context*
A crossword game, involving the use of parts of speech, to form sentences on a nine by nineteen square board. Stimulating and amusing. Can be

played at two levels, elementary and advanced. Takes under an hour for two to four players; suitable for seven years upwards. By Airfix.

(ii) *Crack*
A board word game using coloured tiles and squares. Bonus given for achieving colour words. For eight upwards, playing time variable. By Peter Pan Playthings.

(iii) *Foil*
Each player is dealt ten letter cards; the aim basically is to scramble other players' words in three minutes. Simple rules. From six years to adult, two to four players and takes between one and two hours. By 3M.

(iv) K. R. Krupar *Communication Games,* Collier Macmillan, 1973.
A book consisting of thirty-three English games, for individual pupils.

(v) *My Word*
Printed grids with column of eleven test-word spaces of unequal letters lengths. Build up to longer words. Scoring in large numbers. Well presented. For two players from ten to adult. Time, one hour. By Gamut of Games, USA.

(vi) *Storypacks*
Comprehensive simulation and role play material (ready to cut out) for English teachers. Two packs. One, *Cokerheaton,* deals with an industrial town and the second, *Rushbrook,* with a village. Useful for middle school pupils age nine to thirteen. From Evans Bros., Montague House, Russell Square, London WC1.

Foreign Languages

(i) *Domino Quelle Heure Est-il?*
Practice, in French, of telling the time. Illustrations help to make this attractive for primary children. From European School Books, 100 Great Russell St., London WC1.

(ii) *Spanish Chatter*
(iii) *French Chatter*
This game is a form of rummy, using graded phrase cards illustrations. For young players, eight upwards, as a reinforcement for language learning. Playing time about two hours. By Intellect Games.

Geography

(i) *Cities and People*
The second of three units of work of the Schools Council Geography for the Young School Leaver Project, directed by R. A. Beddis and T. H. Dalton. Each theme consists of 35 units. The fifth one here involves role playing and the solution of urban problems e.g. to improve the area of Rochdale, Lancashire and plan the future growth of Washington D.C. Published by T. Nelson and Sons, 36 Park St., London W1.

(ii) J. P. Cole and N. J. Benyon *New Ways in Geography* Blackwell, 1969–72
Four books, for primary and lower secondary age students, which pioneered the way in using simulation and games in geography. Good value.

(iii) J. M. Haigh *Geography Games* Blackwell, 1975
Contains five new games, with notes for pupils and teachers, on fishing, shipbuilding, tourism, transport and new towns.

(iv) *High School Geography Project*
An American project started in 1961 to reliven the teaching of geography at secondary level. Makes much use of simulations. One, the game of *Section,* is described in *Journal of Curriculum Studies* May 1971.

(v) *Longman Geography Games*
Consists of 15 units contributed by several authors, including Rex Walford. Only three of them—Motorway, Urbanisation and Super-Port—involving role-playing. A separate unit is provided for this purpose. For all ages, specified in the instructions. Available on subscription only from Longman Group Resources Unit, 9/11 The Shambles, York.

(vi) *Railway Rivals*
(vii) *Oil Distribution Game*
The first game deals with railway routes in USA, Canada and Britain. It is concerned with construction and competition between companies. For up to eight players. The second deals with industrial location and is played in pairs. Takes from a half to two hours. Clear instructions and cheap. From D. G. Watts, 32 Eastleigh Drive, Milford Haven, Pembs, Wales.

History

(i) *Destiny*
(ii) *Discovery*
(iii). *Division*
Three simulations for up to a whole class of upper secondary pupils on various events in the history of the USA. *Destiny* concerns the Cuban Crisis of 1898; *Discovery* looks at early American colonisation; and *Division* examines the political issues dividing the nation in the 1850–60 period. The first lasts up to eight hours, the other two up to fifteen hours. From Interact, PO Box 262, Lakeside, California, USA.

(iv) *Longman History Games Series*
Twelve games, for the full secondary range which provide insights into historical process. The Norman Conquest, Development of the Medieval Town, Trade and Discovery, Frontier Ironmaster, Canals, Congress of Vienna, Harvest Politics, Railway Mania, Village Enclosure, Scramble for Africa and General Strike. There is also a Teacher's Unit. Obtainable by subscription from Longman Group, Resources Unit, 9–11 The Shambles, York. Two of the authors D. Burt and J. Nichol describe further games in *Games and Simulations in History* 1973, Longman.

(v) *Saga*
An historical version of Monopoly. Values are placed on 'events' and participants have to plan their resources and strategy. For children of nine and upwards. By Epic, London.

(vi) *The Workhouse Game*
From the Schools Council History and Geography and Social Science 8–13 project unit on Poverty. Pupils are divided into groups of five. Four pupils from the group are chosen to be head of a family who lived in the town about a hundred years ago. A family's circumstances are traced,

195 with help of chance cards and the use of a board, over a period of four months. For whole class and takes two periods. Details in the project's *Games and Simulations in the Classroom* 1975 pp. 16–19.

Mathematics

(i) P. Epps and J. Deans, *Mathematical games 1 and 2.* Macmillan Educational. 1972, 1976
Thirty-five well designed board games with a developing mathematical content. Well produced, but expensive. For primary and lower secondary age.

(ii) *Mastermind*
Set up a code with coloured pegs and challenge your opponent to break it. For two players of almost any age or intelligence. From toyshops, or from Invicta Plastics, Oadby, Leicester.

(iii) *Sequence Blocks, The OP-game, The L-game*
Three games to develop skill in thinking. Devised by Edward de Bono. For one or two players, aged eight upwards. From Invicta Plastics, Oadby, Leicester.

(iv) *Equations*
Played with dice by between two and six players. Ingeniously devised. For primary age upwards. Fifty-five page handbook describes how rounds vary according to the experience of players. From Science Systems, 173 Southampton Way, London SE5 7EJ and Wff'n Proof Inc., Box 71, New Haven, Connecticut, USA.

(v) *Numbers Up*
A numerical version of Scrabble. Each player shakes fifteen numbered dice and has three minutes to build up a number sequence on a grid. By Waddington.

(vi) T. Rice *Mathematical Games and Puzzles,* B and T. Batsford, 1973
A book explaining more than forty types of puzzles and games. The final section deals with games for one or more players. Attractively set out. For primary school pupils upwards.

(vii) *Commercial games suitable for Middle and Secondary School Mathematics*
A list by Peter Dean of about one hundred games and their suppliers. In *Mathematics in School,* March 1976.

Science

(i) *Animal Lotto*
Requires primary pupils of five to ten years to match photographs to names: in three languages. Takes up to half an hour and for four players. From Educational Supply Association, PO Box 22, The Pinnacles, Harlow, Essex. CM19 5AY.

(ii) *Ionics*
Cards which combine to make ionic formulae or equations. For two to five players aged thirteen upwards. From Science Systems, 173 Southampton Way, London SE5 7EJ and Wff'n Proof Inc., Box 71, New Haven, Connecticut, USA.

(iii) *Cheminoes*
The principles of chemical formulae based on the game of dominoes. For upper secondary pupils. From Chemical Teaching Aids, Letham, Ladybank, Fife, Scotland.

(iv) *Circuitron*
A board game for teaching electric circuits. Different symbols represent cells, switches in the open position, etc. Played in groups of four. For fourteeen years upwards. From Griffin and George, 285 Ealing Road, Wembley, Middlesex.

(v) *Longman Science Games*
Eighteen games in two packs: one pack with eight biology and one general science and the second, eight physics and one chemistry. For two or more players from ten years upwards. By subscription only. Longman Resources Unit, 35 Tanner Row, York.

(vi) *British Birds*
Card game based on Happy Families. Age eight upwards. For two or more players. By Pepys.

Organizations

(i) *Association for the Teaching of the Social Sciences*
This Association disseminates news of teaching materials and advice on teaching methods related to the social sciences. It produces a journal *The Social Science Teacher* five times a year with some references to simulations, e.g. Vol. 4 No. 2 Winter 1974–5, and organises weekend and annual conferences. Details from the Secretary, Chris Brown, West Midlands College of Education, Walsall, Staffs.

(ii) *Cockpit Arts Workshop*
Gateforth Street, Marylebone, London NW1
The Cockpit, administered by the Inner London Education Authority, is a specialist group activity youth centre for the 15–25 age range. It devises simulations for sale, including Raftonbury, Problo and Who's to Blame?

(iii) *Community Service Volunteers*
237 Pentonville Road, London N1
Produces a number of community simulation games which can be obtained for an annual subscription.

(iv) *General Studies Association*
Longman Group, Subscription Enquiries, Journals Division, 43/49 Annandale St., Edinburgh, Scotland. Publishes a quarterly magazine *General Education* focussing on this aspect of the curriculum in schools. Also issues free to members from time to time documents on a variety of topics including simulations and games.

(v) *Media Resources Centre, Inner London Education Authority*
Highbury Station Road, Islington, London N1
Produces a range of material, notably Nine Simulations (1975). These are packs of documentary material covering a variety of situations and take the form of diaries and letters. The simulations are primarily intended to give practice in communication skills. Some of the titles are Survival, The Azim Controversy, Action for Libel and Airport Controversy.

197 (vi) *One World Trust*
Concerned with the World Studies Project which contains simulations.
37 Parliament Street, London SW1.

(vii) *Oxfam*
274 Banbury Road, Oxford
Specialises in materials concerning the Third World e.g. Aid Committee
Game and the Poverty Game.

(viii) *Schools Council*
A national body, consisting of representatives of the Department of
Education and Science, local education authorities and teachers. The
Council sponsors curriculum research projects on a large scale. Some of
the material developed contains sections on simulation and games. The
Project Files and Index, issued annually, gives details of all projects.
Contact Schools Council Project Information Centre, 160 Great Portland
Street, London W1.

(ix) *Shelter*
Shelter Youth Education Programme, 86 Strand, London WC2
The best known simulation which has been produced so far is
Tenement.

(x) *Society for Academic Gaming and Simulation in Education and
Training* (SAGSET)
Centre for Extension Studies, University of Technology, Loughborough,
Leics.
Besides producing a journal, this society organizes an annual conference
and local one-day courses. Details are given in the journal. Details of
membership available from the Secretary.

(xi) *Town and Country Planning Association*
17 Carlton House Terrace, London SW1
The Education Unit of the Association issues a monthly magazine with
the acronym BEE (Bulletin of Environmental Education). Much relevant
information. May 1972 issue was given over to games and simulations.

(xii) *Voluntary Committee on Overseas Aid and Development*
(VCOAD)
Education Unit, Parnell House, 25 Wilton Road, London SW1
This is a co-ordinating agency for information about the education work
of such bodies as Save the Children Fund, Christian Aid, Freedom from
Hunger Campaign, Council for Education in World Citizenship. Details
of simulations available from the above address. The Development
Puzzle is one of the very sound publications.

(xiii) *Youth Service Information Centre*
17–23 Albion St., Leicester, Leics.
Loans (only) a number of games and simulations connected with youth
service leadership e.g. Mock-Up, Decision Game and Anoton.

USEFUL BOOKS ON GAMES AND SIMULATIONS

1 General

(i) C. C. Abt *Serious Games* The Viking Press. N.Y., 1970.
Covers a wide field of interests, including games for disadvantaged
children, for occupational training and for many areas of the school
curriculum.

198 (ii) T. Brennan and J. E. Brown (eds.) *Teaching Politics: Problems and Perspectives.* BBC, 1975.
The final part of this short book deals with the application of games and simulations to a relatively new area of the curriculum.

(iii) M. Chesler and R. Fox *Role-Playing Methods in the Classroom,* Science Research Association, Maidenhead, Berks, 1966.
A short and useful introduction to this aspect.

(iv) G. Elliott, H. Sumner and A. Waplington *Games and Simulations in the Classroom* Collins, 1975.
Small (32 pages) book published in connection with the Schools Council Project History, Geography and Social Science 8–13.

(v) G. I. Gibbs *Handbook of Games and Simulation Exercises* E. and F. N. Spon, 1974.
An exhaustive bibliography of games, listing almost 2000 together with details of content, suppliers and audience.

(vi) C. Longley (ed) *Games and Simulations* BBC, 1972.
The handbook was intended to accompany a series of ten broadcasts in 1972. It surveys some aspects of gaming but does not claim to be comprehensive.

(vii) P. J. Tansey and D. Unwin. *Simulation and Gaming in Education.* Methuen Educational, 1969.
One of the earliest British books on the subject. It gives a good general guide to simulations at both school and teacher training levels.

(viii) P. J. Tansey and D. Unwin. *Simulation and Gaming in Education Training and Business: A Bibliography.*
Education Centre, New University of Ulster, Coleraine, N. Ireland, 1969. Republished by SAGSET. Centre for Extension Studies, Univ. of Technology, Loughborough, Leics. A compact guide to over 400 references on games and simulations in books and articles.

(ix) J. L. Taylor and R. Walford. *Simulation in the Classroom.* Penguin, 1972.
A good introduction to role play, games and simulations. It contains a detailed account of six games and a useful list of some material for the classroom.

2 More Advanced

(i) R. H. R. Armstrong and J. L. Taylor (eds) (i) *Instructional Simulation Systems in Higher Education* 1970. (ii) *Feedback on Instructional Simulation Systems.* 1971. Both by Cambridge Institute of Education.
These volumes contain 33 contributions which deal with both practical and theoretical dimensions. Not for the beginner.

(ii) E. Berne *Games People Play* Penguin, 1968.
Deals with the psychology of human relationships in a games context. Amusingly written but with a serious message.

(iii) M. Inbar and C. S. Stoll *Simulation and Gaming in Social Science* Free Press, N.Y. 1972.
The majority of the book is devoted to case studies of a number of simulations. Chapter 17 deals with the problem of designing a simulation.

199 (iv) P. J. Tansey (ed) *Educational Aspects of Simulation* McGraw-Hill, 1970.
Eleven articles by distinguished workers in the field from Britain and the USA. Meant as a reference book rather than as a primer.

(v) J. L. Taylor *Instructional Planning Systems* Cambridge U. P. 1971.
Directed towards instructional simulation in the field of urban studies.

Journals

(i) *Games and Puzzles*
A monthly magazine dealing with many aspects of games. The evaluation of new commercial games is a useful feature. It also carries advertisements by leading stockists. 11 Tottenham Court Road, London W1.

(ii) *Programmed Learning and Educational Technology*
Includes articles on simulations. Special issues devoted to the topic, e.g. July 1973 and July 1974. Also news of conferences. Bimonthly. Kogan Page Ltd., 116A Pentonville Road, London N1.

(iii) *SAGSET Journal*
The journal of the Society for Academic Gaming and Simulation in Education and Training. Includes information on new games and helpful advice in devising them and a good section on book reviews. Published by Kogan Page Ltd., 120 Pentonville Rd., London N1.

(iv) *Simulation and Games*
Its subtitle, 'An International Journal of Theory, Design and Research' indicates its scope. It is issued quarterly by Sage Publications, 28 Banner Street, London EC1Y 8QE and Beverly Hills, California, USA.

(v) *Simulation/Gaming/News*
Published in America. This bi-monthly journal gives details of mainly new unpublished games. A useful journal. From Box 3039, University Station, Moscow, Idaho 83843, USA.

(vi) *Social Education*
The journal of the National Council for Social Studies, with a majority of its articles concerned with schools, issued monthly. A number of articles deal with the evaluation and description of simulations, see e.g. January 1972, January 1974 and February and March, 1975. 1515 Wilson Boulevard, Arlington, Virginia, 22209, USA.

(vii) *Teaching Geography*
A recent journal (1975) issued quarterly for schools. Simulations described e.g. Planaforest, an afforestation simulation, January 1976. Published for the Geographical Association by Longman, Journals Division, Longman House, Burnt Mill, Harlow, Essex.

(viii) *Teaching History*
Sponsored by the Historical Association and issued twice yearly with details of games e.g. May 1972 (two articles) and May 1974. The Historical Association, 59A Kennington Park Road, London SE11.

(ix) *Teaching Sociology*
A rather more advanced twice yearly journal but which contains interesting descriptions of simulations e.g. 'The bureaucratization

200   process and its effects', October 1974; 'Simulation in teaching research methods', October 1975. Sage Publications, 28 Banner St., London EC1Y 8QE, and Beverly Hills, California, USA.

(x) *Journal of Recreational Mathematics*
A quarterly journal, first published in 1968. Each issue contains articles both for the intelligent reader and for the mathematics specialist. Baywood Publishing Company, 43 Central Drive, Farmingdale, New York, 11735.